Humanitarian Logistics
Meeting the challenge of preparing for and responding to disasters

Edited by
Martin Christopher and
Peter Tatham

The Chartered Institute of
Logistics and Transport (UK)

KoganPage

LONDON PHILADELPHIA NEW DELHI

First published in Great Britain and the United States in 2011 by Kogan Page Limited

120 Pentonville Road	1518 Walnut Street, Suite 1100	4737/23 Ansari Road
London N1 9JN	Philadelphia PA 19102	Daryaganj
United Kingdom	USA	New Delhi 110002
www.koganpage.com		India

© Martin Christopher and Peter Tatham, 2011

The right of Martin Christopher and Peter Tatham to be identified as the authors of this work has been asserted by them in accordance with the Copyright, Designs and Patents Act 1988.

ISBN   978 0 7494 6246 8
E-ISBN   978 0 7494 6247 5

British Library Cataloguing-in-Publication Data

A CIP record for this book is available from the British Library.

Library of Congress Cataloging-in-Publication Data

Christopher, Martin.
   Humanitarian logistics : meeting the challenge of preparing for and responding to disasters / Martin Christopher, Peter Tatham. – 1st ed.
      p. cm.
   ISBN 978-0-7494-6246-8 – ISBN 978-0-7494-6247-5 1. Humanitarian assistance. 2. Emergency management. 3. Business logistics. I. Tatham, Peter. II. Title.
   HV553.C55 2011
   363.34068'7–dc22
                                        2011003435

Typeset by Saxon Graphics Ltd, Derby
Print production managed by Jellyfish
Printed and bound in the UK by CPI Antony Rowe

CONTENTS

List of figures and tables ix
List of contributors x

Introduction 1
Martin Christopher and Peter Tatham

01 **Risky business: what humanitarians can learn from business logisticians – and vice versa** 15
Paul D Larson

Abstract 15
Introduction 16
A brief review of recent literature 17
The players and the stage 20
Supply chain risk management in the humanitarian world 23
Conclusion 27
References 30
Acknowledgements 31

02 **Impacts of funding systems on humanitarian operations** 33
Tina Wakolbinger and Fuminori Toyasaki

Abstract 33
Introduction 33
Structure of funding systems 35
Impacts of financial flows on disaster response 36
Incentives provided by donors 41
Summary and recommendations 43
References 44
Acknowledgement 46

03 **The importance of information technology in humanitarian supply chains: opportunities and challenges in the Helios project** 47
Martijn Blansjaar and Charl van der Merwe

Abstract 47

Introduction 48
The relevance of supply chain information 49
Some recent history 52
The Helios initiative 54
A brief overview of the ILPPM journey 57
Reflections on the ILPPM project 59
Further growth: inter-agency efforts 60
Concluding remarks 62
References 63

**04   Humanitarian logistics metrics: where we are and
how we might improve** 65

Peter Tatham and Kate Hughes

Abstract 65
Introduction 66
Humanitarian logistics 67
Performance measurement in commercial supply networks 68
Performance measurement in 'not for profit' supply networks 69
Academic perspectives 70
Practitioner perspectives 73
The recipient's perspective 76
Conclusion 79
References 80
Notes 84

**05   Humanitarian logistics and the cluster approach:
global shifts and the US perspective** 85

Nezih Altay and Melissa Labonte

Abstract 85
Introduction 86
Background 87
Change afoot – the cluster approach and implications for humanitarian
logistics 89
Business as usual or… ? 92
US perspectives on humanitarian logistics, the CA and the LC 95
Conclusion 98
References 99
Notes 101

06   The 2004 Thailand tsunami reviewed: lessons learned 103

Stephen Pettit, Anthony Beresford, Michael Whiting and Ruth Banomyong

Abstract 103
Introduction 104
What happened on 26 December 2004? 104
Hazard event response in Thailand 107
Reflections and lessons to be learned 112
Conclusions 116
References 118
Notes 119

07   The journey to humanitarian supply network management: an African perspective 121

Paul SN Buatsi

Abstract 121
Introduction 122
Types of disaster 122
The nature and incidence of disasters in Africa 123
Disasters and sustainable development in Africa 123
The scope and role of humanitarian logistics 124
Unpredictable demand and supply 125
Efficiency of disaster response 125
Critical success factors in the context of humanitarian aid supply
    chains 126
Disaster risk management and contingency planning in Africa 127
Institutional frameworks and policies 128
Multiplicity of actors: the critical roles of inter-agency
    communication, collaboration and coordination 129
The role of technology in humanitarian logistics in Africa 131
Human capacity building for disaster risk management in
    Africa 133
Challenges of humanitarian logistics in Africa 134
Conclusion 136
References 137

08   Humanitarian logistics in the United States: supply chain systems for responding to domestic disasters 141

Jarrod Goentzel and Karen Spens

Abstract 141
Introduction 142

Overview of US emergency response 143
Florida division of emergency management 145
Supply chain strategies 158
Conclusions 160
References 162
Notes 162
Acknowledgements 163

09   The supply network's role as an enabler of development 165

Deborah Ellis

Abstract 165
Introduction 166
1 Improving access to essential medicine 166
2 Reliable supply links and economic development 173
A final word – the supply chain as an enabler 176
References 177
Notes 178

10   Humanitarian logistics professionalism 179

David M Moore and David H Taylor

Abstract 179
Context and background 179
Understanding logistics: commercial best practice; supply chain
    management as the evolutionary development of logistics 180
Further application of supply chain management: military adaptation – the
    use of commercial best practice in the defence logistics environment 181
Humanitarian logistics: an opportunity to develop and adapt commercial
    and military approaches 182
Challenges of, and for, humanitarian logistics 184
Gaining knowledge: the basis of professionalism in humanitarian
    logistics 192
Professionalism – the response for, and of, humanitarian logistics 195
Summary 197
Conclusion 198
References 199

11   Humanitarian logistics: a cultural perspective 201

Rachel A Dowty

Abstract 201
Hierarchy of needs 202
Sourcing humanitarian aid 204
Transporting humanitarian aid 205

Distributing humanitarian aid 206
The importance of local knowledge 208
References 212

12   The impossible interface? Combining humanitarian logistics and military supply chain capabilities 215

Jersey Seipel

Abstract 215
Introduction 216
Humanitarian and military logistics 217
Humanitarian principles and ideology 219
A strategic-level decision 221
The joint logistics and supply chain interface: function defines form? 222
Recommendations 228
Conclusion 229
References 230

13   Disaster agencies and military forces – not such strange bedfellows after all! 233

Tim Cross

Abstract 233
Introduction 234
From cold to hot wars: the growth in humanitarian operations/ complex emergencies 235
The turning point 236
The players and their roles 236
The good, the bad and the ugly 238
Accept these realities – and move on 242
There is more to this than war-fighting and military victories 244
Both sides need each other 245
So, what? The need for a widely understood doctrine 246
The example of logistic supply chains 247
The time for change is now 248

14   So where next? Developments in humanitarian logistics 249

Gyöngyi Kovács

Abstract 249
Introduction 250
From inter-agency coordination to relationship building in the supply chain 250

Technology development and the pragmatism of humanitarian operations
  research (OR) 255
Questioning disaster taxonomies and the humanitarian-development
  divide 256
Units of analysis – taking the strategic view 256
Addressing sustainability 257
Concluding remarks 259
References 260
Notes 262

Index 265

FIGURES AND TABLES

FIGURE 0.1   The two generic categories of risk 9

FIGURE 1.1   Articles on supply chain risk management, 1998–2009 17

FIGURE 1.2   Dormant and active supply chains 24

FIGURE 1.3   Active, lean and dormant, agile supply chains 26

FIGURE 4.1   A comparison of measurement frameworks for humanitarian supply networks 71

FIGURE 8.1   Organization chart including the SERT sections and Emergency Support Functions (ESFs) 151

FIGURE 8.2   The Logistics Operation Center is set up 24/7 at the SLRC and ready to make IMTs productive immediately upon arrival 152

FIGURE 8.3   Example of a Time Phased, Force and Deployment Data List (TPFDDL) 155

FIGURE 8.4   Communications systems used by the state and federal government 157

FIGURE 8.5   Laptop computer cache ready for deployment by the Florida Department of Emergency Management 158

FIGURE 10.1   Military organizations' supply chain 182

FIGURE 10.2   Humanitarian logistics operations supply chain 183

FIGURE 10.3   Knowledge acquisition 193

FIGURE 10.4   Cognitive growth process 195

TABLE 1.1   Six types of supply chain 22

TABLE 2.1   Main objectives and challenges in fund management 40

TABLE 5.1   Organization of disaster assistance/response 96

TABLE 6.1   The Asian tsunami disaster, December 2004: casualties by country 105

TABLE 6.2   Tsunami-susceptible areas in Thailand 108

TABLE 6.3   Cluster responsibilities and lead organizations in humanitarian emergencies 114

TABLE 8.1   SLRC base stock levels and the derived rations of immediate response 159

CONTRIBUTORS

Nezih Altay is an Associate Professor of Operations Management at DePaul University. He received his PhD in Operations Management from Texas A&M University. Living through the 1999 Turkey earthquake drew his attention to operational problems in disaster preparedness and response. His first paper on this issue – a call to the OR/MS community – appeared in the *European Journal of Operational Research*. He is specifically interested in the issues in humanitarian logistics and in the impact of disasters on firms and supply chains.

Ruth Banomyong is currently an Associate Professor in the Department of International Business, Logistics and Transport Management at the Faculty of Commerce & Accountancy, Thammasat University in Thailand.

He received his PhD in 2001, in the field of International Logistics within the Logistics & Operations Management Section (LOMS) at Cardiff Business School (UK). He was the winner of the James Cooper Cup in 2001 for the best PhD dissertation in logistics from the Chartered Institute of Logistics and Transport (CILT) in the United Kingdom.

Ruth's main research interests are in the field of multimodal transport, international logistics and supply chain performance measurements. He has published over 70 papers and reports in such journals as *International Journal of Physical Distribution and Logistics Management*, *International Journal of Logistics Research and Application*, *Asia Pacific Journal of Marketing and Logistics*, *Journal of Applied Sciences*, *Maritime Policy and Management*, and he has co-authored 10 books.

Since 1995, Ruth has been a consultant for international agencies such as the United Nations Conference on Trade & Development (UNCTAD), the United Nations Economic and Social Commission for Asia and the Pacific (UN-ESCAP), The World Bank, The Asian Development Bank (ADB), The Association of South East Asian Nations (ASEAN).

Anthony Beresford, Reader, Transport and Shipping Research Group, Cardiff Business School, Cardiff University, UK.

Having graduated with a BA Honours degree in Geography from Manchester University in 1977, Anthony was awarded his PhD in Environmental Sciences at the University of East Anglia in 1982. He has travelled widely in an advisory capacity within the ports and transport fields in Europe, Africa, Asia and North America. He has been involved in a broad range of transport-related research and consultancy projects including: Transport Rehabilitation, Aid Distribution and Trade Facilitation for

UNCTAD and for the Rwandan government (1995, 1998); Cost Structures on Multimodal Transport Corridors in South East Asia (1998–2006); and Improvement of Transit Transport Systems in Africa, Asia and Latin America, 1999 (UNCTAD). Most recently he has been working on humanitarian supply chain operations in the context of man-made emergencies and natural disasters. He is a member of the Cardiff–Cranfield Humanitarian Logistics Initiative, a research group developing research interests in the area of humanitarian aid distribution.

Martijn Blansjaar is Head of Logistics and Supply in OXFAM GB's International Division.

He first entered the field of humanitarian logistics when he joined MSF-Holland in 1987, in Uganda. Having spent several years in a variety of field-based positions, for a number of organizations, he relocated to MSF-H's head quarters in Amsterdam, assigned to evaluate special operations. Among these were MSF's extensive pharmaceutical distribution projects in Former Yugoslavia, and the major crisis interventions in Rwanda and Zaire. He was also involved in the redesign of MSF's supply and programme approach to food aid. Martijn combined his hands-on experience with a study of integrated logistics management, followed by undertaking an MBA in the late 1990s. In 1997 he was appointed Coordinator for Technical Support in MSF-Holland, and in 2001 he became MSF-Holland Director of Logistics.

Martijn is a member of the Executive Committee of the Humanitarian Logistics Association, a Board member of the Helios Foundation for supply chain, and member of the Advisory Committee that works with the Fritz Institute and the Chartered Institute of Logistics and Transport (CILT) to develop and maintain a professional Certification for Humanitarian Logistics. He regularly appears as a guest lecturer and contributed to research and curriculum development of various institutions including MIT Zaragoza, Cranfield, USI Lugano, INSEAD and Hanken.

Prof **Paul SN Buatsi** is the Managing Consultant of Omega Strategic Resources Ltd (Accra, Ghana). He is a Professor of Marketing and International Business with research interest in humanitarian logistics. He is a former Chief Director of the Ministry of Education (Ghana), Dean of the Graduate School of Business at the Ghana Institute of Management and Public Administration (Accra, Ghana), and the founding Dean of the KNUST School of Business, Kwame Nkrumah University of Science and Technology (Kumasi, Ghana). He is also a founding member of the HUMLOG Group of humanitarian logistics.

Martin Christopher is Emeritus Professor of Marketing and Logistics at Cranfield School of Management. His work in the field of logistics and supply chain management has gained international recognition. He has published widely and his recent books include *Logistics and Supply Chain*

Management and *Marketing Logistics*. Martin Christopher co-founded the *International Journal of Logistics Management* and was its joint editor for 18 years. He is a regular contributor to conferences and workshops around the world.

At Cranfield, Martin Christopher chairs the Advisory Board of the Centre for Logistics and Supply Chain Management, the largest activity of its type in Europe. In addition to leading a number of ongoing research projects in logistics and supply chain management, Martin Christopher is active as an advisor to many organizations and is non-executive Director of LCP Consulting, a specialist consulting service in the fields of logistics and supply chain management.

Martin Christopher is an Emeritus Fellow of the Chartered Institute of Logistics and Transport. He is also a Fellow of the Chartered Institute of Purchasing & Supply and a Fellow of the Chartered Institute of Marketing. In 1988 he was awarded the Sir Robert Lawrence Gold Medal for his contribution to logistics education, in 1997 he was given the USA Council of Logistics Management's Foundation Award, and in 2005 he received the Distinguished Service Award from the USA Council of Supply Chain Management Professionals. In 2007 he was appointed a Foundation Professor of the UK Chartered Institute of Purchasing & Supply and in 2008 he was awarded the Swinbank Award for Lifetime Achievement by the same Institute.

He is Visiting Professor/Guest Professor at the University of Hull, England; Instituto Empresa, Madrid; IESE, Barcelona; Macquarie University, Australia; the Kuehne Logistics University, Hamburg; and Chalmers University, Gothenburg.

Major General (Retired) **Tim Cross** CBE was commissioned into the British Army in 1971. He has commanded at every level, from leading a small bomb disposal team in Northern Ireland in the 1970s to commanding a Division of 30,000 in 2004/07. He completed a tour with the UN in Cyprus in 1980/81 before attending the Army Staff Course in 1983, returning as a member of the teaching staff in 1987. After an operational deployment to Kuwait/Iraq in 1990/91, he attended the Higher Command and Staff Course in early 1995 before serving as a Colonel in Bosnia in 1995/96 and 1997. In 1999, as a Brigadier in command of 101 Logistic Brigade, he deployed to Macedonia, Albania and Kosovo and was appointed CBE in the subsequent operational awards for his work in leading the NATO response to the humanitarian crisis.

Handing over command in 2000 he attended the Royal College of Defence Studies and then, in 2002, he became involved in the planning for operations in Iraq; he subsequently deployed to Washington, Kuwait and Baghdad as the Deputy in the US-led Office of Reconstruction and Humanitarian Affairs, later re-titled the CPA (the Coalition Provisional Authority). He returned to the UK in 2003, took over a key staff appointment before assuming command of one of the three Divisions of the UK Field Army from October 2004, retiring in January 2007.

He is now a Director of two International Aid Agencies, a Visiting Professor at three Universities, a Defence Adviser to the UK House of Commons Defence Committee and a number of UK/International Companies, and a Trustee of a number of charities.

Rachel A Dowty is an Assistant Professor – Research, at Louisiana State University's (LSU's) Department of Geography and Anthropology and Co-Director of LSU's Disaster Science and Management (DSM) Program in the School of Humanities and Social Sciences. She received her PhD from Rensselaer Polytechnic Institute in the field of Science and Technology Studies (STS), researching how culture shapes scientific and technological standards for rational decision making. She developed low-impact methods for response to oil spill crises in Louisiana marshlands while earning her MS in wetlands ecology from Southeastern Louisiana University. Prior to receiving her PhD in STS, she served as a faculty member of biological sciences and environmental sciences at Southeastern Louisiana University, the State University of New York (SUNY) at Plattsburgh and at Clinton Community College.

Deborah Ellis is a supply chain consultant based in Sydney where, since 1990, she has conducted projects in Australia, Asia and Europe in a wide range of industries including industrial, FMCG, retail, resources and banking. Her consulting practice, Carpenter Ellis, has in recent years undertaken logistics reviews, network modelling projects and a series of ground-breaking projects for the banking industry applying supply chain principles to the distribution of cash. She has also collaborated with Dr John Gattorna on the Dynamic Alignment framework for supply chains, and on industry-level engagements for the Australian coal industry, the Textiles, Clothing and Footwear industry and the Australian Meat and Livestock industry. Earlier in her career Deborah held line responsibility for logistics operations with Master Foods (Mars Corporation), and in third-party perishable distribution with Frigmobile (Swire).

Deborah is now expanding her focus into non-commercial supply chains, particularly those that support development in resource-poor countries. She is currently undertaking a PhD at Macquarie Graduate School of Management (MGSM) in the high-reliability supply chains needed to improve access and availability to life-critical medications such as insulin, and has convened discussions in 2010 in a cross-sector seminar on Humanitarian and Development Supply Chain issues.

Jarrod Goentzel received a PhD from the School of Industrial and Systems Engineering at the Georgia Institute of Technology, a MS in Applied Mathematics from Colorado State University and a BA in Mathematics from Tabor College with studies at the Technical University of Budapest (Hungary). He is currently the Executive Director of the MIT Supply Chain Management Program. In this role, he is responsible for design and management of the nine-month professional Master's degree program, including admissions, curriculum, placement and alumni relations. He has developed graduate-level courses in supply chain finance, international operations and humanitarian logistics. He is also Research Director of the Humanitarian Logistics Initiative and the Renewable Energy Delivery project at the MIT Center for Transportation & Logistics.

Previously, Dr Goentzel directed the MIT-Zaragoza International Logistics Program, leading MIT's role in developing novel education, research, and outreach programmes with the Zaragoza Logistics Center in Spain. Before joining MIT in 2003, Dr Goentzel held senior management positions in supply chain consulting and product development with a large ERP company and technology startups. He has also worked with humanitarian and global health organizations such as World Food Programme, Oxfam, International Rescue Committee, Partners In Health and USAID to develop supply chains that effectively meet needs.

Kate Hughes is a business consultant with extensive experience in managing research projects sponsored by industry, government and not-for-profits over the past 10 years. Her primary focus is on supply chain management, marketing and industry clusters. She is employed part-time at the Macquarie Graduate School of Management (MGSM) as a Research Associate to promote research clusters and support university–business collaboration and funding. Her academic qualifications include a Bachelor of Science (Honors) and a Masters of Applied Science from the University of New South Wales, and an MBA from MGSM. Kate is currently completing a PhD focusing on managerial decision-making in humanitarian supply chain response, also at MGSM. She can be contacted at kate.hughes@hughes-scm.com.

Gyöngyi Kovács (DSc (Econ)) is the Director of the Humanitarian Logistics and Supply Chain Research Institute (HUMLOG Institute) that has been established by the Hänken School of Economics and the (Finnish) National Defence University. She is also the co-editor of the *Journal of Humanitarian Logistics and Supply Chain Management* and one of the European editors of the *International Journal of Physical Distribution and Logistics Management*. Her research interests include humanitarian logistics as well as corporate responsibility in the supply chain, industrial ecology and questions of research design and methods. She can be reached at: kovacs@hanken.fi; Humanitarian Logistics and Supply Chain Research Institute (HUMLOG Institute), Hanken School of Economics, PO Box 479, 00101 Helsinki, Finland.

Melissa Labonte is Assistant Professor of Political Science at Fordham University. She received her PhD in Political Science from Brown University. Her research interests include humanitarian politics, inter-governmental and non-governmental organizations, peace-building, conflict resolution, and human rights. Her most recent publication is *Jus Post Bellum*, Non-State

Actors, and Peacebuilding: Lessons from Afghanistan, in (eds) E Heinze and B Steele, *Ethics, Authority, and War: Non-state actors and the just war tradition* (Palgrave-Macmillan, 2009). She is currently finalizing a book manuscript entitled *The Promise and Peril of Implementing the Responsibility to Protect: Back to the future?*

Fordham University, Department of Political Science, 441 E. Fordham Road, Bronx, NY 10458, USA; tel: +1 718 817 3959; e-mail: labonte@fordham.edu

Paul D Larson PhD is the CN Professor of SCM at the University of Manitoba. He is Head of the SCM Department and Director of the Transport Institute. From 1979 to 1981, he worked in Fiji, as a United States Peace Corps Volunteer. In October 2009, he organized and hosted a conference on relationship building in humanitarian supply chains in Ottawa, Canada. He has consulted on and conducted executive seminars in Europe, North and South America, Australia, the Caribbean and China. Dr Larson serves on the Editorial Review Boards of the *International Journal of Physical Distribution and Logistics Management*, the *Journal of Business Logistics*, the *Journal of Humanitarian Logistics* and the *Journal of Supply Chain Management*. His research interests include supply chain risk management, supply chain sustainability and humanitarian logistics.

David M Moore is a Director of the Centre for Defence Acquisition with Cranfield University at the Defence Academy of the United Kingdom. He worked in purchasing, logistics and supply chain management in public sector and commercial organizations before entering academia. After a period at the University of Glamorgan, he joined Cranfield University in 1997 where he developed a number of Masters programmes. He has undertaken extensive education, training and consultancy assignments in the UK, USA, Europe, Middle East and Far East. Particular interests include outsourcing, the use of contractors for service provision, developing effectiveness through professionalism and humanitarian logistics (especially the contribution that can be delivered from joint military, commercial and NGO cooperation). He has written a number of books and book chapters plus conference and journal papers, and served in the RLC (TA) until 1999 in the rank of Lieutenant Colonel.

Stephen Pettit graduated with a BSc Honours degree in Maritime Geography from Cardiff University in 1989 and was awarded a PhD from the University of Wales in 1993. Subsequently he has been involved in a range of transport-related research projects including a groundbreaking project for the Department of Transport studying the UK economy's requirements for people with seafaring experience. His most recent research work has considered aspects of the logistics of humanitarian aid delivery. He first worked on a project that was funded by the Chartered Institute of Logistics and Transport through their Seedcorn Grant scheme and was co-researcher with Dr Anthony

Beresford. Stephen has contributed to many academic papers, conference papers and reports; his broad research interests include port development, port policy and the logistics of humanitarian aid delivery. He is a member of the Cardiff–Cranfield Humanitarian Logistics Initiative, a research group developing research interests in the area of humanitarian aid.

Jersey Seipel is a Lecturer in Humanitarian Logistics and Supply Chain Management at both Massey University in New Zealand, and at the University of Sydney, Australia.

Following training as logistician for Médecins sans Frontières, he spent nearly a decade in various humanitarian aid roles, supporting relief missions in Africa and Asia. His assignments included South Sudan, Congo, Burundi, Cambodia, Afghanistan and Indonesia, where he was involved in the Boxing Day 2004 tsunami recovery phase as logistics delegate for the Red Cross in Sumatra. He also gained valuable experience as project manager and head of mission in Phnom Penh and Kabul, which he is now employing in his role as a university lecturer and researcher.

Karen Spens is Professor of Supply Chain Management and Corporate Geography at Hanken School of Economics in Helsinki, Finland. She has written several book chapters and published in logistics and supply chain journals such as *International Journal of Physical Distribution and Logistics Management*, *International Journal of Logistics Management* and *Supply Chain Management: An International Journal* as well as in other journals such as *Disaster Prevention and Management*. She has also edited several special issues for various journals, such as *Management Research News*, and is currently co-editor of the *Journal of Humanitarian Logistics and Supply Chain Management*. Her research interests include humanitarian logistics, healthcare-related research and methodological issues in logistics and supply chain management.

Peter Tatham joined the Royal Navy in 1970 and served in a variety of appointments during his career of some 35 years during which he rose to the rank of Commodore. Highlights include Logistics Officer of the Aircraft Carrier HMS *Invincible* in 1994/5 during operations in Bosnia against the Former Republic of Yugoslavia, and Chief Staff Officer responsible for all high level personnel and logistics issues emanating from the 10,000 sailors and 30 surface ships in the Royal Navy (1999–2000). His final four years in the Service were spent in the UK's Defence Logistics Organisation where he was responsible for key elements of the internal programme of Change Management (2000–04). Following his retirement from the RN, he joined the faculty of Cranfield University where he lectured in Human Systems and Military and Humanitarian Logistics. He was awarded his PhD in 2009 for research into the issues surrounding the role of shared values within UK military supply networks. Peter has recently joined the faculty of Griffith University in Queensland, Australia, as a Senior Lecturer in Logistics and Supply Network Management.

He has published on defence and humanitarian logistics in a variety of journals and has edited special editions on the latter subject in the *International Journal of Physical Distribution and Logistics Management* (IJPDLM) and in *Management Research News* (MRN). He is the Australian editor of the *Journal of Humanitarian Logistics and Supply Chain Management* and in 2010 he was awarded the Emerald/EFM Outstanding Doctoral Research Award for his investigation of UK military supply networks.

David H Taylor PhD has been involved in logistics and supply chain management for over 20 years, working in manufacturing, consultancy and academia. Between 1997 and 2010 he was Senior Research Fellow in the Logistics and Operations Management Section of Cardiff Business School where he was a member of the Lean Enterprise Research Centre and Co-Director of the Food Process Innovation Unit. His research has involved the development and application of innovative approaches to the application of lean concepts and methodologies to supply chain improvement. He has published three books and over 30 articles on supply chain management in both academic and practitioner journals. David currently holds the position of Visiting Fellow in the Centre for Defence Acquisition at Cranfield University, where he is responsible for a Humanitarian Logistics module on a Masters degree programme. He is also the Director of the Cardiff–Cranfield Humanitarian Logistics Initiative, is a founder member of the Chartered Institute of Logistics and Transport 'HELP' initiative, and is on the board of directors of the Humanitarian Logistics Association.

Fuminori Toyasaki is an Assistant Professor at the School of Administrative Studies, York University, Canada. He has been conducting research in the area of sustainable operations, including closed-loop supply chains and humanitarian logistics. He received an NSERC Discovery Grant for his research project on closed-loop supply chains in 2009. In the humanitarian logistics area, he has researched the fundraising operations for NGO disaster relief projects. He developed the first course on 'Disaster and Logistics' at York University and is expected to teach it from 2012.

Charl van der Merwe is SMS Project Coordinator, Oxfam International. Charl started his career as an Urban Planner after studying for a BSc in Town and Regional Planning in South Africa. Working as an urban planner in South Africa provided exposure to the poverty and injustice in former townships in South Africa. Charl joined Oxfam GB in 2002 during the Southern African Food Crises Response. Since then Charl has been part of Oxfam's emergency response teams working in emergencies such as Darfur and the Asian tsunami. He moved to Oxford in 2005 to join Oxfam GB Head Office in a new role as IS Project Manager for Logistics and Supply. Charl was responsible for the process of migrating Oxfam GB from paper-based supply chain and logistics systems to an integrated web-based supply chain management information system. This resulted in an organizational change process that includes business transformation supported by the implementation of Helios in 2009.

During his time in Oxford Charl obtained his PRINCE 2 Practitioner certification, and is currently working on his dissertation for his MSc in Project Management. In 2009 Charl joined Oxfam International as Project Coordinator for the Oxfam Single Management Structure project.

Tina Wakolbinger is an Assistant Professor at Fogelman College of Business and Economics, University of Memphis. She conducts research in the area of humanitarian and sustainable supply chain management. Her research interests lie in the modelling and analysis of complex decision making on network systems with a specific focus on global issues. She explores the impacts of relationships, information and financial flows on supply chain operations. Her publications include articles in *International Journal of Production Research*, *International Journal of Production Economics*, and *Naval Research Logistics*.

Michael C Whiting BA (Hons) is a Fellow of the Chartered Institute of Purchasing and Supply and a Fellow of the Chartered Institute of Logistics and Transport (CILT) with some 47 years of international logistics experience. Michael has a passion for humanitarian logistics, and is the Chairman of the CILT UK Humanitarian Emergency Logistics Professionals (HELP) Forum. He has taken part in the humanitarian response to the Indian Ocean tsunami in 2004, Nias earthquake March 2005, Hurricane Katrina in the USA September 2005, the Yogyakarta earthquake in Indonesia in May 2006, Cyclone Nargis in Myanmar in May 2008, the Haiti earthquake in January 2010 when he worked with USAF, and most recently the Pakistan floods August 2010.

Michael is a Trustee of RedR UK, a founder member of the Cardiff–Cranfield Humanitarian Logistics Initiative, a Stakeholder of ELRHA (Enhancing Learning & Research for Humanitarian Assistance) and a member of the Humanitarian Logistics Association.

Michael has contributed to two books – *Dynamic Supply Chain Alignment* by Professor John Gattorna and Friends, published by Gower, July 2009, and a second collaborative work that is still in production examining humanitarian logistics post-Indian Ocean tsunami 2004. He has written numerous magazine articles and papers on many aspects of humanitarian logistics that have been published in the United Kingdom, Unites States and Australia.

Michael lectures on Humanitarian Logistics at the UK Defence Academy, Chester, and Plymouth Universities.

Introduction

MARTIN CHRISTOPHER AND PETER TATHAM

The global demand for humanitarian assistance, including requests for assistance by national governments, continues to rise. This is triggered and sustained by increased severity of natural hazards, escalating conflict, and a dramatic increase in vulnerabilities caused by the global financial crisis, continuing high food prices, the scarcity of energy and water, population growth and urbanization.[1]

This gloomy prediction from the UN Secretary General underscores the massive challenge facing the world and its population as we reached the end of the first decade of the 21st century. Indeed, even if global peace were to break out tomorrow, the reality is that an increasing population (and individuals' associated rising expectations) is putting enormous pressures both on the world's resources and on the generic infrastructure supporting them. It is no wonder, therefore, that disasters frequently strike those countries that are the least prepared, both economically and socially, to deal with them. Indeed, as Kahn[2] succinctly observes, the per capita GDP is a key indicator of disaster casualty rates.

Although it would be wonderful if such challenges could be solved via the stroke of the editors' pens – this is, of course, not the case. It will take far more than the thoughts of those involved in this volume to alter the social, political and environmental trajectory of the world. So, faced with the reality of an annual occurrence of some 350 natural disasters,[3] what insights *can* those involved in the preparation for, and response to, such events bring to bear?

More specifically, and as betrayed by its title, this volume seeks to understand the nature of the challenges facing those who are involved in the management of the logistics of disaster relief, and to offer some potential solutions that can be developed in the near and longer term. Many of those contributing have spent considerable periods thinking about such issues, be this in a commercial, a humanitarian or a military context. We aim, therefore, to try to bring these perspectives together as a means of offering ways in which particular aspects of this complex and evolving problem might be tackled.

But why focus on logisticians? The answer is simple – be it in the context of a rapid- or slow-onset disaster – the imperative is to procure and move the required materiel (water, food, shelter, clothing, medicines, etc) from point A to point B in the most efficient and effective way possible. But although simply stated, the reality is hugely complicated and, indeed, costly – not least because of the difficulty of forecasting when and where the next crisis will occur. It is unsurprising therefore, that recent estimates would suggest that as much as 80 per cent of the expenditure of aid agencies is on logistics[4] (as described above). Given that the overall annual expenditure of such agencies is of the order of US $20 billion, the resultant logistic spend of some US $15 billion provides a huge potential area for improvement, and consequential benefit to those affected by such disasters.

In the light of these almost self-evident observations, it is really quite surprising that, until relatively recently, the challenges of humanitarian logistics have not attracted serious consideration by the academic community at large. Certainly a number of important contributions have been made, with one of the earliest by Douglas Long and Donald Wood in 1995,[5] however, it is suggested that the South East Asia tsunami of 2004 really provided the catalyst for the current sustained level of interest. Not least, the publicity surrounding this catastrophic event underlined the importance of the logistics challenge as exemplified by the reported remarks of a European ambassador who observed in the immediate aftermath: 'We don't need a donors' conference, we need a logistics conference.'[6]

Arguably, however, the timing of this recognition of the importance of the logistic element of a humanitarian response has had a fortuitous aspect. By the early part of the millennium, the processes underpinning the operation of the fast-moving consumer goods (FCMG) retail business within the developed world had reached a significant degree of sophistication. This reflected the cumulative learning over the previous 20 years and, as a result, a number of key principles had been developed and understood. Thus, to many observers, the post-tsunami challenges (and, indeed, those of subsequent disasters such as the Pakistan earthquake and the series of hurricanes that devastated parts of the southern United States in 2005, Cyclone Nargis in the Bay of Bengal (2008) and most recently the 2010 earthquake in Haiti and flooding in Pakistan), have the potential to be mitigated through the application of appropriate tools and techniques that have proved beneficial in a commercial context.

But, of course, the challenges of humanitarian logistics have a number of key aspects that clearly differentiate them from those of the commercial world. First and foremost among these is the massive uncertainty surrounding, in particular, rapid-onset events. Thus, while we know that such events will unquestionably occur, their timing and location is hugely difficult to predict with any significant degree of certainty. Second, the humanitarian field faces the challenge of a de-coupling of financial and material flows. As a result, aid agencies are placed in the difficult position of having to second guess the needs of the beneficiaries who are frequently solely focused on the business of staying alive – and yet, at the same time, the agencies must satisfy the increasingly demanding governance requirements of the donor community. Therefore, while many management gurus would argue strongly that the voice of the customer should always be paramount in an organization's thinking, the absence of clarity over the identity of the humanitarian logistician's customer remains unhelpful and can lead to perverse behaviour.

Third, almost by definition, the infrastructure surrounding the disaster will be devastated to a greater or lesser extent. Thus, generic prescriptions such as the substitution of information for inventory face a particular challenge in this environment. Finally, of course, the price of failure in terms of unnecessary loss of life or prolonged hardship is significantly greater than that of reduced profits.

Fortunately, all is not gloom and this edition represents part of the effort of the academic and practitioner community to develop novel solutions to these challenges. In doing so, it reflects the growing determination of these communities to bring together their knowledge and experience and to build on the increasing body of thought that is being exposed through a broad range of journals, conferences and international groups, such as the 'HUMLOG initiative;[7] in Australia through the Australia/New Zealand Academy of Management (ANZAM) supply chain special interest group; and, in the UK context, the collaboration between Cardiff and Cranfield Universities, which have pooled their logistic expertise in a common effort to overcome some of the issues outlined above.

However, in setting the scene for this volume, we propose to begin by exploring the challenge of how to manage supply networks when future requirements are manifestly uncertain – which is, of course, one of the most challenging aspects of humanitarian relief programmes.

Managing supply networks under conditions of uncertainty

One of the distinguishing features of modern supply networks – both in the world of business as well as in the humanitarian arena – is that they are characterized by uncertainty and, hence, unpredictability. For some time now commercial supply-network managers have become accustomed to the idea that they can no longer rely on the traditional rules and techniques that have allowed them to plan ahead with a degree of confidence.

Thus, although conventional supply-network management typically assumes a degree of stability with planning horizons that extend some months into the future, the last few decades have seen a considerable increase in turbulence in the wider business environment. Demand can no longer be easily forecast and supply conditions have become more volatile in almost every industry. As a result of this uncertainty new business models have emerged to enable organizations to make the transition from the classic 'forecast-driven' approach to a much more 'event-' or 'demand-driven' capability.

Organizations doing business in turbulent markets have learned that one of the key elements to ensure survival is 'agility'. This can be defined as the ability to respond rapidly to unexpected changes in demand or supply conditions – and, indeed, to changes in the wider business environment.

It can thus be argued that the logistical capabilities required by aid agencies and others to deal successfully with large-scale, sudden-onset disasters are not dissimilar to those required in commercial organiszations faced with rapidly changing conditions. There is, therefore, an excellent opportunity to learn from the experiences of companies who have become adept in responding rapidly to unpredictable events.

Because all organizations are part of a wider network of suppliers, intermediaries and customers, it is important to recognize that agility is not just about achieving internal responsiveness, but rather about how the end-to-end supply network can become more agile. Thus, the concept of agility has significant implications for how organizations within the supply/ demand network relate to each other, and how they can best work together to maximize the efficiency and effectiveness of the network as a whole. It has been suggested that there are a number of key prerequisites to the design and management of such agile supply networks.[8] Specifically, agile organizations tend to exhibit certain characteristics; agility implies that they are demand- or event-driven, they are network-based, they are process oriented and they are virtually integrated through shared information.

Demand- and event-driven

Traditional management practice has been based upon the principle of planning ahead, usually based upon a forecast. In conditions of turbulence and unpredictability, however, the challenge is to create a capability to facilitate a rapid response to events as they happen. A fundamental enabler of demand/event-driven responsiveness is time compression. Much of the time that is consumed in supply networks could be termed 'non-value adding time'. In other words this is time when nothing is happening to achieve the goal of the 'right product in the right place at the right time'. Sometimes this non-value adding time is incurred because of cumbersome planning and decision-making processes. At other times it may arise because of queues at bottlenecks, or because of inadequate coordination across the different stages in the supply network. As a result, many commercial organizations have transformed their responsiveness by a strong focus on what has been called 'business process re-engineering'[9] whereby every underpinning process in the supply network is put under the spotlight with the intention of squeezing out as much non-value adding time as possible.

Demand- and event-driven supply networks are also often characterized by their strategic use of inventory and capacity. Conventional wisdom is often driven by the desire to follow 'lean' principles of reducing inventory and eliminating idle capacity. Agile supply networks on the other hand recognize that in conditions of uncertainty – both on the demand side and the supply side – a certain level of 'slack' is essential. Ideally, such strategic inventory is held as far upstream as possible and in a generic form to enable 'risk pooling' – in other words, rather than disperse the inventory in its final form and run the risk of having the wrong product in the wrong place, it is held centrally, shipped and configured on a just-in-time (JIT) basis. Clearly this approach will incur a cost penalty compared to the 'leaner' alternative, but that is the price of responsiveness.

Network-based

One way that organizations can enhance their agility is by making use of the capacity, capabilities and resources of other entities within the network. It could be financially crippling for one organization to have to carry enough capacity and inventory to, for example, cope with any demand eventuality. However, if close working relationships can be established with other organizations that can provide access to their own resources, then a real opportunity exists for creating high levels of flexibility in the supply network.

A good example of how network partners can enable a more agile capability in the commercial world is provided by the Spanish clothing manufacturer and retailer, Zara. Because Zara competes in a market characterized by unpredictability and short product life cycles, the need for agility is high. One way that Zara achieves this agility is by making use of a network of small, independent workshops that do the final sewing of many of their products. Zara has established strong working relationships with these suppliers and regards them as part of their 'extended enterprise'. These external workshops reserve capacity for Zara even though they will not know the precise requirements until a few days before the garment is to be manufactured.

In other cases organizations can benefit by sharing resources across a network even with competitors. Thus, for example, petrol companies such as Shell, BP and Total will often share refinery capacity, while in the airline industry different airlines will pool their inventory of service parts and position these strategically around the world. In a similar way, the Armed Forces of the NATO countries use a common parts identification system that facilitates an equivalent approach.

Indeed, in the world of humanitarian logistics, such a resource-sharing model has recently been created to enable access to a common inventory, with the United Nations Humanitarian Response Depot (UNHRD) network, which is coordinated by the World Food Programme (WFP) in Italy, being a case in point.

Process-oriented

One feature of organizations that can respond rapidly to unpredictable events is that they have achieved a high level of cross-functional working. Most conventional businesses tend to be organized around functions, eg the production function, the distribution function, etc. This type of organizational structure may be administratively convenient, but it often leads to an inwardly focused 'silo' mentality. It also means that there are usually multiple 'hands-offs' from one department to another. The end result is that the decision-making process is lengthy, and that lead-times are extended.

The alternative is to break down the silos by adopting a cross-functional team-based approach that reflects the key business processes – particularly the supply-network processes. Processes are the horizontal, market-facing sequences of activities that create value for customers. In the context of supply networks they include such key underpinning processes as order-to-delivery, capacity and demand management, and supplier management. For each of these processes a 'process owner' should be appointed whose task is to bring together a cross-functional team and to seek to create a seamless and more rapid achievement of the process goals. Thus, for example, the order-to-delivery process will consider how a customer's requirement can be met in shorter timeframes with more reliability by 'project managing' the order from the moment it is captured until it is delivered. Usually when processes are managed in this way, opportunities for process simplification and improvement quickly become apparent.

Furthermore, if the supply network is to work effectively across multiple independent entities, it is critical that processes are aligned across organizational boundaries. A good example of such process alignment is provided by the concept of vendor-managed inventory (VMI). Under a VMI arrangement, the sales outlet (say a supermarket) does not formally place an order on the supplier; rather they provide the supplier with regularly updated information (usually extracted from the point of sale systems) on the rate at which the customer's inventory of the product in question is being depleted. The supplier then automatically replenishes the inventory. It is akin to a closed-loop supply network process.

Virtually integrated

By definition, for global supply networks to achieve high levels of agility there must be a corresponding level of *connectivity*. Historically, such connectivity may have been achieved through ownership and control – a state often described as 'vertical' integration. Today, the likelihood is that the supply network will be fragmented and dispersed with each entity independent from the others. However, the need for integration is still as vital as ever, but now the essential integration is not achieved through ownership and control but rather through shared information and collaborative working. This type of connectivity is often called 'virtual integration'.

The underpinning idea of virtual integration is that an agile capability can be enabled through enhanced visibility. Ideally all parties in the network should share information in as close to real time as possible. This information will include the actual requirement from the field (demand), current inventory dispositions, the supply schedule and event management alerts.

Many traditional supply networks have poor upstream and downstream visibility with little shared information. Hence they are prone to mismatches of supply and demand at every interface – a situation made worse by the so-called 'bullwhip' effect that amplifies disturbances in the demand signal as orders are passed up the supply network. Bullwhips can be dramatically reduced or even eliminated if the different echelons in the supply network can be linked through shared information.

The barrier to improved visibility is, however, no longer technological. The tools exist to enable the highest levels of connectivity in even the most fragmented global network. The real challenge is the reluctance that still exists within some organizations to share information across boundaries – be these internal or external. The most agile supply networks are typified by a mindset of collaborative working with other partners in the network based upon a spirit of trust and shared goals.

Lessons from best practice

It may sometimes seem banal or inappropriate to ask the question 'what can humanitarian logistics learn from best practice in the commercial sector?' Although there can be no question that the challenge of saving lives is significantly more important than improving on-the-shelf availability of consumer products in a retail outlet, we would argue that there *are* lessons that can be learned and through which humanitarian logistics practice can be improved.

We have suggested that the key connection between the worlds of commerce and humanitarian logistics is that of uncertainty, and we have highlighted how, to a certain extent, such uncertainty can be conquered through agility. But one of the biggest remaining barriers to supply network agility is complexity. In a global supply network this complexity comes in many forms, but one of its most potent manifestations is in the multitude of nodes and links that constitute the network.

As Figure 0.1 suggests, what are often referred to as 'supply chains' are not really chains; rather they are networks or webs of inter-connected and inter-dependent entities. The resulting complexity can be considerable and, unless a means is found of managing across these nodes and links, the system will be prone to disturbance and disruption. The challenge is to synchronize activities across the network so that a more agile response to changes in demand can be achieved. One idea that is attracting attention is the concept of supply network 'orchestration', and a good example of such orchestration is provided by the Hong Kong-based company, Li & Fung.

Li & Fung work on behalf of clients, mainly retailers, who are seeking to source products made to their own specification. Thus, for example, the global retailer Wal-Mart might decide that for the next winter season in the USA they want to introduce a range of low-priced ski wear. Acting on their behalf, Li & Fung will identify the appropriate designers, they will source the different fabrics, fasteners and zips, they will contract with appropriate manufacturers, and manage the whole supply network from raw materials through to Wal-Mart's stores. Li & Fung's capability as an orchestrator comes from their specialist knowledge of the industry, their long-standing relationships with suppliers, and their information systems that enable them to coordinate and synchronize the flows of material and product across a complex network.

Sometimes the supply network orchestrator is termed a Lead Logistics Provider or a 4PL (Fourth Party Logistics) provider, and companies such as DHL, UPS and FedEx are increasingly taking on this role on behalf of global corporations. For example, Cisco, one of the world's leading suppliers of communication network equipment, use UPS to coordinate a large part of their global network of contract manufacturers, distribution service providers and component suppliers to enable a high level of synchronization in what has become a very volatile marketplace. Again, this synchronization is greatly enabled by real-time information that is shared across the partners in Cisco's global network.

The way forward

It seems that the common thread running through agile supply networks is a focus on synchronization enabled by shared information. Clearly there are other enablers of agility such as process alignment and collaboration across inter- and intra-organizational boundaries, but 360° visibility appears to be the critical element. Given that meeting the challenges facing the humanitarian logistic community would seem to demand the ultimate in

FIGURE 0.1 The two generic categories of risk

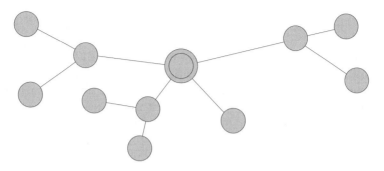

- Supply chains comprise nodes and links

- Nodes – organizational risk
- Links – connectivity risk

agile response, it is heartening to recognize that, as reflected in the contributions contained within this book, this message is now gaining traction and that there is a growing commitment to breaking down the barriers to much closer collaboration across organizational boundaries.

In approaching the challenge of developing a volume on humanitarian logistics, as editors we were especially keen to present as diverse a set of perspectives as was practicable. In particular, we believed that an improved understanding of the challenges and solutions could be gained by garnering contributions from both a geographically diverse community as well as from practitioners (as distinct from academics). It is, however, a sad reality that the real world events of 2010 conspired against us as a succession of major events, including the Haiti earthquake, the Pakistan flooding and the Indonesian volcanic eruption made for an even more frenetic year that usual for the disaster-response community. As a result, and to their considerable regret, a key contribution from George Fenton of World Vision International and Mike Goodhand of British Red Cross was never able to make it onto the written page – although they have promised to do better for the 2nd edition!!

In line with our theme that there are potential lessons that humanitarian logisticians can develop from emerging business best practice, *Professor Paul Larson* from the University of Manitoba, Canada, explores these issues more fully in Chapter 1. In particular, Paul reflects on the potential for an approach that considers the application of commercial and academic models of risk management to the humanitarian logistics network. In doing so, he powerfully reminds us that, ultimately, the supply network is operated by individuals who must endure considerable hardship and discomfort in carrying out their tasks for which much of the reward is in terms of self-satisfaction rather than in a tangible financial sense. Sadly, and all too frequently, such unsung heroes pay the ultimate price and, in that sense, this book can be seen as a small contribution to the global efforts to achieve a fairer and more just society.

In Chapter 2, *Dr Tina Wakolbinger* from the University of Memphis, USA, and *Dr Fuminori Toyasaki* of York University, Canada, reflect on a second of the key challenges facing the humanitarian logistic system as a whole. This emanates from the basic structure of the system for funding the preparation and response mechanisms, and these authors underline the importance of investing in logistic systems in the round. In doing so, they underline one of the key premises of this anthology, which is that significant improvements in the humanitarian response to disasters are, to a significant degree, conditional on achieving advantages in logistic practice and, preferably, transformation to supply network management with concomitant embodiment of the practices that have led to such massive improvements in the business environment.

As has been discussed earlier, a robust and comprehensive end-to-end communications system is one of the key ingredients underpinning the advances in commercial supply network management. Unsurprisingly, this is equally true of humanitarian logistics systems; however, persuading NGO management to invest in such a 'back office' (as distinct from 'front line') function has proved extremely difficult – notwithstanding the weight of evidence from other fields. Perhaps this reflects the very nature of non-profit organizations where the absence of the profit motive removes a key indicator that will inform strategic decision making. Nevertheless, a number of major NGOs such as Oxfam are making a concerted effort to improve the information systems supporting their supply networks. The challenge that this presents is explored by Oxfam GB's head of supply chain management *Martijn Blansjaar* and his colleague *Charl van der Merwe* in Chapter 3. Through a historical discussion of the various intertwined change programmes within Oxfam GB, this chapter powerfully demonstrates the importance of focusing on the organizational and interpersonal dimensions of the problem as well as those relating to the computer technology. The chapter also offers a tantalizing glimpse of the humanitarian supply network of the future that is underpinned by a common software package that significantly eases the cooperation and coordination challenges that have bedevilled the field.

Not least as a result of the absence of data relating to profit/loss in the humanitarian arena, the challenge of developing appropriate management metrics is particularly difficult in a non-profit environment. *Dr Peter Tatham* from the Graduate Business School of Griffith University, Australia, and *Kate Hughes*, a Res Associate at Macquarie University, Australia, explore this issue in Chapter 4. These authors note that, although there is a welcome improvement in the use of metrics to understand the efficiency of the supply network, achieving a better understanding of the outcome (or effectiveness) of the operation as a whole and specifically focusing on the aid beneficiaries, remains remarkably elusive.

The final chapter relating to the major issues facing those who wish to improve the humanitarian logistic response has been written by *Dr Nezih Altay* of De Paul University in the USA and his colleague *Dr Melissa Labonte* of Fordham University, also in the USA. Given that the response to many disasters sees a large number of UN agencies and NGOs operating in close geographic proximity, achieving coordinated action to meet the needs of those affected has long been recognized as one of the most significant challenges facing the humanitarian community as a whole. The most recent initiative to achieve a resolution to the resulting inefficiency has been developed through the United Nations Cluster system, and this is analysed in depth through the work of these two authors in Chapter 5.

In line with the approach to this book that has been outlined earlier, Chapter 6 is the first of three that take regional perspectives on a broad range of humanitarian logistic issues. Authored by *Dr Stephen Pettit* and *Dr Anthony Beresford* of Cardiff University, UK, *Mike Whiting* who both lectures at Cranfield University, UK, and is regularly deployed in the aftermath of disasters to assist in the management of helicopter and fixed-wing assets, and *Dr Ruth Banomyong* from Thammasat University, Thailand, this chapter takes a retrospective view of the 2004 SE Asia tsunami as it affected Thailand, and through this reflects on the logistic lessons identified and the associated progress towards their resolution. In doing so, it underlines many of the themes that have been touched on in this opening chapter, including the necessity for good communications and for appropriate coordination mechanisms.

Professor Paul Buatsi who, until recently, was the Dean of the Kwame Nkrumah University of Science and Technology in Ghana has kindly contributed Chapter 7, which draws on his extensive expertise in the management field. This essay emphasizes the extent to which the development of efficient and effective logistics processes is equally applicable in the environment of a developing country. Indeed, the absolute level of improvement generated by even limited advances in the practice of supply network management underscores the importance of working with local agencies and individuals to deliver transformational change in a way that is appropriate to the specific geographic and cultural context.

In stark contrast to the previous contribution, Chapter 8 contains a case study of the State of Florida that is used by *Dr Jarrod Goentzel* (from MIT) *and Professor Karen Spens* (of Hanken School of Economics, Finland) to describe the current arrangements for responding to disasters that affect that part of the USA. Indeed, given that the frequency and severity of the wind storms that strike Florida each year, it will be readily appreciated that these can only be loosely described as *uncertain* future events. As a result, the enormous scale and scope of the dormant preparation and response mechanism reflects the reality of the threats the population faces. In particular, however, this case study underlines the benefits of adopting a multi-agency approach, and of the need to fund the associated training and equipment in order to turn a powerful theoretical concept into reality.

Although not entirely focused on the problems of preparing for and responding to rapid-onset disasters, Chapter 9, which is the work of *Deb Ellis*, a researcher based in Sydney, Australia, reminds us that successful management of supply networks is equally important in the development field. Through a number of broadly based cases studies she expands the book's discussion significantly and demonstrates how important supply networks are to the ongoing delivery of support to populations that are facing a broad range of challenges. Conversely, she demonstrates that the failure to leverage the supply network in the case of those individuals suffering from diabetes clearly results in unnecessary death or prolonged suffering.

If one was to summarize many of the themes that this book has touched on at this stage, one might use the single word 'professionalization', and this is the theme of Chapter 10 contributed by *Dr David Moore* of Cranfield University, UK, and *Dr David Taylor* who, until recently, was a Senior Research Fellow at Cardiff University, UK. In a powerfully argued contribution, these authors discuss what is implied by the desire to increase the professionalization of humanitarian logistics and humanitarian logisticians and, in doing so argue strongly for the development of a 'body of knowledge' that records, criticizes, codifies and contextualizes the field. Although the authors fully recognize the enormity of such a challenge, they rightly observe that such a process, which can be found in many other walks of life, is a sure way to achieve improved performance – and, at least in part, this volume can be seen as a contribution to this goal.

In his book *Logistics and Supply Chain Management*, one of the editors of this volume has observed that key to a successful supply network is: 'The management of upstream and downstream relationships with suppliers and customers to deliver superior customer value at less cost to the supply chain as a whole.'[10] This theme of the importance of interpersonal relationships is taken up by *Dr Rachel Dowty*, from Louisiana State University in the USA in Chapter 11. In particular, she emphasizes the need for humanitarian logisticians to be aware of the cultural challenges that they face – be these related to those affected by a disaster, or to the differences that are manifest by different organizations that will meet up in the field.

This latter aspect of potential cultural dissonance is taken up in Chapter 12, which is the first of two that discusses the challenge of the humanitarian military interface. Written by *Jersey Seipel* from Massey University, New Zealand, this chapter reflects the author's significant experience and expertise as a logistician working for, among others, Médecins sans Frontières (MSF), Action Contre La Faim (ACF), the German Red Cross and Caritas in Sudan, Cambodia, Indonesia and Afghanistan. Reflecting on the benefits and challenges of improved humanitarian/military cooperation, the chapter recommends an approach that develops the interface through engagement in the form of discussions, training exercises and scenario planning prior to a disaster. Building on the resultant improved understanding and respect, it is argued that improvements in logistic cooperation are most likely to occur in the aftermath of rapid-onset disasters where the military's strengths of speed, equipment and training are most beneficial. From this, there is the potential to develop the interfaces to allow similar engagement in more troubling areas that, in particular, present significant challenges to the principles underpinning humanitarian actions.

This theme is taken up in Chapter 13 by *Major General (Ret'd) Tim Cross*, a Visiting Professor at Cranfield University, UK, and former senior logistician within the UK Army. Adopting a perspective based on his many years of experience in field operations that have often seen him working alongside humanitarian agencies, the chapter discusses the similarities and differences between NGOs and the military. Concluding that there are, in practice, more areas of agreement than disagreement, the author challenges the system as a whole to work towards the development of common processes and procedures that will play to the strengths of both communities in the delivery of humanitarian logistic support.

The final chapter of this collection of contributions by humanitarian logistic practitioners and academics has been written by *Dr Gyöngyi Kovács,* from the HUMLOG Institute at Hanken University, Finland. Universally acknowledged as one of the thought leaders in the humanitarian logistic field, she has risen to the editors' challenge of peering into the mythical crystal ball in order to discern and capture the emerging trends. In doing so, not only has she touched on many of the key themes that have been considered in several of this book's chapters, but she has also uncovered her view of the next series of obstacles that await the humanitarian logistician (and, indeed, the humanitarian movement as a whole). In particular, she underscores the extent to which the emerging need for sustainable supply networks will interface with those responding to the needs of those affected by disasters in the shorter term. This sustainability perspective is, unquestionably, one that will play an increasingly dominant role in the thinking of the humanitarian logistician as the next decade of this century rolls forward.

A final thought

In inviting contributions to this book, as the editors we were keen to stress that authors were at liberty, if not positively encouraged, to offer unusual or controversial viewpoints. Inevitably, therefore, the book will contain perspectives that can be contrasted or may even be thought to be in downright opposition. We have not sought to ameliorate these – indeed, to do so would seem to imply a degree of arrogance as it would suggest that we are aware of the correct and proper approach to a particular challenge.

Certainly this is not the case; rather we hope that this volume will provide some tangible assistance to those tasked with prosecuting the enormously complex business of humanitarian logistics. What we would, however, claim is that we have yet to meet a 'wicked problem' in this field that cannot be at least partially tamed through the application of prescriptions drawn from the commercial environment.

Notes

1 UN (United Nations) (2009) Strengthening of the coordination of emergency humanitarian assistance of the United Nations. Report by the Secretary General to the General Assembly Economic and Social Council dated 28 May. At: http://www.reliefweb.int/rw/RWFiles2009.nsf/FilesByRWDocUnidFilename/ SNAA-7U67T3-full_report.pdf/$File/full_report.pdf [accessed 27 Jan 2010].

2 Kahn, ME (2005), The death toll from natural disasters: The role of income, geography and institutions, *The Review of Economics and Statistics*, 87(2), pp 271–84.

3 Rodriguez, J, Vos, F, Below, F and Guha-Sapir, D (2009) Annual Disaster Statistical Review 2008: The numbers and trends. *CRED* (Center for Research on the Epidemiology of Disasters). At: http://www.cred.be/sites/default/files/ADSR_2008.pdf [accessed 27 Jan 2010].

4 Van Wassenhove, LN (2006) Humanitarian aid logistics: Supply chain management in high gear, *Journal of the Operational Research Society*, 57 (5), pp 475–589.

5 Long, DC and Wood, DF (1995) The logistics of famine relief, *Journal of Business Logistics*, 16(1), pp 213–29.

6 Shane, S and Bonner, R (2005) UN chief urges immediate aid for tsunami-torn countries, *New York Times*, 6 Jan 2005.

7 The HUMLOG group consists of 11 universities and other institutions, the aim of which is: 'to research the area of humanitarian logistics in disaster preparedness, response and recovery with the intention of influencing future activities in a way that will provide measurable benefits to persons requiring assistance'. (www.humloggroup.org)

8 Christopher, MG (2005) *Logistics and Supply Chain Management*, Pearson Education: London, UK.

9 Hammer, M and Champy, J (1993) *Re-engineering the Corporation*, Nicholas Brealey Publishing: London, UK.

10 Christopher, MG (2005) *Logistics and Supply Chain Management*, Pearson Education: London, UK, p5.

01
Risky business
what humanitarians can learn from business logisticians – and vice versa

PAUL D LARSON, UNIVERSITY OF MANITOBA

Emergency response is extremely costly. It is estimated that every dollar spent on prevention today saves four dollars in emergency response tomorrow. There is no economic sense in spending money on emergency response alone. Years of investment can disappear in minutes if risk reduction and prevention are ignored. (IFRC, 2008: 14)

Abstract

This chapter is inspired by the premise that humanitarian logisticians have much to learn from their commercial counterparts. There has been limited knowledge transfer between business people and humanitarians, and aid agencies are thought to be many years behind large corporations in adopting modern supply chain practices. Although there are a number of areas in which humanitarians could learn from the commercial sector (eg preparedness, responsiveness, coordination and partnerships), supply chain risk management (SCRM), the focus of this chapter, may be the ultimate area for such learning, SCRM literature is growing in the business journals – and humanitarians are involved in 'risky business'. Commercial logisticians can also learn SCRM lessons from the humanitarians, who have tremendous experience in preparing for and responding to disasters of all types.

Introduction

Humanitarian logisticians have much to learn from their commercial counterparts. Pettit and Beresford (2005: 314) observe that: 'There are clear parallels between business logistics and relief logistics, but the transfer of knowledge between the two has been limited and the latter remains relatively unsophisticated.' According to the Fritz Institute, the humanitarian aid agencies are 20 years behind the large corporations in adopting today's fundamental tools of logistics and SCM (Spring, 2006).

In their recent assessment of the state of the humanitarian system, Harvey *et al* (2010) identify a number of areas in which humanitarians could learn from the commercial sector, including leadership; needs assessment; preparedness and responsiveness, to customers/beneficiaries; coordination and partnerships, among NGOs and other agencies; monitoring and evaluation; safety; human resource management; and disaster risk reduction (DRR). Supply chain risk management (SCRM), the focus of this chapter, may be the ultimate area for humanitarians to learn from the business sector. In the last few years, there has been a fair amount written on this topic in the business academic journals. Moreover, humanitarians are involved in truly 'risky business'.

As noted by Van Wassenhove (2006), commercial logisticians can also learn from humanitarians. Again, SCRM is an area of especially high potential for cross-learning, as humanitarians have tremendous experience in responding to disasters of all types. Still, the primary purpose of this chapter is to explore what humanitarian logisticians can learn from business logisticians, with a focus on SCRM.

The chapter is organized into four more sections. The first section presents a brief review of recent literature in the area of SCRM. The second section describes several of the main humanitarian players and their stage. Their perilous work includes the delivery of both development aid and disaster relief. Next, the third section addresses SCRM in the humanitarian world, offering an extension of a framework on active and dormant supply chains proposed by Kovács and Tatham (2009). The final section provides a summary and conclusions, including implications for practitioners and an academic research agenda.

FIGURE 1.1 Articles on supply chain risk management, 1998–2009

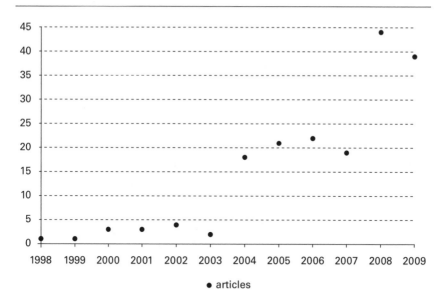

● articles

A brief review of recent literature

Figure 1.1 is a plot of articles published on supply chain risk management from 1998 to 2009. Articles were identified using the ABI/INFORM Global™ database, (arguably) the most comprehensive business database available. It covers more than 3,000 periodicals, and provides full text for over 2,000 of these. Users enjoy access to published information on business conditions and trends, management practices and theories, corporate strategies and tactics etc (see http://www.proquest.com). The plot reflects a search of *scholarly journals* for articles with the following terms in their citations or abstracts: 'supply chain' and 'risk management'. While the first article appeared in 1998, a total of 187 articles were identified, including 10 in the first near-half of 2010.

Given the state of the world, and the globalization of supply chains, it is not surprising to see that the SCRM literature is growing. A surprise comes if 'humanitarian' is added as a third search term. This trims the literature (on humanitarian SCRM) to a single article, by Kovács and Tatham (2009). Though disaster relief may be the ultimate 'risky business', the database search found only one article devoted to the topic!

According to Manuj and Mentzer (2008: 192), 'Global supply chains are more risky than domestic supply chains.' This statement makes it clear that nearly all the supply chain risk management literature is written for American business-men and -women, and their counterparts in other developed countries. Often, in the humanitarian world, the global portion of the supply chain is the least risky portion. It is the domestic 'last mile' of the supply chain where shipments are hijacked, logisticians are murdered, and customers or beneficiaries remain in need.

In his fifth chapter, Paulsson (2007) provides a thorough review of the SCRM literature up to 2007. Since nearly all the literature is written for the commercial realm, this brief review focuses on possible transference of learning across three areas of contribution: (1) identifying and categorizing types of risk; (2) developing SCRM processes; and (3) creating and adapting tools for SCRM.

Rao and Goldsby (2009) review the SCRM literature and develop a typology for the identification of risk factors. They differentiate three broad risk categories: *environmental*; *industry* (eg inputs – labour and material, demand shifts, competition); and *organizational* (eg labour, material, credit, product liability, production process). The environmental risk variables include political instability; government policy shifts; macroeconomic uncertainties (eg volatility in oil prices and currency exchange rates); social uncertainties (terrorism); and natural uncertainties (eg earthquakes, floods and fires). Based on interviews with global supply chain managers, Manuj and Mentzer (2008) found four categories of risk: supply, demand, operational, and security risks. Specific risk events most salient to their interviewees were currency volatility, transit time variability, forecast accuracy, quality, safety, business disruption, survival, inventory (and asset) ownership, cultural differences, dependency and opportunism, oil price fluctuations, and other risk events affecting suppliers and customers.

Inspired by 9/11, Williams *et al* (2008) focus on supply chain security, ie protecting assets (personnel, products, facilities, equipment and information) from theft, damage or terrorism and preventing illicit use of supply chain assets for smuggling contraband, people or weapons of mass destruction. The article includes a short history lesson in supply chain security. In the 1800s, American railroads had a security problem. Thieves would stop some trains, pillaging their goods and passengers. To protect goods and passengers, and in absence of effective law enforcement, the railroads created a private police force. Given the perilous nature of their work (Stoddard *et al*, 2009), should the humanitarian community consider creating such a force?

Williams *et al* (2008) also discuss the possible role of inter-organizational relationships – with supply chain members; public-sector and not-for-profit entities (eg government agencies and non-government organizations (NGOs), such as the Red Cross); and even competitors – in supply chain security. In considering these 'strange bedfellows' type of relationships, commercial logisticians may have much to learn from their humanitarian counterparts (Larson, in press).

Turning to catastrophes, Knemeyer *et al* (2009) suggest supply chains are becoming more vulnerable, partly due to implementation of lean techniques and globalization policies. They define a catastrophic event, such as a hurricane or terrorist attack, as something having a very low probability of occurrence but very severe consequence if it does occur. This 'low probability' trait of catastrophes may be unique to the commercial sectors in certain regions of the world. Humanitarian relief work commences shortly after a catastrophic event and at the site of the event. Development aid work is often undertaken in places where catastrophic events are likely to occur. Manuj and Mentzer (2008) note that most companies develop plans to protect against low-impact, recurrent risks; but they ignore high-impact, low-likelihood risks. Humanitarian organizations (and militaries) differ from these companies in that they face high-impact, high-likelihood risks, all in a day's work.

Like the World Economic Forum (2010), Knemeyer *et al* (2009) study supply chain risks in terms of severity (or business impact) and likelihood (or probability). Their process for SCRM proactive planning can be paraphrased by the following steps: 1) identify locations and threats; 2) estimate probabilities and loss potential, by location; 3) evaluate alternative countermeasures (eg relocation, building redundancy, redesigning facilities, enhancing flexibility, buying insurance, increasing inventory, and surveillance); and 4) select countermeasures to prevent or mitigate the threats and/or their effects. The supply chain risk evaluation and management (SCREAM) process takes a step back and starts by asking: Who are your stakeholders? What are you doing for them? These questions are followed by team formation, supply chain mapping and identification of vulnerabilities, based on the likelihood X impact concept (Larson, 2009).

Pujawan and Geraldin (2009) develop a framework they call the 'house of risk', combining the house of quality and failure mode and effect analysis from the quality management literature. They make the useful distinction between operational and disruption risks. Whereas operational risks are due to inherent features of supply chains, such as demand, supply, and cost uncertainties, disruption risks are caused by natural and man-made disasters, eg floods, earthquakes, drought, and economic crisis. In their case study, the top 10 risks identified, in terms of likelihood X severity, were all operational risks rather than disruptions. While natural disasters ranked 15 out of 22 on the risk list, terrorist attacks were not on the list. Similar to Stokes (2008), the Pujawan and Geraldin (2009) proactive model starts with supply chain mapping to identify exposure to risk events. The house of risk approach then assesses risk events in terms of severity of impact and likelihood of occurrence, identifies preventive actions, and estimates the difficulty and effectiveness of those actions. Stokes's tool focuses on estimating possible monetary losses due to relevant risk events, and then determining insurance requirements.

To prepare for supply chain disruptions, Yang and Yang (2010) recommend two basic approaches: adding redundancy and building flexibility. Adding redundancy involves maintaining extra resources, such as inventory and capacity. Although this provides some protection against sudden disruptions, excess resources are expensive to maintain. Flexibility can be enhanced with a multi-skilled workforce, more versatile equipment, and closer relationships with certain supply chain members. Postponement also provides flexibility by delaying final processing or movement of material until customer requirements are known. Postponement is linked to the *push–pull boundary* concept: forward deploy or push assets to the boundary; keep the assets there until when, where, and how much questions about customer requirements are answered; and then let this information pull the assets further forward based on the known needs of customers. Thus, postponement is another tool for SCRM.

Yang and Yang (2010) suggest that postponement requires tight coupling of supply chain entities and reduction of 'interactive complexity' (through standardization of items and effective information exchange). They cite the case of Dell computers during and after the 1999 Taiwan earthquake, which disrupted the worldwide supply of memory chips. Dell's postponement strategy played a prominent role in protecting the company against that disruption.

Christopher and Lee (2004) propose another conceptual 'tool' for managing supply chain risk. They suggest that high risk often brings lack of confidence, which further increases risk exposure (the 'risk spiral'); eg demand uncertainty leads to higher inventory which increases risk of obsolescence. Many types of risk – more volatile demand, shorter product life cycles, wars and terrorism, labour strikes, outbreak of disease, mistrust, distorted information, strategic shifts (eg globalization, lean supplier reduction, outsourcing) – can lead to erosion of confidence. The risk management tool is *confidence* created via visibility and information sharing. Of course, the information must be accurate and accessible.

Whether the concern is Icelandic volcanoes, Sudanese insurgencies, American pandemics or all of the above, SCRM is about minimizing interruptions through avoidance or effective response. While the literature is almost exclusively focused on commercial supply chains, the next section explores the humanitarian context, (arguably) the ultimate in 'risky business'. Humanitarians need the knowledge (topics, tools and techniques) available in the commercial supply chain literature. In return, they have rich, hands-on risk management experience. They have a message for the business world.

The players and the stage

Kovács and Spens (2007) describe a variety of actors in the humanitarian aid network, including donors, aid agencies and other non-governmental organizations (NGOs), governments, military units and logistics service providers. The supply chain also includes suppliers of goods and other services, 'customers' or beneficiaries, and communities. For the purposes of this chapter, aid agencies and NGOs are the critical, focal entities.

World Vision International (WVI) is involved in three primary activities: 1) development – transforming communities; 2) relief – responding to disasters; and 3) advocacy – seeking global change (see http://www.wvi.org). In 2009, WVI spent US $2.63 billion working to fulfill its mission. Across the three activities, 2009 expenditures break out as follows: international development ($1.53 billion, 58.0 per cent); relief and rehabilitation ($0.73 billion, 27.7 per cent); and fundraising, administration and advocacy ($0.37 billion, 14.3 per cent). Thus, WVI is globally and heavily involved in both development aid and disaster relief, spending a little over twice as much on development compared to relief.

Similarly, Oxfam works with local partner organizations and people living in poverty in the following critical areas: 1) development – working on long-term programmes to eradicate poverty and combat injustice; 2) emergency relief – providing immediate life-saving assistance to people affected by natural disasters or armed conflicts, and helping to build their resilience in anticipation of future disasters; and 3) campaigning/advocacy – raising public awareness of the causes of poverty, encouraging people to take action for a fairer world, and influencing leaders to change policies and practices that reinforce poverty and injustice (see http://www.oxfam.org/en/about/what). In addition, Oxfam conducts policy research, which draws on experiences in the field and supports the other three areas of activity.

For reporting purposes, CARE USA divides its activities broadly into programme activities (90.7 per cent of the 2009 total operating budget of US $708.4 million) and support services/fundraising (9.3 per cent of the budget). Of total programme activity spending in 2009, $503.8 million went toward community development/lasting solutions to poverty (78.4 per cent); while the remaining $138.7 million was spent on emergency (relief) and rehabilitation (21.6 per cent). Thus, CARE spent approximately $3.63 on development aid for every dollar spent on disaster relief (CARE, 2009).

McLachlin *et al* (2009) develop a framework in which differences between commercial and humanitarian supply chains largely follow from two dimensions: motivation (profit/not-for-profit) and environment (uninterrupted/interrupted). Commercial actors have the profit motive and generally operate in uninterrupted environments. Interrupted environments are rare exceptions, usually thrust upon the business by disasters or emergencies. Conversely, humanitarian actors are typically not-for-profit organizations and interrupted environments are the norm, especially in the case of disaster relief as opposed to ongoing development aid operations. Development aid is often delivered in places where disruptions are likely, ie in environments that are likely to transition from uninterrupted to interrupted, and back again. Table 1.1 classifies six types of supply chains, with commercial, humanitarian and military organizations engaged in uninterrupted or interrupted environments. Commerce is 'business as usual', humanitarians provide development assistance, and soldiers are at peace – until the disaster or crisis occurs.

TABLE 1.1 Six types of supply chain

Organization	Environment	
	Uninterrupted	Interrupted
Commercial	*Business as usual*	*Business at risk*
Humanitarian	*Development aid*	*Disaster relief*
Military	*Peace*	*War*

ADAPTED FROM: McLachlin *et al* (2009)

Working in more than 160 countries, the United Nations Development Programme's (UNDP) mandate is to reduce poverty, promote democratic governance, prevent and recover from crises, and protect the environment and combat climate change. In 2009, UNDP spent more than US $4.1 billion delivering its programmes (UNDP, 2010a). The earthquake on 12 January 2010 affected at least 3 million Haitian citizens, destroyed much of its capital region, and devastated fragile development gains made during recent years. Among the more than 200,000 lives lost were 101 UN staff members – the single greatest loss in UN history. UNDP headquarters in Haiti was destroyed and many ongoing development programmes suffered serious setbacks.

In response to the March 2010 murders of six aid workers during an attack on its office in Mansehra district, north-west Pakistan, WVI suspended its operations in that country. WVI was working in the area to provide ongoing assistance to survivors of the deadly earthquake that struck Pakistan in October 2005, leaving 3 million people homeless. UN Secretary General Ban Ki-moon insisted: 'all the armed actors in the country must ensure the safety of aid workers'. Previously, 12 UN staff members had been killed and 12 others injured in four separate, violent incidents since January 2009, including a suicide attack on the World Food Programme (WFP) office in Islamabad in October 2009 that killed five people. Despite these enormous risks, the UN and its partners provided 4.3 million Pakistani people with food aid in 2009 (UN News Centre, 2010). In 2008, all over the world, 260 aid workers were killed, injured and/or kidnapped during targeted attacks (Stoddard *et al*, 2009).

Although the frequency and impact of disasters seems to be rising, there is not a lot of literature on managing natural disasters, terrorist attacks, pandemics, oil shocks, etc. A scan of sources to support this chapter discovered only several articles; such as Perry (2007), on natural disaster management planning and Burke (2005), on managerial implications of global terrorism and threats to security.

Kovács and Tatham (2009) observe that humanitarian and military organizations specialize in responding to disasters. While humanitarians deliver aid to people in need, militaries wage war and engage in peacekeeping missions. In contrast to the business case, interruptions are inevitable; the disaster's the thing. As depicted in Figure 1.2, they also suggest that humanitarians and militaries both transition from dormant to active once disaster or disruption strikes. During the dormant, preparation phase, the focus is on lean or efficient operations. Once disaster strikes, the active phase is inspired by the need for agility or responsiveness.

During complex emergencies, where armed conflict often accompanies natural disaster, disease or drought, humanitarians (unarmed, funded by multiple public and private sector donors, and on a social mission) and militaries (armed, government-funded, and on a political mission) often work in close proximity. Unfortunately, this can be an additional source of risk for humanitarian NGOs, as local insurgents and saboteurs treat both groups as unwelcome guests.

The next section covers humanitarian supply chain risk management. Two central themes are coordination between development aid and disaster relief, and creation of local capabilities in the developing world. Development aid workers can contribute to the preparedness of their disaster relief colleagues, as well as participate in disaster relief. In many cases, the three phases of disaster relief – preparation, immediate response, and reconstruction (Kovács and Spens, 2007) – occur within a bigger picture, ie development aid. Development is interrupted by disaster. At some point after the disaster, development commences anew.

Supply chain risk management in the humanitarian world

Bartle argues that moving from disaster relief to development aid requires a transformation, rather than a slight shift along a continuum. In more detail, he suggests:

> It sounds reasonable: after a disaster you provide emergency response for survival, then recovery, then rehabilitation, then development. It is called 'The Continuum', and it sounds like a smoothly transitional set of steps (or 'gears' in a car). It is not. The transition from providing emergency response (using a charity methodology) to providing development assistance (using an empowerment methodology) is not a neat series of steps in the same direction. It is a radical transformation, almost a complete reversal of methods. An empowerment methodology is based upon the concept that any organism needs to exercise (expend energy) or 'struggle' in order to become stronger, whereas if it only (lies) back and waits for outside help, it becomes weaker. (Bartle, 2007)

FIGURE 1.2 Dormant and active supply chains

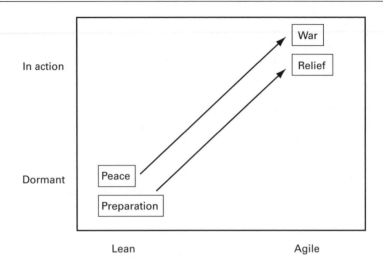

Adapted from Kovács and Tatham (2009: 217)

Despite the need for different methods – and perhaps different personnel – in disaster relief vis-à-vis development aid, there are opportunities for greater coordination between these two activities, especially in the area of SCRM.

'Disasters put development at risk' (UNDP, 2004). At a minimum, disasters put the brakes on development work, posing a threat to achievement of the Millennium Development Goals (MDGs). 'For the poor more than others, incomes are likely to be adversely affected by conflict, natural disasters and economic fluctuations, as well as the recent increases in food prices and the increasingly visible effects of global warming' (United Nations, 2008: 5). In the worst-case scenario, natural disasters and human conflicts can wipe out many years of development effort. According to UNDP (2004), annual economic losses due to natural disasters averaged US $659.9 billion during the 1990s. In turn, development aid can have a very large impact on disaster risk. Development can both cause and reduce disaster risk. For instance, risk can accumulate over time because of inappropriate development activities. By including disaster risk considerations into development decisions, odds are reduced that efforts to increase social and economic well-being will unexpectedly increase disaster risk. Strategic integration of SCRM within development planning can contribute to achieving the MDGs.

The UNDP (2004) draws a distinction between prospective and compensatory risk management. *Prospective* disaster risk management is integrated into development aid planning; programmes and projects are carefully reviewed regarding their potential to either reduce or increase vulnerability to disasters. This is about long-term disaster risk reduction. *Compensatory* disaster risk management focuses on reducing current vulnerability that has accumulated in part through past development work. This is about reducing contemporary risk. This is the opportunity for greater coordination between development aid and disaster relief planners in the area of preparedness and response.

Regarding the need for greater coordination between development aid and disaster relief planning, Harvey *et al* (2010: 31) state that:

> There is a growing focus on the need to increase investments in DRR (disaster risk reduction) and to better link development and humanitarian work in this area. DRR [is] a growing area of policy and programmatic investment for NGOs, and some positive knock-on effects have come from this, including a greater focus on partnerships and community engagement, and an increased awareness of the need for risk reduction work in development programming.

For a variety of reasons, SCRM and disaster risk reduction need to become central elements of ongoing development aid policy and disaster relief preparedness. By coordinating their efforts, development aid and disaster relief units can both be more effective.

Local presence and community response are critical factors in enabling people to reduce disaster risk. As early as 1998, the IFRC *World Disasters Report* suggested that local authorities are the most important actor for reducing the impact of natural and man-made disasters in urban areas. The Red Cross/Red Crescent is a leader in creating local presence. They are often the first to arrive on the scene of a disaster – and the last to depart. There are now 186 National Red Cross and Red Crescent Societies around the world, employing nearly 300,000 people and drawing on the skills of 97 million volunteers (http://www.ifrc.org). National Societies in many countries around the world enable Red Cross/Red Crescent volunteers, who live in the communities they serve, to be the first responders (IFRC, 2008).

Figure 1.3 is a modification of the Kovács and Tatham (2009) framework on military and humanitarian supply chains. They suggest that such supply chains transition from a dormant, lean phase of peace and preparation to an active, agile phase of war and disaster relief. However, these supply chains could (and should) also include an active, lean phase as well as a dormant, agile phase.

Although 'military intelligence' has been labelled an oxymoron, intelligence gathering is often used in advance of warfare to learn about the enemy and the theatre, and to increase the effectiveness of any possible future waging of war. Intelligence gathering can also facilitate diplomacy and perhaps reveal alternatives to warfare. Intelligence is lean, since large amounts of equipment or personnel are neither required nor desired. Thus, intelligence gathering implies an active, lean military supply chain.

FIGURE 1.3 Active, lean and dormant, agile supply chains

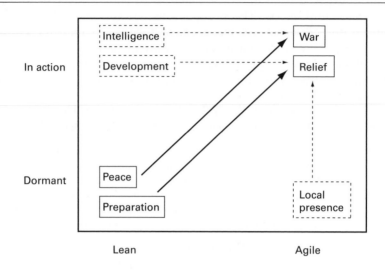

Adapted from Kovács and Tatham (2009: 217)

The potential of an active, lean approach is even more compelling in humanitarian supply chains. As noted above, there is often ongoing development work being done in disaster-prone places, eg Haiti. This work is enabled by active supply chains. Development aid supply chains can also be lean, with labour and materials arriving just in time to meet project schedules. While disaster relief needs rapid response to save lives and ease suffering, development focuses on building a better future. In-country development workers can be fountains of knowledge about the needs of the communities where they live, both before and after disaster strikes.

SCRM for development aid needs to be coordinated with the preparation phase of disaster relief. Proper development can reduce the likelihood that catastrophic events will occur and/or reduce the severity of their impact. Coordinated SCRM between development and relief personnel includes having a plan in place to recover from the disaster as quickly as possible. 'Building back better', a phrase coined by the former American President Bill Clinton following the 2004 Asian tsunami, is about reducing the severity of the next disaster during recovery from the current disaster. In order to achieve real, long-lasting impact, building back better must be integrated with disaster risk reduction and disaster preparedness measures (IFRC, 2008). This is strategic integration of disaster relief and development aid.

While Kovács and Tatham (2009: 223) anticipate the disaster relief/ development aid connection by recognizing the potential of 'local presence', such as local chapters or national societies (eg IFRC), they neglect the fact that many of the humanitarian NGOs are engaged primarily in development aid – as opposed to disaster relief. Disaster relief personnel may only remain in-country a short time. However, development workers are more enduring. By maintaining a local presence, humanitarian organizations can have a dormant, agile capability in place. Local presence implies there are trained personnel, ready to respond to disaster at a moment's notice. This is the essence of agility. Both Perry (2007) and Burke (2005) recognize the important role of locally led inclusiveness and the people most directly affected by disaster in making a difference in recovery. As noted above, Red Cross/Red Crescent is a global leader in maintaining a dormant, agile local capability.

Conclusion

This final section provides a summary of the chapter in the form of practitioner implications and a research agenda.

Practitioner implications

NGOs and other agencies have an opportunity to include SCRM in development planning to reduce the likelihood and severity of disasters. They should consider adopting a risk management perspective on disasters and establishing the 'business case' for allocating resources to SCRM and preparedness. When development work neglects risk reduction, communities become more vulnerable to disaster. The absence of effective preparedness and mitigation plans (eg early warning systems, evacuation routes, shelters, relief stockpiles, trained response teams, public awareness) increases vulnerability further. IFRC (2002) has identified the following barriers to more effective disaster risk reduction: the fragmented, unorganized risk reduction 'community'; risk reduction treated as a separate area, rather than integrated with development and humanitarian programming; and lack of donor support for risk reduction as opposed to disaster relief. Despite strong evidence on the value of disaster prevention, over 90 per cent of international relief aid is still dedicated to disaster response. A compelling financial case is needed to move towards investment in risk reduction and prevention (IFRC, 2008). The 'building back better' approach to disaster recovery is a good start.

The humanitarian community also has the opportunity to be better prepared. Development aid workers could coordinate their plans with disaster relief colleagues by providing intelligence to support early warning and post-disaster needs assessment. Development and relief personnel would benefit from training in the tools and techniques of SCRM. NGOs and other agencies should seek development aid/disaster relief supply chain integration opportunities. Although the 'goods' may be different, suppliers and logistics service providers may be the same. Strategic postponement can increase operational efficiency and reduce exposure to risk, without sacrificing flexibility and responsiveness. Opportunities for supply chain integration may be intra-organizational or inter-organizational, ie involving greater collaboration with other NGOs, UN agencies, etc. Finally, NGOs should not forget the prominent role of local presence in anticipating and mitigating disastrous events.

Humanitarian logisticians are advised to access the commercial literature on SCRM tools, topics and techniques; along with the humanitarian disaster risk reduction literature (IFRC, 2002; UNDP, 2004). It is loaded with ideas. NGOs and other agencies could also create a knowledge management (KM) system (Kovács and Tatham, 2009) to harness the wisdom and experience of those 595,000 aid workers in the field (Harvey *et al*, 2010). The objective is to help humanitarians do even better, through information sharing.

Here is a challenge to the business or for-profit sector. Perhaps as an element of corporate social responsibility (CSR), leading commercial firms should sponsor an event bringing business, humanitarian and military logisticians together for an open exchange of ideas and experiences in SCRM. The business logisticians could describe various risk management tools they have developed and implemented, and then discuss adaptation of these tools and techniques for the humanitarian sector. The humanitarians could share their rich, hands-on experience. Hopefully, such a forum would include a discussion on the shrinking humanitarian space and the humanitarian/military interface in the field.

Finally, let's take back the humanitarian space! Theoretically, the humanitarian space is a zone of tranquility where civilians and aid workers are protected from hostilities so they can move about and operate freely (Van Wassenhove, 2006: 478). This space has been shrinking, to the peril of humanitarian workers. On Thursday, 5 August 2010, 10 humanitarian aid workers were murdered in a remote area of northern Afghanistan: Mahram Ali, Cheryl Beckett, Daniela Beyer, Brian Carderelli, Dr Tom Grams, Ahmed Jawed, Glen Lapp, team leader Dr Tom Little, Dan Terry and Dr Karen Woo. They were there to provide health care to villagers who otherwise would have none. They knew the risks (Nordland, 2010). They were with International Assistance Mission, whose core values are: dependency on God, love for all, teamwork, accountability, learning and quality work (http://www.iam-afghanistan.org/our-mission-values). Let us remember them, and all the other fallen humanitarians, by taking back the space.

Building peace, establishing security and reinforcing justice are essential for achieving the MDGs. In conflict-afflicted countries, government authority and the developmental process itself are sometimes violently contested. This makes progress on the MDGs extremely challenging (UNDP, 2010b: 19–20). To make a difference, aid and relief workers need their humanitarian space.

Research agenda

Although there are many aspects of humanitarian SCRM in need of research, this final sub-section briefly discusses three areas: 1) the role of intra- and inter-organizational relationships in disaster risk reduction; 2) the impact of empowerment versus charity approaches to humanitarian aid; and 3) the *humanitarian space* problem.

There are a variety of worthwhile research questions on the role of closer relationships in disaster risk reduction. The hypothesis is that greater coordination – within NGOs, among NGOs and between NGOs and other actors – can reduce disaster risk and improve humanitarian effectiveness. Some more specific research questions include the following: How can development aid/disaster relief coordination facilitate risk reduction, and smooth the transitions from preparation to response and from recovery to development? To what extent is there coordination between development and relief within the NGOs? Are there opportunities for greater coordination? To what extent is there coordination among NGOs in the areas of development and relief? Can a more coordinated effort help make the case for funding of preparation and SCRM? Is there a role for commercial firms and military units in humanitarian SCRM?

Another hypothesis is that the empowerment aid model (as opposed to the charity model) is more conducive to a proactive (versus reactive) approach to SCRM. Bartle (2007) provides considerable detail on differences between empowerment and charity models and Larson (2009) contrasts proactive and reactive approaches to risk management. The proactive versus reactive decision should be made on the basis of likelihood of disaster occurrence and severity of impact. High likelihood/high impact disasters call for a proactive, 'be prepared' approach. On the other hand, low likelihood/low impact disasters can be handled with a reactive, 'bring it on' approach. One problem with the charity model is its likely affinity for a reactive approach to risk management: disaster strikes, charitable funds pour in, and then we respond. The big-picture research question is: could the empowerment model to aid delivery be the key to convincing humanitarian NGOs (and their donors) to adopt a proactive approach to SCRM?

The final issue for brief consideration here is the *humanitarian space* problem. Why is the space shrinking? What conditions make aid workers particularly vulnerable? How can this phenomenon be measured and documented? How can this trend be reversed? Under what circumstances should leaders of the humanitarian NGOs and agencies make the decision to pull their people, particularly the foreigners, out of a situation? Are military units the cause of this problem? Could they be part of the solution? Have humanitarian organizations lost touch with the communities they try to serve? Are some NGOs more vulnerable than others? Researchers and field workers alike should ask the question: If the humanitarian space vanishes, can we still make a difference?

References

Bartle, P (2007) *From Disaster to Development,*
http://www.scn.org/cmp/modules/dis-int.htm

Burke, RJ (2005) International terrorism and threats to security: implications for organizations and management, *Disaster Prevention and Management,* **14**(5), pp 639–43

CARE (2009) *Annual Report,* http://www.care.org

Christopher, M and Lee, H (2004) Mitigating supply chain risk through improved confidence, *International Journal of Physical Distribution & Logistics Management,* **34**(5), pp 388–96

Harvey, P *et al* (2010) *The State of the Humanitarian System: Assessing performance and progress,* Active Learning Network for Accountability and Performance (ALNAP), London

IFRC (2002) *World Disasters Report: Focus on reducing risk,* International Federation of Red Cross and Red Crescent Societies, Geneva, http://www.ifrc.org/publicat/wdr2002/index.asp

IFRC (2008) *Annual Report,* International Federation of Red Cross and Red Crescent Societies, Geneva, http://www.ifrc.org/Docs/pubs/who/ar2008-en.pdf

Knemeyer, AM, Zinn, W and Eroglu, C (2009) Proactive planning for catastrophic events in supply chains, *Journal of Operations Management,* **27**, pp 141–53

Kovács, G and Spens, KM (2007) Humanitarian logistics in disaster relief operations, *International Journal of Physical Distribution & Logistics Management,* **37**(2), pp 99–114

Kovács, G and Tatham, P (2009) Responding to Disruptions in the Supply Network – from Dormant to Action, *Journal of Business Logistics,* **30**(2), pp 215–29

Larson, PD (2009) SCREAM! (Supply Chain Risk Evaluation and Management), APICS Annual International Conference, Toronto, 5 October

Larson, PD (in press) Strategic partners and strange bedfellows: Relationship building in humanitarian supply chains, in *Relief Supply Chain Management: Humanitarian aid and emergency logistics,* eds G Kovács and K Spens, IGI Global

Manuj, I and Mentzer, JT (2008) Global supply chain risk management strategies, *International Journal of Physical Distribution and Logistics Management,* **38**(3), pp 192–223

McLachlin, R, Larson, PD and Khan, S (2009) Not-for-profit supply chains in interrupted environments: The case of a faith-based humanitarian relief organization, *Management Research News,* **32**(11), pp 1050–64

Nordland, R (2010) Afghan aid leader recalls talk of risk, *The New York Times,* 9 August

Paulsson, U (2007) *On managing disruption risks in the supply chain – the DRISC model,* doctoral dissertation, Lund University, Sweden

Perry, M (2007) Natural disaster management planning: a study of logistics managers responding to the tsunami, *International Journal of Physical Distribution & Logistics Management,* **37**(5), pp 409–33

Pettit, SJ and Beresford, A (2005) Emergency relief logistics: an evaluation of military, non-military and composite response models, *International Journal of Logistics: Research & Applications,* **8**(4), pp 313–31

Pujawan, IN and Geraldin, LH (2009) House of risk: a model for proactive supply chain risk management, *Business Process Management Journal*, **15**(6), pp 953–67

Rao, S and Goldsby, TJ (2009) Supply chain risks: a review and typology, *International Journal of Logistics Management*, **20**(1), pp 97–123

Spring, S (2006) Relief when you need it: can FedEx, DHL and TNT bring the delivery of emergency aid into the 21st century?, *Newsweek International Edition*, 11 September

Stoddard, A, Harmer, A and DiDomenico, V (2009) *Providing Aid in Insecure Environments: 2009 update*, Humanitarian Policy Group (HPG) Policy Brief 34, April

Stokes, R (2008) Understanding supply chain risk, *Risk Management*, **55**(8), pp 54–57

United Nations (2008) *The Millennium Development Goals Report*, UN, New York

UNDP (2004) *Reducing Disaster Risk: A Challenge for Development*, UNDP, New York

UNDP (2010a) *Delivering on Commitments: UNDP in Action 2009/2010*, UNDP, New York, May

UNDP (2010b) *What Will It Take to Achieve the Millennium Development Goals? An international assessment*, United Nations Development Programme, New York, June

UN News Centre (2010) Safety of aid workers crucial, UN officials say after murders in Pakistan, 11 March

Van Wassenhove, LN (2006) Humanitarian aid logistics: supply chain management in high gear, *Journal of the Operational Research Society*, **57**, pp 475–589

Williams, Z, Lueg, JE and LeMay, SA (2008) Supply chain security: an overview and research agenda, *International Journal of Logistics Management*, **19**(2), pp 254–81

World Economic Forum (2010) *Global Risks 2010: A global risk network report*, World Economic Forum, Geneva

WVI (2009) *World Vision International 2009 Review*, http://www.wvi.org

Yang, B and Yang, Y (2010) Postponement in supply chain risk management: a complexity perspective, *International Journal of Production Research*, **48**(7), pp 1901–12

Acknowledgements

The author wishes to thank the Social Sciences and Humanities Research Council of Canada (SSHRC) for supporting the research program that includes this chapter.

02
Impacts of funding systems on humanitarian operations

TINA WAKOLBINGER AND FUMINORI TOYASAKI

Abstract

Funding systems and financial flows play an important role in humanitarian operations. They directly and indirectly affect the scope, speed, effectiveness and efficiency of disaster response. Despite their importance, constraints imposed by funding systems are often not considered in models of humanitarian supply chains. This chapter explores the interdependence of financial flows and material flows in humanitarian relief operations. Specifically, this chapter shows how the structure of funding systems and the characteristics of financial flows impact humanitarian operations. Based on insights concerning the link between funding systems and humanitarian operations, we provide recommendations concerning future research projects.

Introduction

The occurrence and impact of natural disasters are expected to strongly increase in the future (Thomas and Kopczak, 2005). In order to respond to increasing needs, improving the efficiency of response systems is essential (Altay and Green, 2006; Oloruntoba and Gray, 2006). Due to the realization of the necessity of improved response systems, the area of humanitarian supply chain management emerged. Humanitarian supply chain management is typically defined as 'the process of planning, implementing and controlling the efficient, cost-effective flow and storage of goods, materials, and money, as well as related information from the point of origin to the point of consumption for the purpose of alleviating the suffering of vulnerable people' (Thomas and Kopczak, 2005: 2). Logistics plays a very important role in humanitarian supply chains and accounts for a large portion of costs. Reducing inefficiencies in humanitarian logistics operations can, hence, lead to large costs savings. Recently, OR/MS researchers started applying techniques used in the corporate sector to increase the efficiency of logistics operations in humanitarian supply chains (Van Wassenhove, 2006).

Inefficiencies in humanitarian operations have many causes. Current funding systems are one of the causes that have been cited in the literature (Thomas and Kopczak, 2005). Funding systems limit the scope of humanitarian response and they directly and indirectly affect the speed, effectiveness and efficiency of disaster response. The impact of funding systems is increasing as aid agencies are currently facing multiple changes and challenges in their environment: increasing demand for disaster relief, increasing numbers of aid agencies leading to more intense competition for donations, increasing earmarking among private and official donors, new funding mechanisms such as the Central Emergency Response Fund (CERF), Common Humanitarian Funds (CHFs), and Emergency Response Funds (ERFs), and donors that are more demanding in terms of performance, accountability, quality and impact (Thomas and Kopczak, 2005; Beamon and Balcik, 2008; Street, 2009).

Only recently have researchers started analysing the link between logistics and funding (Jahre and Heigh, 2008). Topics that have been addressed are the importance of sufficient amounts of money allocated to different stages in the disaster response (Balcik and Beamon, 2008; Jahre and Heigh, 2008) and the impact of earmarked funds on humanitarian operations (Martinez *et al*, 2010; Toyasaki and Wakolbinger, 2010). Further exploring this interaction is of utmost importance, especially, since humanitarian relief operations have many of the characteristics of complex systems (Goncalves, 2008).

In this chapter, we explore the interaction between funding systems and humanitarian relief operations from the perspective of a non-profit organization. Although previous papers have highlighted some of these interactions, this chapter will be the first one to provide a comprehensive overview of the impact of funding systems on humanitarian operations. We expect to see more papers in the future that address the interaction between money flows and product flows in humanitarian operations. We hope that this chapter contributes to increasing this important research stream.

This chapter is organized as follows: first, we provide an overview of the structure of humanitarian funding systems. Then, we describe how characteristics of financial flows impact the efficiency and effectiveness of humanitarian operations and we show how incentives provided by donors can lead to misallocation of resources. Based on insights concerning the link between funding systems and humanitarian operations, we provide recommendations concerning future research projects.

Structure of funding systems

Funding systems typically involve multiple stakeholders with diverse objectives. The structure of the humanitarian funding system and the number of stakeholders involved impacts the characteristics of funding flows and the power of the stakeholders. Furthermore, it affects the percentage of donations that reaches beneficiaries since intermediaries typically keep a percentage of the money as transaction costs and, thereby, reduce the amount of money that can be used for beneficiaries (Walker and Pepper, 2007).

Funds to deal with the effects of disasters usually come from public or official sources. Traditionally, governments provided a big portion of funds; therefore, they had a strong influence over the sector (Thomas and Kopczak, 2005). In recent years, contributions from foundations, individual donors and the private sector increased in importance (Thomas and Kopczak, 2005; Kovàcs and Spens, 2007).

Donors need to decide how to allocate their money. Funds are either provided directly to providers of aid or they are channelled through intermediaries (Macrae, 2002). Providers of aid include international aid agencies, local non-governmental organizations (NGOs) and community-based organizations (Oloruntoba and Gray, 2006). International aid agencies can be divided into three categories: entities operating under the United Nations umbrella, international organizations such as the International Federation of the Red Cross and Red Crescent Movement (IFRC), and global NGOs (Thomas and Kopczak, 2005). Intermediaries include the World Bank, international organizations or non-governmental organizations (Macrae, 2002). Administrative costs involved in allocating funds play an increasingly important role in the allocation decision of official donors. These considerations led to increasing amounts of resources being allocated to new funding mechanisms like CHFs (Street, 2009).

Besides deciding how to allocate money, donors and intermediaries also need to decide on restrictions that they impose on the use of financial funds and reporting requirements. Accountability is of increasing concern to many donors and increases reporting requirements for aid agencies. Restrictions imposed on the use of donations strongly impact the efficiency and effectiveness of humanitarian operations, as the next section will show.

Impacts of financial flows on disaster response

Financial flows are an important input in humanitarian supply chain operations and, therefore, humanitarian operations are strongly affected by the characteristics of the funding flows (Development Initiatives, 2009a). When analysing the impact of financial flows, traditionally, a lot of emphasis has been put on the total amount of donations received. However, speed and timing, fluctuation and predictability, and flexibility of funds also influence the efficiency and effectiveness of disaster response, and, hence, these characteristics strongly impact the value of donations from the perspective of an aid agency.

Volume

Although funds available for humanitarian relief are increasing, they are not large enough to cover humanitarian need (Development Initiatives, 2009b). Given the increasing need for disaster response, this situation is not likely to change. Aid agencies need to compete for the resources that are available. The amount of funds that an aid agency receives determines the scope of the relief operations that an aid agency can conduct. Large amounts of donations provide aid agencies with the opportunity to take advantage of economies of scale and to gain influence and negotiation power with suppliers. Furthermore, large amounts of resources provide aid agencies with visibility to donors. Given the importance of financial funds, there is a large literature on fundraising strategies and issues.

Traditionally, fundraising issues have been analysed by researchers in the area of economics. Only recently have they also been investigated by researchers in the area of operations research and computer science. Most previous empirical (see for example, Kingma, 1989; Khanna and Sandler, 2000; Okten and Weisbrod, 2000; Ribar and Wilhelm, 2002; Andreoni and Payne, 2003; Thornton, 2006; Barman, 2008) and theoretical research papers (see for example, Fisher, 1977; Rose-Ackerman, 1982; Andreoni, 1998; Bilodeau and Slivinski, 1997; Vesterlund, 2003; Andreoni, 2006; Starke, 2007; Casteneda *et al*, 2009; Aldashev and Verdier, 2010) focus on fundraising activities of the non-profit sector in general and do not explicitly consider the challenges of fundraising for sudden-onset disaster relief projects. The issue of disaster relief fundraising is addressed by Bennett and Kottasz (2000) and Oosterhof *et al* (2009). The empirical analysis of Bennett and Kottasz (2000) determines factors that impact the effectiveness of disaster relief fundraising activities. Oosterhof *et al* (2009) analyse social cognitive factors for donations to relief campaigns. Both papers stress the impact that mass media has on donors' willingness to donate money for disaster relief projects.

When analysing the impact of increased donation amounts, it is very important to distinguish between donations that are earmarked and donations that are not. Earmarking/restricting donations means that donors put conditions on their gifts and select what projects or activities to fund within the recipient organization (Barman, 2008). In the case of earmarked funds, increasing donation amounts is not always desirable for aid agencies, as too much money is allocated to certain emergencies. This is especially true for emergencies with a lot of media attention that receive large amounts of earmarked donations. In these situations, aid agencies sometimes discourage donors from donating money, eg Doctors Without Borders discouraged donors from donating money for the 2004 Indian Ocean earthquake and tsunami.

Fluctuation and predictability

Fluctuations in funding levels can be observed in funding from private and government donors. Private donation levels are strongly impacted by the amount and type of news coverage (Bennett and Kottasz, 2000; Tomasini and Van Wassenhove, 2009). The 2004 Indian Ocean earthquake and tsunami, for example, led to a huge response from the donor community while other emergencies that were neglected by the media received few resources. In the case of government donations, money that has been pledged is not always delivered. In the refugee crises in Darfur, Western Sudan and after Hurrican Mitch, for example, aid agencies only received a third of promised funds (Oloruntoba, 2005).

Strong fluctuation with respect to donations makes it very difficult for aid agencies to efficiently use their resources. A sudden inflow of financial resources might overload an aid agency's capacity to handle these resources while very limited donations might force an aid agency to reduce valuable resources and capacities. Furthermore, strong fluctuations also make it very difficult for aid agencies to plan their activities. Kovàcs and Spens (2007) divide disaster relief operations into three phases: preparation, immediate response and reconstruction. Adequate funding for the preparation stage is very important and strongly determines how quickly and efficiently an aid agency can respond to a disaster (Jahre and Heigh, 2008). However, strong fluctuation concerning occurrence and impact of disasters as well as availability of financial resources make it very difficult for aid agencies to decide on adequate investment in capacity and resources.

Speed and timing

Once a disaster occurs and an aid agency decides to provide aid, an immediate response is critical and time delays can lead to loss of lives (Kovàcs and Spens, 2007; Beamon and Balcik, 2008). How quickly an aid agency can respond to a disaster depends on how well it is prepared. However, it also depends on how quickly the aid agency is able to receive money to set up operations.

Some aid agencies have resources that they can use to pre-finance their operations before they get aid from outside sources (Development Initiatives, 2009a). The IFRC, for example, has a Disaster Relief Emergency Fund. The Fund is used immediately after a disaster and allows the IFRC to respond quickly in many emergencies, for example, in the case of the Gujarat earthquake (Chomilier *et al*, 2003). Even if aid agencies have resources to pre-finance their operations, long waiting times increase the risk of not being fully reimbursed for their operations. Aid agencies that do not have the financial resources to pre-finance their operations need to wait until they receive the aid before they can respond, resulting in costly time delays of their response.

While many donors are aware of the importance of quick aid, they are also increasingly concerned about financial accountability. The increasing desire for financial accountability slows down the process of releasing funds from official sources, which can take up to 40 days (Walker and Pepper, 2007).

Flexibility

Aid agencies receive earmarked and un-earmarked donations. Government aid is often earmarked with respect to regions and use. Private donations are also often earmarked for a certain disaster; however, they are typically not earmarked concerning how an aid agency needs to spend the money and private donors are typically willing to reallocate donations if the need arises (Development Initiatives, 2009a).

Earmarked donations reduce aid agencies' flexibility in their allocation decisions. Aid agencies might be forced to allocate money and resources to emergencies, activities and projects that provide little benefit to them and reduce the efficiency and effectiveness of their operations.

Allocation to emergencies

Private as well as government donors frequently earmark donations with respect to the emergency that it should be used for. Resources are often not allocated according to need but according to donors' preferences, which are often driven by media attention in the case of private donors and political and strategic considerations in the case of government donors. Many resources, for example, were used to respond to the 2004 Indian Ocean earthquake and tsunami.

Too many resources allocated to one area not only take away from resources being used in other areas, but they can also lead to increased competition, increased prices and wasted resources (Van Wassenhove, 2006; Beamon and Balcik, 2008). Furthermore, donations that are earmarked for certain areas also restrict aid agencies' flexibility concerning their allocation of resources. Postponement strategies have been shown to potentially lead to large cost savings in humanitarian supply chains (Oloruntoba and Gray, 2006; Jahre and Heigh, 2008). Earmarked donations severely restrict the use of postponement strategies.

Allocation to resources and activities

Donor funding tends to focus on direct programme and project inputs and does not provide enough funding for disaster preparedness, infrastructure, information and logistics systems (Gustavsson, 2003; Thomas, 2007; Beamon and Balcik, 2008). IFRC, for example, found it challenging to obtain funds for disaster preparedness and capacity building (Chomilier *et al*, 2003). Besides too little funding for the preparation phase there is also often too little funding for the long-term phase of reconstruction (Kovàcs and Spens, 2007).

Resources need to be available in the right amounts in each one of the phases of disaster relief – preparation, immediate response and reconstruction. A very strong focus on short-term relief leads to a lack of planning, capacity building and investment in infrastructure and employee training as well as a lack of long-term reconstruction (Kovàcs and Spens, 2007; Oloruntoba, 2007; Perry, 2007; Beamon and Balcik, 2008; Goncalves, 2008; Jahre and Heigh, 2008). Lack of planning leads to high competition for available resources, overuse of expensive and unsafe transportation modes, and high supply chain costs (Oloruntoba, 2007; Jahre and Heigh, 2008). Not enough investment into computer systems and employee training leads to wasted time, reduced efficiency and increased costs (Perry, 2007; Beamon and Balcik, 2008).

Aid agencies also benefit from flexibility concerning changing the allocation of resources at any time. The situation in the emergency areas frequently changes. Hence, it is important to be able to change the allocation of resources accordingly. Donors' increasing desire for financial accountability has led to a large amount of funding being allocated against requests for proposals, which has strongly limited aid agencies' flexibility in their allocation decisions (Walker and Pepper, 2007).

Volume, speed, fluctuation, predictability and flexibility of funds from different donors and intermediaries determine how desirable they are for aid agencies. Private funds, for example, are typically preferable to official funds with respect to the speed with which they are available as well as the flexibility with which they can be used (Development Initiatives, 2009a). Not every aid agency values these characteristics equally. The speed of financial flows, for example, is more important for small organizations that do not have enough money to pre-fund activities than large organizations with funding reserves. Also, the importance of these characteristics differs with respect to the phase of the disaster relief. Speed of aid provision, for example, is very important for immediate disaster relief; therefore private funds are often used in this phase. Jahre and Heigh (2008) describe preferred funding models for each disaster relief phase differentiating between earmarked and non-earmarked as well as long- and short-term funds highlighting the importance of flexibility and speed in the response phase of disaster relief. Table 2.1 provides an overview of the main objectives of fund management

TABLE 2.1 Main objectives and challenges in fund management

Disaster Response Phase	Main Objectives	Challenges
Preparation Phase	Forecast costs and needs for various disaster scenarios	Volume: Shortage of funds because of donors' lack of interest
	Allocate resources to prepare for future disasters and disaster response	Uncertainty concerning future needs
Immediate Response Phase	Quickly secure adequate amount of funds for disaster response under limited information concerning need	Speed: Slow disbursement of government funds
		Predictability: Strong role of media and strong fluctuation in private funds
		Flexibility: Increasing earmarking of private and official funds
Reconstruction Phase	Allocate funds to long-term projects considering need, impact and cost-effectiveness	Volume: Shortage of funds because of donors' lack of interest
	Consider interaction between reconstruction phase and immediate response phase, especially for areas where emergencies occur frequently	Predictability: Reallocation of funds if new emergencies arise
		Different agencies and funding streams for disaster relief and long-term development make coordination difficult

and their associated challenges with respect to the characteristics discussed in this section.

Aid agencies need to determine the optimal portfolio of funding sources based on the characteristics of funds from different sources, their specific needs, the type of disaster they respond to, as well as the phase of the disaster response. Some previous papers analyse the importance and trade-offs between some of these characteristics. Toyasaki and Wakolbinger (2010) analyse the trade-off between size and flexibility. Jahre and Heigh (2008), Balcik and Beamon (2008) and Martinez *et al* (2010) highlight the importance and value of flexibility. Further exploring of the trade-offs between these characteristics is an important area for future research projects.

Incentives provided by donors

As the previous section highlights, donors can directly influence how their donations are used. Besides this direct impact, donors also indirectly strongly influence how aid agencies use their resources. When aid agencies make decisions concerning resource allocations, they need to consider how these decisions impact donors' perception of their work and future donation streams. Hence, donors strongly influence aid agencies' allocation decisions by the way they make their own allocation decisions.

Donors are interested in making sure that their donations are used in the best possible way; however, they cannot directly measure the impact that their donations make. Although there are current efforts to measure the performance of aid agencies, this is not an easy task due to the intangibility of services offered and characteristics of humanitarian operations (Beamon and Balcik, 2008). Since donors cannot directly observe the quality of an aid agency's work, they need to rely on indicators of the quality of aid agencies' operations. Examples of indicators that are currently used are visibility, fundraising cost percentage and overhead costs. These indicators have the potential to provide aid agencies with incentives for inefficient resource allocations.

Visibility

Aid agencies that want to make sure that their efforts are noted by donors, especially private donors, need to focus their activities on emergencies and activities with high donor visibility. Aid agencies' desire for visibility leads them to provide aid in areas with a lot of media coverage, which are typically areas that receive a lot of aid (Oloruntoba, 2007). Furthermore, it leads aid agencies to focus their activities on the response phase, since it provides more possibilities for activities with high visibility than the preparation phase (Jahre and Heigh, 2008) and it encourages aid agencies to participate in projects and activities with high donor visibility, for example, provision of food as opposed to infrastructure development. In addition, the need to be visible to donors can also reduce collaboration and coordination between aid agencies (Tomasini and Van Wassenhove, 2009) since aid agencies want to emphasize their own contribution.

Financial indicators

Government and private donors increasingly focus on financial accountability. In the case of government donors, this leads to slower disbursement of donations and reduced flexibility for aid agencies as discussed in the previous section. Private donors who want to make informed decisions when donating money often base their decisions on financial indicators including low overhead costs and fundraising cost percentages. Overhead costs include support activities. By supporting aid agencies that have low overhead costs, donors encourage aid agencies to focus on the response phase and they discourage them from allocating sufficient amounts of money to the preparation phase with all the negative consequences discussed in the previous section. Furthermore, competition to lower costs might lead to underreporting of administrative expenses (Krishnan *et al*, 2006).

The fundraising cost percentage is defined as total fundraising costs divided by total funds raised. This indicator is typically reported by aid agencies. It represents the percentage of donations that cannot be directly used for disaster relief activities. Donors and policy makers generally do not like a high fundraising cost percentage and prefer aid agencies that have a low fundraising cost percentage (Sargeant and Kaehler, 1999; Hopkins, 2002). However, when looking at fundraising cost percentages, one must consider that dollars raised for unpopular emergencies typically need more fundraising activity than fund-raising for popular emergencies. Trying to reach a low fundraising cost percentage might encourage aid agencies to focus their fundraising activities on popular emergencies. Hence, this might lead to a further emphasis on emergencies that already receive a disproportionate amount of aid. This problem is further increased due to the increasing amount of private funds that are earmarked for certain disasters as well as donors' increasing willingness to enforce these allocation decisions.

A strong donors' focus on visibility and financial accountability can provide aid agencies with incentives to use their resources in an inefficient way. It can potentially encourage aid agencies to provide aid for emergencies that are already crowded with relief groups and it can encourage them to focus on short-term objectives instead of long-term goals. Donors are starting to realize that visibility and financial indicators do not always reflect the quality of aid agencies' work. However, better indicators are still largely missing. The development of better measurement for aid agencies' performance, need in different regions, the impact of improvements in logistics systems and time value of money, are of utmost importance.

Summary and recommendations

Due to increasing demand for disaster relief and limited resources, it is important that aid agencies use the available resources in the most efficient and effective way. Currently, misallocation of resources reduces efficiency and effectiveness of humanitarian operations.

Resource misallocations are partly caused by aid agencies' difficulty in determining the optimal allocation of resources. People working for aid agencies often are not aware of the value of logistics and information systems and, therefore, do not invest enough in these areas. Researchers in the area of OR/MS are working on projects that highlight the value of logistics operations and information systems. Furthermore, models are developed that help aid agencies allocate appropriate resources to different phases and activities in humanitarian operations. Very often these models do not consider financial constraints. Considering the reality in which many aid agencies work, including financial constraints into models of logistics operations and analysing their impact is of utmost importance.

Resource misallocations are also partly caused by funding systems and they will not disappear until funding systems are improved and donors are educated about the consequences of their decisions. Donors provide resources for aid agencies and, hence, have a strong influence on the allocation decisions that aid agencies make. On the one hand, donors can directly impact allocation decisions by earmarking donations for certain emergencies or activities. On the other hand, they can provide incentives that guide aid agencies towards a certain decision. Currently, donors frequently explicitly and implicitly provide incentives for aid agencies' behaviour that leads to too many resources being allocated to direct response instead of preparedness and reconstruction and to too many resources being provided for emergencies with a lot of media attention while others are largely neglected.

Aid agencies, UN agencies, and donors are aware of the shortcomings of the current funding systems. They are re-evaluating their previous approach to humanitarian funding and they are trying to improve the system, as many initiatives such as the Good Humanitarian Donorship (2003) Initiative indicate. Operations researchers and operations research tools could significantly contribute to establishing sound humanitarian funding systems. System dynamics models can highlight the interaction between money and product flows as well as trade-offs between short-term and long-term goals (Goncalves, 2008). Principal-agent models (Seabright, 2001) can provide insights concerning how to align the interests of the different stakeholders in the humanitarian supply chain. Development of indicators of need and quality of response (Beamon and Balcik, 2008) can reduce the information asymmetry between donors and aid agencies. Optimization models can highlight the trade-offs between different characteristics of funding flows and they can allow aid agencies to create the appropriate funding portfolios.

We expect to see more research papers in the future that address these issues.

References

Aldashev, G and Verdier, T (2010) Goodwill bazaar: NGO competition and giving to development, *Journal of Development Economics*, **91**(1), pp 48–63

Altay, N and Green, WG III (2006) OR/MS research in disaster operations management, *European Journal of Operational Research*, **175**(1), pp 475–93

Andreoni, J (1998) Toward a theory of charitable fund-raising, *Journal of Political Economy*, **106**(6), pp 1186–213

Andreoni, J (2006) Leadership giving in charitable fund-raising, *Journal of Public Economic Theory*, 8(1), pp 1–22

Andreoni, J and Payne, A (2003) Do government grants to private charities crowd out giving or fundraising?, *The American Economic Review*, **93**(3), pp 792–812

Balcik, B and Beamon, BM (2008) Facility location in humanitarian relief, *International Journal of Logistics: Research and Applications*, **11**(2), pp 101–21

Barman, E (2008) With strings attached, *Nonprofit and Voluntary Sector Quarterly*, **37**(1), pp 39–56

Beamon, BM and Balcik, B (2008) Performance measurement in humanitarian relief chains, *International Journal of Public Sector Management*, **21**(1), pp 4–25

Bennett, R and Kottasz, R (2000) Emergency fund-raising for disaster relief, *Disaster Prevention and Management*, 9(5), pp 352–60

Bilodeau, M and Slivinski, A (1997) Rival charities, *Journal of Public Economics*, 66, pp 449–67

Casteneda, M, Garen, J and Thornton, J (2009) Competition, contractibility and the market for donors to non-profits, *Journal of Law, Economics and Organization*, 24, pp 215–46

Chomilier, B, Samii, R and Van Wassenhove, LN (2003) The central role of supply chain management at IFRC, *Forced Migration Review*, 18, pp 15–18

Development Initiatives (2009a) Public support for humanitarian crises through aid agencies, United Kingdom; available at http://www.globalhumanitarianassistance. org/Projects.htm [accessed 21 April 2009]

Development Initiatives (2009b) GHA Report 2009, United Kingdom; available at: globalhumanitarianassistance.org [accessed 21 October 2009]

Fisher, FM (1977) On donor sovereignty and united charities, *American Economic Review*, **67**(4), pp 632–38

Goncalves, P (2008) System dynamics modeling of humanitarian relief operations, working paper, MIT Sloan Research Paper No 4704–08

Good Humanitarian Donorship (2003) 23 principles and practices of good humanitarian donorship; available at: http://www.goodhumanitariandonorship.org (accessed 10 June 2010)

Gustavsson, L (2003) Humanitarian logistics: context and challenges, *Forced Migration Review*, 18, pp 6–8

Hopkins, BR (2002) *The Law of Fundraising*, Wiley, New York

Jahre, M and Heigh, I (2008) Does failure to fund preparedness mean donors must prepare to fund failure in humanitarian supply chains?, NOFOMA Proceedings, Helsinki, Finland

Khanna, J and Sandler, T (2000) Partners in giving: the crowding-in effects of UK government grants, *European Economic Review*, 44(8), pp 1543–56

Kingma, BR (1989) An accurate measurement of the crowd-out effect, income effect, and price effect for charitable contributions, *The Journal of Political Economy*, 97(5), pp 1197–207

Kovàcs, G and Spens, KM (2007) Humanitarian logistics in disaster relief operations, *International Journal of Physical Distribution & Logistics Management*, 37(2), pp 99–114

Krishnan, R, Yetman, M and Yetman, R (2006) Expense misreporting in nonprofit organizations, *The Accounting Review*, 81(2), pp 399–420

Macrae, J (2002) The bilateralisation of humanitarian response: trends in the financial, contractual and managerial environment of official humanitarian aid. A background paper for UNHCR; available at: http://www.odi.org.uk/resources/download/3197.pdf [accessed 10 October 2009]

Martinez, AP, Stapleton, O and Van Wassenhove, LN (2010) Field vehicle fleet management in humanitarian operations: a case-based approach, INSEAD Working Paper No 2010/38/TOM/INSEAD Social Innovation Centre

Okten, C and Weisbrod, BA (2000) Determinants of donations in private nonprofit markets, *Journal of Public Economics*, 75(2), pp 255–72

Oloruntoba, R (2005) A wave of destruction and the waves of relief: issues, challenges and strategies, *Disaster Prevention and Management*, 14(4), pp 506–21

Oloruntoba, R (2007) Bringing order out of disorder: exploring complexity in relief supply chains, in *Proceedings 2nd international conference on operations and supply chain management: regional and global logistics and supply chain management*, ed U Laptaned, Bangkok, Thailand

Oloruntoba, R and Gray, R (2006) Humanitarian aid: an agile supply chain?, *Supply Chain Management*, 11(2), pp 115–20

Oosterhof, L, Heuvelman, A and Peters, O (2009) Donation to disaster relief campaigns: underlying social cognitive factors exposed, *Evaluation and Program Planning*, 32(2), pp 148–57

Perry, M (2007) Natural disaster management planning, a study of logistics managers responding to the tsunami, *International Journal of Physical Distribution and Logistics Management*, 37(5), pp 409–33

Ribar, DC and Wilhelm, MO (2002) Altruistic and joy-of-giving motivations in charitable behavior, *The Journal of Political Economy*, 110(2), pp 425–57

Rose-Ackerman, S (1982) Charitable giving and 'excessive' fundraising, *The Quarterly Journal of Economics*, 97(2), pp 193–212

Sargeant, A and Kaehler, J (1999) Returns on fundraising expenditures in the voluntary sector, *Nonprofit Management and Leadership*, 10(1), pp 5–19

Seabright, P (2001) Conflicts and objectives and task allocation in aid agencies: general issues and application to the European Union, in *The Institutional Economics of Foreign Aid*, ed B Martens, Cambridge University Press

Starke, C (2007) Social entrepreneurs, lead donors, and the optimal level of fundraising, in *Operations Research Proceedings 2007*, eds J Kalcsics and S Nickel, pp 237–41, Berlin Heidelberg: Springer

Street, A (2009) Review of the engagement of NGOs with the humanitarian reform process, synthesis report commissioned by the NGOS and Humanitarian Reform Project; available at: http://www.icva.ch/doc00003914.pdf

Thomas AS (2007), Humanitarian logistics: enabling disaster response, Fritz Institute, San Francicso, CA

Thomas, AS and Kopczak, LR (2005) From logistics to supply chain management: The path forward in the humanitarian sector, white paper, Fritz Institute, San Francicso, CA

Thornton, J (2006) Nonprofit fund-raising in competitive donor markets, *Nonprofit and Voluntary Sector Quarterly*, 35(2), pp 204–24

Tomasini, R and Van Wassenhove, LN (2009) *Humanitarian logistics*, Palgrave Macmillan, Hampshire, UK

Toyasaki, F and Wakolbinger, T (2010) Impacts of Earmarked Private Donations for Disaster Fund-raising, working paper [under review]

Van Wassenhove, LN (2006) Humanitarian aid logistics: supply chain management in high gear, *The Journal of the Operational Research Society*, 57(5), pp 475–89

Vesterlund, L (2003) The informational value of sequential fundraising, *Journal of Public Economics*, 87(3–4), pp 627–57

Walker, P and Pepper, K (2007) Follow the money: a review and analysis of the state of humanitarian funding, background paper for the meeting of the Good Humanitarian Donorship and Inter Agency Standing Committee, 20 July, Geneva; available at: http://www.reliefweb.int/rw/lib.nsf/db900SID/AMMF-75MGSC/$FILE/Tufts-July2007.pdf [accessed 1June 2010]

Acknowledgement

This work was partially funded by a Summer Research Grant from the Fogelman College of Business and Economics, University of Memphis, and a Start-up Fund at Faculty of Liberal and Professional Studies, York University. This support is gratefully acknowledged.

03
The importance of information technology in humanitarian supply chains
opportunities and challenges in the Helios project

MARTIJN BLANSJAAR AND CHARL VAN DER MERWE

Abstract

After a long period of hesitation, there appears to be a positive change in attitude in humanitarian organizations towards engaging with information systems/information technology (IS/IT) to support their supply chains. This chapter discusses the specific case of such a project within Oxfam GB; its challenges and what it aspires to achieve.

In addition, the chapter reviews the opportunities presented by the Helios project to provide a relatively cheap and simple IS solution to many of the standard humanitarian logistic information management challenges. It argues that engagement with the development of Helios will not only provide NGOs with an improved understanding of their internal supply chain dynamics but, more importantly, it will encourage agencies to think beyond their own needs and reflect on the benefits that standardization and common IS platforms can bring to their aid programmes and the people they try to assist.

Introduction

The aim of this chapter is to discuss the development of humanitarian logistic information systems within the non-government organization (NGO) Oxfam GB and, in doing so, to reflect on the current challenges facing many similar organizations engaged in the provision of emergency relief to those affected by disasters. As an introduction to the discussion, the chapter will first consider the management of supply chain information in the context of (humanitarian) emergency relief efforts. To achieve this, however, it is necessary to provide an explanation of the subjective use of terminology, before we briefly introduce Oxfam GB as the organization that is the subject of this case study.

Thus, when speaking of 'the sector' we refer to the group of UN Agencies, International Organizations and private International Non Governmental Organisations (INGOs), as well as their local partners and counterparts, that are engaged in the provision of (humanitarian) emergency relief in response to a crisis. Importantly, it should be noted that, for the majority of these organizations, emergency relief is but one part of a broader portfolio containing a mix of development, policy, advocacy and campaigning work, largely aimed at assisting in the betterment of living conditions of people in the poorer parts of the world.

Oxfam GB itself was founded in 1942 as the 'Oxford Committee for Famine Relief' in an effort to assist famine victims in Greece during the Second World War. It has since grown to a £250 million/year portfolio of campaigns, development and emergency aid programmes delivered across some 60 countries, making it the largest INGO in the UK and one of the 10 largest INGOs in the sector as a whole. During the 1980s Oxfam GB started to reach out to similar organizations around the world to form an international confederation. As a result, Oxfam International was started in 1995 and is currently made up of 14 national affiliates working increasingly closely together in the delivery of their programmes and fundraising.

The relevance of supply chain information

Current humanitarian supply chain improvement initiatives

Disasters create chaos. Existing structures break down, authority is dispersed and many people are left to fend for themselves in critical conditions. An effective disaster response should, therefore, at least mitigate the chaos and, ideally, overcome it. However, considering that over 1,200 (I)NGOs were part of the response to the 2004 tsunami response in Indonesia, and a similar number were registered with the United Nations Office for the Coordination of Humanitarian Affairs (UNOCHA) in Haiti in the third month after the earthquake, it is clear that sheer weight of numbers is not the answer.

Indeed, the ability of local authorities and relief providers to restore order in the aftermath of a disaster is probably the most important current discussion topic in and about the aid sector. Much has been achieved, for example the establishment of the cluster system in the main sectors of activity (such as protection, health, education, shelter, etc) has provided a hugely valuable mechanism for agreeing the division of work, obtaining a broad overview, passing essential instructions and discussing the programme approaches being adopted by participants.

Within the cluster system mentioned above, the World Food Programme (WFP) has assumed the role of lead agency for logistics. As such, the cluster coordination role focuses on infrastructure updates, managing bottlenecks such as international ports of entry, secondary (air/road) hubs, and the provision of capacity for logistics activities and/or infrastructure repair. In addition, a number of Humanitarian Response Depots (HRDs) and other prepositioning facilities hold stocks of relief materials in strategic locations across the globe. UNOCHA also keeps central registers of those organizations within the sector that are holding stocks of key materials and equipment, and this information is regularly published for general use.

These examples do not represent an exhaustive list of the efforts being undertaken to facilitate and coordinate supply chain activities across the sector, but they do reflect some of the more important initiatives that are designed to manage scarce resources more effectively and they also emphasize the increasing appreciation of the importance of logistics operations to the delivery of aid in general.

However, as demonstrated by the recent Cluster Evaluation Report (Stoddard *et al*, 2007), there is also much that still needs to be done. Within this chapter, we want to focus specifically on the opportunities that would be delivered by the harmonization of ways-of-working between agencies within the sector and the consequential facilitation of critical information exchange. It is argued that such harmonization has the potential to provide a massive improvement both in the general efficiency and effectiveness of humanitarian programmes as well as in the management of the associated supply chains.

Humanitarian supply chain planning and management

Having outlined some of the key initiatives aimed at improving humanitarian supply chain management, and recognizing that they are, as yet, insufficient to deliver the performance improvements that we seek, the next section of this chapter steps back and considers at a more basic level how the flow of goods itself is planned and managed within the humanitarian field.

In essence, there are two ways in which aid organizations go about planning material requirements for their programmes. The first is situational, in which non-standard materials are used and the quantities and types to be supplied are based on a detailed understanding of the precise requirements for a specific activity in a particular context. It will be quickly appreciated that this approach requires a very good knowledge of the local context and market and is, thus, normally used when there is ample lead-time for project planning.

The second method is that of employing a standardized approach that is based on consolidated experience of the agency in regard to the type of programmes (eg medical aid or water distribution) it deploys. This enables the provision of a generic activity template that can be set up in a very short timeframe. In response to a disaster, organizations that specialize in emergency relief typically use the second method to execute template interventions. Through these, they push materials (such as water purification equipment or kits for the treatment of cholera patients) into the affected area or, as Oxfam often does, they use a slightly more responsive approach based on a core 'menu' of emergency material that their programme staff can choose to call forward. An alternative approach employed by some NGOs is to use more loosely defined lists of standard items, sometimes in combination with knowledge of the local market, to help them put together the services they provide for more specific disaster scenarios. Meanwhile, those that get caught up unprepared have to make it all up on the spot!

Agencies that have off-the-shelf 'template' response programmes or situation-specific scenarios have a definite advantage in the immediate aftermath of rapid-onset disasters. Their ability to push pre-selected materials and teams into the crisis area allows them to hit the ground running. However, as soon as the disaster timeline moves beyond life-saving first aid, search and rescue and some emergency distributions, such responders are faced with the challenge of early recovery and reconstruction, and generally finding appropriate ways forward for that specific event and context. This is becoming even more urgent as the general view within the sector of what constitutes a good response is evolving towards the integration of immediate life-saving work with 'early recovery', which, in turn, merges with longer term rehabilitation efforts.

Thus, although programme templates may be resilient and effective in the immediate onset of a disaster, they do not remain appropriate for long. Situation-specific scenarios can take more account of the environment and last longer but, unfortunately, the level of detail required to give them operational value also makes them more sensitive to changes in critical variables. And when a disaster hits there are plenty of these – for example, local markets will be severely disrupted so that prior knowledge and supplier relations are no longer quite the assets they used to be. Meanwhile, the count of people affected changes every day, priorities shift with new agencies arriving and coordination mechanisms kicking in, while security or other problems arise overnight and demand that plans are adjusted.

In short, template programmes take considerable time and effort to create, have a limited lifespan due to, for example, the development of new programme approaches and/or materials, and they have limited generic applicability. For example, programme templates built on extensive experience in providing for the sanitation requirements of refugee populations in rural areas from the 1980s and 1990s are of little practical use in an urban disaster in 2010. By the same token, situation-specific scenarios need to be continuously monitored and updated to stay relevant.

In practice, therefore, we see that standard or template responses are very necessary, but also of limited use, both in a particular emergency as well as in the long run. As a result, when facing new contexts and when making the inevitable and necessary shift from 'pushing' materials to that of allowing programme staff to formulate more appropriate requirements, the supply chain needs to become responsive and run on demand. However, the obvious challenge when attempting to supply 'on demand' in the immediate-response context is to match short-cycle programme planning reviews with appropriate lead-times for the materials requested. It is a volatile environment, and tailoring to demand is only useful if delivery can be achieved in quick and timely fashion.

From this brief discussion of the challenges of meeting the needs of the beneficiaries in the aftermath of a disaster, we hope that the crucial role of supply chain information becomes immediately apparent. Put simply, in order to support a realistic planning process for relevant programme activities, the humanitarian logistician requires a continuous and dynamic view of needs, and of progress in meeting them, together with the associated availability and lead-time information across a broad range of commodities.

It is against this background that the aim of this chapter is to discuss the work within Oxfam GB to resolve these challenges through a systems development project known as 'Integrating Logistics in Project Planning and Management' (ILPPM). It will also discuss the broader approach within the sector as a whole by considering the Helios project, which is aimed at the development of a supply chain information systems solution that can be applied across a number of organizations. However, before considering these two initiatives in detail, it is necessary to draw a brief sketch of the background and current state of supply chain management, and its associated information systems, within the sector.

Some recent history

At the January 2004 Humanitarian Logistics Conference (HLC) hosted by Fritz Institute in Geneva, the senior supply/logistic managers of around 40 UN agencies and INGOs discussed their efforts to develop supply chain information systems as part of a broader review of the state of supply chain management in the sector. The objective of the discussion was to 'see if there are opportunities to share cost in future developments, build sustainable tools and create a common platform through collaboration' (Fritz Institute, 2004).

This session was held against the background of emergency and distress relief funding that has, according to the OECD Annual Reports, risen from some US $350 million in the mid-1980s to 7.3 billion/year in 2003. This was accompanied by a significant increase in the demand for improved accountability and transparency of aid agencies. In respect of the latter, historically, donors might have asked for a simple overview of what had been provided to whom and when; but today they require a detailed account of how the activities were carried out, and at what cost particular outputs were achieved.

Within organizations themselves, growth has not just meant more work and more donor requirements, but it has also stimulated the development of professional practice and a drive to systematically embed improvements both internally and within the system as a whole. Such efforts to improve programme quality and coordination in response to major emergencies have, in turn, increased the demand for real-time information. In addition, commercial firms and the armed forces have begun to take a more prominent place among the providers of international aid. Thus, agencies that want to maintain a leading position within the sector need not only to have good programme concepts, but they also increasingly require good internal systems that are capable of meeting ever-increasing standards and, ideally, contributing to their development.

Because their operations are largely in resource-poor settings where, historically, infrastructure was weak or non-existent, computer literacy low and the set-up and network cost of portable technology high, aid organizations have generally exhibited a relatively low interest in the use of IT/IS applications as part of their programmes, preferring to use the 'proven and tested' over innovative approaches. However, the 2004 HLC meeting coincided with a rapid expansion of mobile telephone networks and a parallel reduction in the cost of data communications networks – even in the poorer countries of the world. In addition, reliability is improving and there appears to be no shortage of computer-literate staff who are able to support such programmes.

As a result, some of the larger agencies have global IS projects under way and even though smaller ones often still focus on 'paper and spreadsheet' approaches, everyone agrees not only on the importance of supply chain (information) management for effective humanitarian operations, but also shares concerns over the difficulty of obtaining broad support for the investments required.

Why should this be? Arguably the nub of the problem is that supply chains remain 'undervalued' and, in simple terms, are still not considered critical to the success of aid programmes. So while there is good understanding that supply chains represent a significant area of project expenditure (which has, in turn, fed demands for control and (donor) compliance in operations), the realization that the design and management of supply chains might also have a major impact on project results and cost efficiency is only just beginning to emerge. In part, this may well reflect the shortage of senior supply and logistics roles (and suitably qualified personnel), as well as an under-representation of the function in project design and planning stages. Indeed, it is probably realistic to suggest that many agencies view supply chains as a non-core service they would be delighted to outsource while, at the same time, ignoring the need for the tools and skills to control and direct the resultant service provision challenge.

It is also fair to say that the cost of systems development is high, and that discretionary funds are limited. Indeed, the bulk of agency income is 'earmarked', often in the form of grants from institutional donors that are related to a particular programme and are, thus, intended to deliver specific project outputs. That said, in some INGOs, a small percentage of the earmarked funds will be available for project overheads, but this will only cover some of the cost of indirect expenditure on that specific project leaving none available for the more substantial activities required to run the organization. As a result, unearmarked funds (mostly from private donors) need to be used for any investment in innovation or institutional development, and for funding the organization's autonomous programme decisions. However, even in organizations with a relatively high percentage of private income, such unearmarked funds are scarce and their allocation will, in all probability, be a heavily contested area!

Against this background, the 2004 discussion on supply chain systems development can be seen as providing an accurate measure of the state of affairs within the sector. Although participants were clearly in favour of standardization (and even expressed an interest in the possibility to develop a generic system), the absence of a standardized and shared means of evaluating system requirements meant that agencies were unable to overcome the perceived differences in the nature of their programme activities. As a result, each was left working with, at best, only partly compatible ERP purchase modules or other supply packages originating in entirely different industries.

The Helios initiative

A progressive new idea

The initiative for the development of Helios supply management software was taken by Fritz Institute, which is a US non-profit organization based in San Francisco, California. It was founded in 2001 by Mr Lynn Fritz, a social entrepreneur and philanthropist, and the former chairman and CEO of Fritz Companies, a Fortune 1000 global logistics corporation.

Prior to the development of Helios, Fritz Institute and the International Federation of Red Cross and Red Crescent Societies (IFRC) had collaborated in introducing the Humanitarian Logistics Software (HLS) that was specifically aimed at meeting the requirements of the IFRC logistics organization. Indeed, it was the development of HLS that prompted the idea of a more generic supply chain information system that could be used by the majority of agencies in the sector. However, it was only in the aftermath of the 2004 Asian tsunami that Fritz Institute were convinced that such a sector-wide systems solution was an urgent priority. They conducted a baseline study that confirmed the results of their discussions with agencies and this made clear that:

- there was no 'off the shelf' system in the market that meets the requirements of agencies operating in the sector;
- there is a duplication of systems and process efforts across organizations;
- cost is a prohibitive factor in bringing improvement plans to fruition, in particular in medium sized and smaller agencies.

As a result, at the 2005 HLC, Fritz Institute announced their intention to embark on the development of two software solutions, Humanitarian Track and Trace (HTT) and Humanitarian Supply Chain Solutions (HSCS). The former was designed to address the track and trace requirements in the field, and to provide improved stock visibility and accountability. HSCS, meanwhile, would focus on the management of goods from the appeal to the end distribution points, and would include simplified procurement and warehouse modules. Bearing in mind that the systems gap was largest for small and mid-sized agencies, the proposed solutions would be hosted on an Application Service Provider (ASP) model, making it cost-effective and accessible for organizations that might not have the resources necessary to support a system in-house (Fritz Institute, 2005).

Early design

In the first phase of this project, Fritz Institute collaborated with the International Medical Corps (IMC), Merlin UK, the Kenya Red Cross and

World Vision International to define requirements for the intended supply chain information solutions. From this collaboration, it quickly became apparent that the key challenge was that of resolving two issues. On the one hand, the need for internal process improvements within each agency that would deliver their programmes more effectively and efficiently, and on the other, the need for improved coordination to achieve the same effect between agencies.

In relation to the former challenge, the project team had to establish whether they could usefully maintain an approach based on the use of a generic 'best practice' concept which was bedevilled by the multitude of differences in the detail of how the participating agencies worked, and the consequential variation in the improvements that were being sought. To develop better coordination between agencies, the focus would be on good information exchange around supply chain bottlenecks such as entry ports or distribution hubs, and providing overall visibility of plans, progress and pipelines to assist inter-agency decision making.

The original concept of the systems development project was to manage supply chain information in relation to each emergency situation rather than in relation to individual agencies. Although this would have made the system an 'add-on' instead of an integral solution for participating organizations, it was considered the most feasible approach in view of the importance attached in preliminary discussions to differences in ways of working between agencies. As the project developed, however, it became clear that it was not practical for the participating organizations to assume that they would end up using different systems between first phase emergency response and other programmes and/or pursue solutions for certain parts of their supply chains only.

On the other hand, and rather more positively, it transpired through the design process that it was indeed possible to identify a generic 'best practices' approach that could be used by all agencies. As a result, concentrating the project on delivering a standard solution then became the obvious way forward and, once that was achieved, the inter-agency tailoring would be a relatively simple matter of configuring reports and areas of shared information.

The early collaboration concluded with a beta version of one product newly called 'Helios' that was subsequently exposed to the wider sectors through meetings in Nairobi and Brussels. As part of this process, Oxfam GB attended the Brussels meeting (along with 12 other agencies), and was given a comprehensive demonstration of the product. This, inevitably, resulted in further in-depth discussions around supply chain commonalities, the state of systems efforts within various agencies, and the future of Helios itself. Nevertheless, the reception was positive, but it also emphasized the importance of keeping the system field focused, light, simple and user friendly and confirming the need for a hosted solution. As a result, the first (beta) version of Helios was officially finalized in December 2006 and made available to the wider sector for testing and potential implementation.

Process redesign in Oxfam GB

Meanwhile in Oxfam GB, the organization's response to the 2004 Asian tsunami had prompted a critical review of its humanitarian capacity and capability. This led to the launch in December 2005 of the Oxfam GB Humanitarian Investment Plan (HIP). The HIP was a combination of projects, the majority of which targeted the development of specific functional areas (including HR, supply and logistics, and finance) within the organization's Humanitarian Department.

The supply and logistics component of the HIP focused on people, systems and process. It was aimed at increasing the area's capacity through the introduction of new key positions, while reinforcing its capability by providing entry-level supply and logistics 'education' and a more unified systems approach. This was achieved through two key projects; Logistics Education and Development (LEAD) and Field Assets Control and Tracking System (FACTS). The FACTS project was, in reality, a heavily tailored version of a commercial purchasing software, set up in a limited number of locations with a view to strengthening field supply functions – importantly, however, it remained relatively isolated from the finance and programme systems.

The effort to pull these improvement programmes together resulted in the launch (in 2006) of a new internal project known as Integrating Logistics into Project Planning and Management (ILPPM). This was, in essence, an integral business process redesign but with a bias towards the supply and logistics functions in recognition of the shortfalls in agreed process and systems standards in this area. Thus, although the ILPPM was the result of the initiative to strengthen Oxfam's humanitarian response, it had its roots in longer standing problems with the quality and integrity of field programme support and delivery processes.

These reflected the fact that, over time, function–driven maintenance of (field) procedures for programmes, finance and logistics had led to somewhat disconnected and cumbersome processes that were at risk of compromising efficiency, loss prevention and compliance. The ILPPM thus addresses:

- alignment of functional strategies and tactics in programme delivery;
- standardization, harmonization and integration of process embedded in day-to-day operations through operating procedures that provide short instructions to project-based staff;
- the development of human capacity and capability through standardization of management lines and job or role profiles, and providing staff with the opportunity to develop through technical and management training;
- provision of an integrated systems environment for programme and support functions.

The ILPPM project has two key deliverables: 1) providing a project activity planning tool; and 2) designing, sourcing and implementing a global supply chain information system. It also has the explicit aim of tying these two together and ensuring a proper fit with other functional areas such as funding and finance. Thus, the ILPPM is about integrating processes and systems at project level and establishing the role of supply and logistics as a central element based on the vision that integration between project activity planning and supply chain planning is an essential element in delivering more effective projects and programmes.

However, to achieve this, the ILPPM project had to challenge the 'traditional project' (or vertical stovepipes) in which functional processes tend to run in isolation. To achieve the desired result, the Oxfam GB logistics/supply chain team had to start proactively engaging with a wider stakeholder group to understand and define the requirements of stakeholders both internally (within logistics) and externally (finance, funding, internal audit, etc). This required a more creative approach to normal systems development processes.

The ILPPM project consisted of a number of standard systems development processes:

- establishing a working group that can design, implement and manage the ILPPM processes;
- defining requirements for a supply chain information system and evaluating potential suppliers through a request for proposal process;
- engaging with shortlisted suppliers to determine what percentage of their products meets high-level requirements;
- selecting a supplier and configuring a product.

To support these standard processes, Oxfam GB created a fictional end-user called 'Tamina' to ensure that the ILPPM processes remains field-focused. Tamina represented a broad range of diversity as (s)he could, at any time, assume various functional roles, albeit with one constant approach – Tamina works at the 'front line' close to the Oxfam partners, allies and beneficiaries. The Tamina concept has been instrumental in prioritizing end-user requirements, maintaining focus on facilitating programme delivery, and it also helped to define the approach to change used to move to the desired end state.

A brief overview of the ILPPM journey

Given the enormity of the cultural/organizational challenge inherent in ILPPM, the following paragraphs offer a brief overview of some of the processes used to help to ensure the integrity of the outcomes. For example, the ILPPM working group consisted of representatives from supply and logistics, IS/IT, international finance, and programme management. The working group was led by an independent manager who was not part of a key stakeholder group – an important consideration that helped to ensure that the ILPPM processes were accountable and transparent to all key stakeholders.

The requirements-gathering process was guided by one overarching principle. The resulting system must be accessible to staff with medium to low IT literacy and must be field-focused. In practical terms, this meant that it must meet the needs of front-line staff and not head office management requirements!! To achieve this, a User Reference Group was established early in 2007 that represents all functional areas at field level, as well as some regional functions. The user group provided invaluable inputs to all ILPPM processes as well as offering a place to discuss and manage expectations of front-line staff.

The working group delivered an 'options appraisal' document that recommended a shortlist of three potential IT/IS products. These consisted of two in-house application platforms currently used by Oxfam GB and Helios. The options appraisal document also recommended that Oxfam GB pilot Helios. In this respect, it was argued that Oxfam GB already has substantial experience working with the two existing in-house platforms and, thus, has enough information to develop a cost-benefit analysis for the business case. The Helios system is, however, relatively new and untested and developing a cost-benefit analysis of Helios would prove challenging without the benefit of a pilot. Essentially piloting Helios in an operational environment would be the only way to really assess if the system would meet Oxfam's requirements. Importantly, as mentioned earlier, Helios also offered 'best practice' processes built for the sector and provided an opportunity to road-test Oxfam requirements against these. This enabled the ILPPM team to identify unrealistic user requirements and also capture the risk of automating current 'bad' practice.

Based on the recommendations from the ILPPM team it was decided to start an 18-month Helios pilot project. Its objectives were to:

- establish whether the Helios software meets Oxfam GB's supply chain needs for overseas programmes;
- estimate the potential costs and timescales involved in implementing Helios in Oxfam GB;
- assess governance risks associated with Helios ownership and support base.

The software (Helios v1.0) was set up to run alongside existing administration in pilot locations in Indonesia and Sudan. The pilot formally concluded that there is a good degree of process fit between Helios and Oxfam GB supply chain business processes; however, it also made clear that there are a number of minor enhancements and some more major development work required to ensure that Oxfam GB can be confident that Helios-supported processes are robust enough to replace the organization's existing paper-based systems.

In terms of governance, it was agreed with Fritz Institute (the legal owners of Helios), that a charitable foundation would be set up in which current and future users of Helios could participate in managing the product. The foundation is to own the software with the objective of issuing it under open-source licence as part of a wider promotion of the use of IS in supply chain management within the sector. The foundation will also undertake controlled development of Helios, sustaining a generic, quality-assured 'core' of new releases for new agencies to engage with and/or to upgrade existing users.

Within Oxfam GB, the conclusions of the pilot study were factored into a business case comparing three alternative solutions. Helios came out as the best option and, in summary, three main points were made in its favour:

- Despite requiring some development work, Helios would be ready for deployment well ahead of other options and, therefore, it would start to generate the expected returns several years earlier.

- Helios is simple, light, and fit-for-purpose, thus comparatively well suited for deployment in a (field project) environment that has relatively little experience with information systems and a generally weak infrastructure.

- Oxfam subscribes to the benefits pursued for the wider sector but also recognizes that, closer to home, Helios offers opportunities for expanding to Oxfam affiliates and partner organizations more readily than would be the case if it took the more conventional approach of adapting a commercial application for its own use.

Based on the business case recommendations, Oxfam GB's Corporate Management Team decided in early 2009 to develop and roll out Helios over two years to 75 per cent (in budget terms) of its International Division programme. Scope and time restrictions were imposed in light of the early effects of the then unfolding global financial crises. However, the fact that the project was allowed on Oxfam's investment agenda at that time at all can be seen as signalling an important step forward in the recognition of supply chains as a core concern for the organization.

Reflections on the ILPPM project

The expected benefits of Oxfam's ILPPM/Helios project range from improving the quality and speed of programme decision making to reductions of process times and surplus inventory as well as better visibility and control of the flows of goods. Critically, however, although the system makes these benefits possible, the extent to which they are realized in practice depends on changes in the way people behave. If people are to work with a system that expects them to behave differently, change should be introduced in advance and with credible authority to ensure they are able and willing to comply.

Delivering this message is complicated in Oxfam in several ways. First, Oxfam tries to decentralize authority; country programme teams are very diverse and have historically had a great deal of autonomy to define ways of working. Second, supply chain issues are not a common 'top five' concern. In part, the argument is circular here as paper-based administrations provide very limited information and project management involvement is mostly reactive. So unless there is something visibly wrong, and without information to support a case, it can be difficult to get attention. Thus, without the information that Helios would bring, there is little appreciation of the benefits that the system would bring. Third, like many organizations over a certain size, Oxfam has developed a degree of isolation of functions and, as a result, spreading the message across these functions is, inevitably, challenging and time consuming.

So far, however, the project has managed to overcome these obstacles and it is considered that a number of preconditions and elements in the project design are likely to have contributed to this:

- senior management in International Division agreed an overarching strategy for the development of (divisional) competence in supply and logistics;
- all relevant stakeholders and decision makers were involved in the project from an early stage;
- users have been widely consulted throughout the project;
- the project management board represented all key functions.

Indeed, it is clear that, in the current deployment stage, planning and resourcing for change management is at least as important as training system users or ensuring functioning hardware and networks for the system to run on. As part of this recognition, benefit tracking tools have been designed and introduced to keep the project focused on its intended outcomes.

Further growth: inter-agency efforts

The Helios Foundation

From early on in the project a Helios User Group was active in advising Fritz Institute, which, in turn, provided a product manager and administrative support and had contracted the services of an offshore software firm for programming and technical support. When the project was originally set up, World Vision International (WVI), Merlin, International Medical Corps

(IMC) and the Kenya Red Cross all collaborated with Fritz Institute in the development of the initial version of the system. However, for a variety of reasons, not all of these organizations were able to expand internally beyond the initial phase and, as a result, when Oxfam joined the project in 2007 only WVI and IMC remained active in the user group.

Although Oxfam is currently piloting and working on the development of Version 2 of the system, the user group has not expanded. Instead, the Helios Foundation for Supply Chain Management was formally established as a charitable organization in the UK early in 2010 with the aim of promoting the use of information technology in humanitarian supply and logistics. Within the Foundation, WVI, Oxfam and Fritz Institute have provided directors for the Board and made arrangements under the Articles of Association to ensure that future participants in the project can provide additional directors.

A key way of implementing the Foundation's aim is the provision of software. The coordination of its development, and the creation of supporting materials are ways to achieve this. To support this, the intellectual property (IP) rights for the Helios system have been transferred by Fritz Institute and Oxfam to the Foundation and the software has been released under open source licence (AGPL v3). In addition, the Fritz Institute's contract with the software development firm has also passed to the Helios Foundation.

Consortium for British Humanitarian Agencies (CBHA)

The Helios Foundation recently took the opportunity to pursue its objectives under a contract with the Consortium of British Humanitarian Agencies (CBHA) – a network of 15 UK-based NGOs. As part of a larger agreement between the CBHA and the UK Department For International Development (DFID), the Helios Foundation is undertaking software pilots with seven CBHA member agencies of which two – Oxfam and WVI – are already Helios users. Of the remainder, the NGO Merlin has returned to the project after a few years' absence, while Save the Children, Tear Fund, Concern, and the International Rescue Committee are new to Helios.

The project has two stages. In the first stage, the five new agencies will define their requirements and evaluation criteria and perform a limited pilot with Helios business processes and software for an element of their supply chain. This stage ends with the creation of a business case for each organization and a consolidated evaluation in June 2011.

In the second stage, which is due to end in December 2011, two or more of the organizations will engage in a deployment of the software to a common programme location.

The first stage aims to demonstrate, for each agency, the potential of:

- greatly improved visibility of supply chain activity and detailed utilization of funds/donations;

- reduction of operating cost and shorter, more reliable lead times;
- timely and accurate management information.

In the second stage the objective is to explore the possible benefits of:

- joint overviews of material and service components of project plans;
- consolidation of supply chain information;
- operational prioritization and resolution of bottlenecks;
- standardization and harmonization of work process.

The project intends to demonstrate that a common (supply) systems platform will greatly enhance collaboration and coordination in emergency response. The project will also assist in the standardization/harmonization of process, as well as supporting benchmarking to promote best practice. The ultimate aim is to ensure that emergency aid is delivered, and is shown to be delivered, more accurately, faster and cost-effective as a result.

Concluding remarks

As has been demonstrated by the unfolding story related in this chapter, the development of information technology and systems is making progress in humanitarian supply chains and, in parallel, supply chain management is gaining increasing relevance and importance in organizations in the sector. Although the chapter has concentrated on the case of Oxfam GB and the Helios project, similar advances are taking place in other organizations and the overall momentum is growing.

It is also worth mentioning the recent publication of a supply chain reference task model for the sector. With the aim of providing aid organizations with a 'template to describe, manage and communicate the tasks and processes in their supply chains' (Blecken, 2010), Alexander Blecken's study adds substantially to the foundation of a unified, sector-specific approach to supply chain process and systems and makes an important contribution to future modelling and design of supply chains for (humanitarian) aid programmes. This will, unquestionably, lead to further improvements in future increments of Helios and other systems efforts, and it represents an excellent example of the integration of academic and practitioner thinking within the field.

Oxfam GB's experience shows that supply chain transformations such as the ILPPM project are possible, but also that they are far from easy not least as agencies need to commit scarce resources while, at the same time, accepting that success is earned slowly. Meanwhile, Oxfam has made a very important statement of intent through its support for the Helios project, which is already helping to bring resource barriers down by offering a relatively simple way to take up IT in supply chain management. Even more importantly, perhaps, the Helios concept will help build the case, and the associated justification, for standardization, learning and collaboration across agencies and regardless of the success of the software, promote a common language and benchmarking practice between them.

There is, clearly, still some way to go to achieve the establishment of a broad, common supply chain information platform in the sector, but the promise of what it will be able to deliver in improving the provision of aid to the millions of people who will depend on it over the next decennium makes it worth every effort.

References

Blecken, A (2010) *Humanitarian logistics: Modelling supply chain processes of humanitarian organisations*, Kuehne Foundation Book Series on Logistics, No 18, Berne: Haupt

Fritz Institute (2004) Proceedings of the 2004 Humanitarian Logistics Conference; available at: http://www.fritzinstitute.org/prgSC-HLC2004-proceedings.htm [accessed 29 Nov 2010]

Fritz Institute (2005) Proceedings of the 2005 Humanitarian Logistics Conference; available at: http://www.fritzinstitute.org/prgSC-HLC2005-proceedings.htm [accessed 23 Nov 2010]

Stoddard, A, Harmer, A, Haver, K, Salomons, D and Wheeler, V (2007) Cluster approach evaluation: Final report, Overseas Development Institute; available at: http://www.odi.org.uk/resources/download/3820.pdf [accessed 23 Nov 2010]

04
Humanitarian logistics metrics
where we are and how we might improve

PETER TATHAM AND KATE HUGHES

Abstract

The management of a supply network is, by any measure, a complex undertaking, and this is reflected in the broad range of prescriptions found within the literature. As a means of guiding management in subsequent decision making, one might reasonably anticipate that considerable effort would be invested in the design of appropriate performance metrics – but, surprisingly, this does not appear to be the case. Furthermore, in non-profit organizations the challenge is much larger given the absence of a (or, perhaps, the) core metric of profitability. In the humanitarian logistic field, there is a recognition of the need for appropriate metrics, but capturing the data in a robust way is hampered by the particular circumstances of operating in an environment with its inherent limitations on communications and IT. However, such metrics that do exist are, typically, focused on operational data – the number of boxes delivered on time, the associated cost, etc. Such efficiency-based metrics are clearly important, but the authors argue that the key challenge is that of developing outcome or effectiveness metrics so that the achievements of the relief operation as a whole can be more readily understood. It is suggested that this process may be aided through the use of 'quality of life' metrics borrowed from the medical field.

Introduction

The frequency and severity of natural and man-made disasters is increasing, in terms of the numbers of individuals injured or killed, the scale of the financial impact and the cost of response and recovery in relation to these events (EM-DAT, 2008). For example, over 220,000 people are officially estimated to have lost their lives following the January 2010 earthquake in Haiti (OCHA, 2010). Similarly, although the casualty level for Hurricane Katrina of 2005 was relatively low (1,836 deaths), it was the largest natural disaster in the history of the United States with damage recorded in excess of US$100 billion (Dyson, 2006). As neither the human nor financial impact of such events is likely to diminish in the near future, it is clear that there is a role for both academics and practitioners to work together to develop appropriate policies, processes and procedures that will help mitigate their effect.

In this regard, there is a general acceptance that logistics is the cornerstone of emergency response with some estimates suggesting that between 60 and 80 per cent of the expenditure of aid agencies can be classified under this broad heading (van Wassenhove, 2006; Blansjaar, 2009). Indeed, it can be argued that agencies responding to a disaster are actually logistics organizations, albeit with a specific mandate and a target set of beneficiaries. Unsurprisingly, and in the face of recent major challenges such as the response to the 2010 Haiti earthquake, there is increasing pressure to improve the logistics response in order to facilitate the provision of aid to end-beneficiaries in a more effective and efficient manner (Kovács and Tatham, 2009).

However, unlike a normal business model in which the customer exchanges cash for a particular set of goods and/or services, in the humanitarian arena funding is provided by the donor community, while those responding to disasters often act as proxies for beneficiaries who are not in a position to articulate their needs. Furthermore, it has been recognized that the beneficiaries may be reluctant to make any request(s) for fear that, if a particular item or service is not available, they would then receive nothing. Thus, unlike a normal free market model, those affected by a disaster are usually not able to 'shop around' and choose goods and services from alternative suppliers leading to a situation that Beamon and Balcik (2008) describe as an 'unregulated monopoly'. In addition, in the absence of any contractual agreement between the relief agencies and the beneficiaries, not only do the latter have limited means of legal redress if their expectations are not met, they are also not in a position to exit from this dependent relationship as, often, there are few alternatives (Hilhorst, 2002).

This decoupling of financial and material flows (and the consequential ambiguity over the identity of the true customer) represents a key difference between the high-level concepts underpinning the for-profit and the not-for-profit supply networks[1] (Walker and Russ, 2010). Within this context, the aim of this chapter is to consider the fitness for purpose of existing humanitarian supply network metrics and suggest potential ways in which they might be improved and/or supplemented.

To achieve this, the first section will set the scene by briefly outlining our understanding of the scope of humanitarian logistics and this will be followed by a discussion of the approaches to metrics commonly adopted in both commercial supply networks as well as those used by disaster response agencies. This background will underpin our key proposition: that existing metrics are insufficiently focused on the actual beneficiaries of this process, ie, those affected by a disaster. The final section will examine some of the recently developed 'well-being' metrics drawn from research in the healthcare and medical sectors for their potential use in humanitarian supply networks. In doing so, we are guided by the observation that 'People will do what's inspected, not what's expected' (Gattorna, 2009: 51). We argue, therefore, that use of such well-being metrics will assist in giving appropriate emphasis to improvements in the effectiveness of humanitarian supply networks in parallel with the existing measurements that are generally focused on their efficiency.

Humanitarian logistics

Before discussing various approaches to performance measurement, it is important to ground our understanding of the term 'logistics', which has a number of interpretations (Tatham and Kovács, 2007; Beamon and Balcik, 2008). Given that this chapter and, indeed, this book is focusing on logistics in a humanitarian context, we have chosen to adopt the oft-quoted definition from Thomas and Mizushima (2005: 60), that it is: 'the process of planning, implementing and controlling the efficient, cost-effective flow and storage of goods and materials as well as related information, from the point of origin to the point of consumption for the purpose of meeting the end beneficiary's requirements'. From this, it follows that a humanitarian logistician is one who is responsible for the management and operation of some part or all of this process.

Although it could well be argued that the above definition is closer to the commercial concept of supply network management than logistics (see, for example, Larson and Halldórsson, 2004; Larson *et al*, 2007; Halldórsson *et al*, 2008), the humanitarian community as a whole tends to prefer to use the term 'logistics' for such activities. Thus, in this chapter, the terms supply network management (SNM) and logistics are used interchangeably – a perspective that equates to the 're-labelling' model of Larson and Halldórsson (2004) and one that is not uncommon within the commercial arena (Okongwu, 2007).

Performance measurement in commercial supply networks

Unsurprisingly, given the increasing recognition of their importance to businesses, the whole subject relating to identifying metrics to underpin the measurement of supply networks has attracted significant academic and practitioner attention over the past decade. For example, a search conducted in June 2009 using the Emerald database with the string 'supply AND chain AND metrics' resulted in an initial group of 995 papers, while Neely (1999) estimated that some 3,615 articles on the subject had been published in the period from 1994 to 1996. However, and notwithstanding this volume of academic interest, it is unclear how effective current metrics actually are in providing the necessary management information. For example, Morgan (2004: 526) notes that: 'Performance measurement is one of the core elements of managerial activity and the choice of PMS [Performance Measurement System] is central to achieving corporate strategic targets. Because of this, one would expect managers to agonise over the design of their PMS, and yet, there is little research evidence to say that this is so.' In this context, it is important to differentiate between performance management and its measurement. The former is, arguably, what management is all about – but that activity is critically dependent on a successful measurement system that is able to capture the required information on which subsequent decisions are based.

A further analysis of the literature related to performance measurement carried out by Lambert and Pohlen (2001) identifies a number of themes, and these are also substantiated by other researchers as indicated within each of the following sections:

- Every organization's measurement system (including their selection of metrics) will be unique as it must support the achievement of that organization's *equally unique* corporate goals (Neely, 1999; Morgan, 2004; Micheli and Kennedy, 2005).

- Organizations frequently employ too many metrics, and many of these are inappropriate. The challenge is, therefore, to identify the metrics that provide the most relevant information and greatest benefits for the business for the least investment of resources in capturing relevant data (Hilhorst, 2002; Hofman, 2004; Morgan, 2004).

- Most performance measurement systems capture data relating to functional goals rather than integrated business processes, and these are dominated by financial and operational metrics (Morgan, 2004; Christopher and Mangan, 2005), and rarely include intangibles or socio-cultural performance measurements (Gunasekaran and Kobu, 2007).

- Supply network management cuts horizontally across the business and tends to challenge the traditional vertical organizational hierarchies. Unfortunately, metrics that capture how a particular firm drives profitability may actually reduce integration throughout the supply network (Lambert and Pohlen, 2001).

Further to this, Neely *et al*, (2000: 2450) note that 'metrics should be both financial and non-financial' and this reinforces the argument that, for a set of metrics to be relevant, it must include both of the above categories. These should be used in appropriate combination to monitor the internal activities of the business as well as those that are sensitive to customer requirements. Thus, the selected internal controls should be designed to help measure (and, hence, aid the management of) the costs and performance of the organization using metrics such as 'cost per sale'. In parallel, most organizations in the for-profit sector are also likely to benefit from metrics that focus on the customer, including the measurement of activities including the percentage of 'on time deliveries' and 'enquiry response times'.

Performance measurement in not-for-profit supply networks

This distinction between internal and customer-related metrics raises the question of the suitability of adopting such metrics used by for-profit organizations to measure the 'success' of supply network activities in a post-disaster response situation where not-for-profit organizations dominate. However, as mentioned in the introduction to this chapter, the underpinning operation of the humanitarian supply network is, to a large extent, provided through donations from governments, organizations and individuals that enable non-government organizations[2] (NGOs) to meet their particular mandate (Beamon and Balcik, 2008). In reality, while clearly focused on a target sub-set of beneficiaries, NGOs must also ensure that appropriate information is readily available to meet the demands of the donor community.

Given that the beneficiaries of the humanitarian response system cannot, for the reasons articulated above, be directly equated to the end-customers of a commercial supply network, it is unsurprising that the wisdom of simply migrating a suite of business metrics to the not-for-profit environment has not been questioned. However, a further complication reflects a similar challenge to that identified by Morgan (2004) in his discussion of issues surrounding the outsourcing of manufacturing to developing nations. In such situations the use of 'standard' metrics is often unsatisfactory as they often do not adequately account for all the cultural nuances impacting business activities. So, although the overall approach of commercial and humanitarian supply networks to metrics may be similar, it is argued they have some differing requirements.

The reality of the underpinning challenge to the NGO community is clearly laid out by Sawhill and Williamson (2001: 371) who ask: 'How can you measure such an abstract notion as to alleviate human suffering? How can an organization meaningfully assess its direct contribution to such a broadly stated mission? And by whose criteria should success be measured?' The next sections of this chapter will, therefore, consider the current attempts to answer these questions from both an academic and a practitioner perspective.

Academic perspectives

To date, at least in comparison with the commercial environment, only relatively limited attention has been paid to the discussion of metrics for the management of not-for-profit supply networks within academic literature (Moxham and Boaden, 2007; Moxham, 2009). That said, a number of additional key sources in this area include Buckmaster (1999), Hofmann *et al*, (2004), Micheli and Kennedy (2005), Davidson (2006), Beamon and Balcik (2008) and Westveer (2008) all of whom describe both the complexities of performance measurement in this sector and the challenges of developing and applying a suitable measurement framework.

Within this body of research, and accepting that his focus is on not-for-profit organizations in general, Buckmaster (1999) distinguishes between various metrics that measure inputs, processes, outputs and outcomes (Figure 4.1). The distinction drawn between outputs and outcomes is an important one as the former tends to capture the direct products of a specific programme of activities (such as the 'number of food parcels provided', or the 'percentage of the population who have received aid'). In contrast, outcomes reflect the *benefits* received by the recipients of the aid activities, which might include new knowledge, increased skills, changed attitudes, modified behaviour, improved conditions or altered status. We would argue that such a characterization – especially as it refers to improved conditions or altered status – comes closer to the type of metrics that could be most relevant to NGOs in the humanitarian sector when capturing the perspective of the beneficiaries to aid and relief.

Following a review of the (then) current state of practice in the identification of metrics relevant to humanitarian response, Hofmann *et al* (2004) adopt an even wider focus concluding that, in general, NGOs lacked a system for measuring and analysing the impact of their work. In their typology, 'impact' is described as being either positive or negative, direct or indirect, and leading to primary and/or secondary long-term intended or unintended effects. By drawing on this approach, we recognize that it is firmly anchored in the realm of development aid work (as distinct from

FIGURE 4.1 A comparison of measurement frameworks for humanitarian supply networks

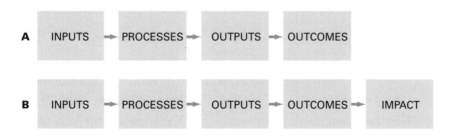

A   INPUTS → PROCESSES → OUTPUTS → OUTCOMES

B   INPUTS → PROCESSES → OUTPUTS → OUTCOMES → IMPACT

SOURCES: Buckmaster (1999) and Hofmann *et al* (2004)

short-term post-disaster response) but, at the same time, the approach of Hofmann and his colleagues draws attention to the need to go beyond 'outcomes' and consider the 'impact' of any humanitarian interventions.

This move towards considering how performance measurement systems could (and should) be improved within the not-for-profit sector is a feature of more recent literature (see, for example, Moxham and Boaden, 2007) but, as recorded by Osborne *et al* (1995: 28), impact monitoring 'is difficult, and therefore occurs less frequently, though conversely it is one of the most significant forms of performance assessment'. Nevertheless, Hofmann *et al* (2004) describe an increasing focus on the need for impact assessments in the humanitarian sector which, as a part of a broader results-based management culture, is driven by both governments and donors. Despite this, however, an analysis of academic literature indicates that while there are many examples of process and output indicators, there is significantly less focus on those metrics that go further to identify and track the outcomes and/or impact of humanitarian activities (see Figure 4.1).

As an example, an analysis of the supply network and metrics supporting the work of the International Federation of Red Cross and Red Crescent Societies (IFRC) was completed by Davidson (2006). In this context it should be noted that the IFRC won the coveted European Supply Chain Excellence award in 2006 and, hence, the organization is likely to possess an above-average set of management metrics. According to Davidson (2006), the overall IFRC system is primed by requests from the field that are entered into a 'Mobilization Table' within their Humanitarian Logistic Software which is used to capture and manage data. This data drives the downstream processes that are managed by four key indicators:

- Appeal Coverage – which calculates both the number of items required that have been covered by donations and the number of items reaching beneficiaries as a percentage of the total number requested in the appeal.

- Donation-to-Delivery Time – which captures the throughput speed of goods in the supply network.

- Financial Efficiency – which relates to the cost of providing goods to beneficiaries.

- Assessment Accuracy – which measures the extent to which the budget for a particular disaster changes over time. This is a reflection of the accuracy (or lack thereof) of the initial assessment of the event.

It will be seen that, although elements of each of these metrics have some relevance to measuring the outcomes or impact of the humanitarian supply network, they do not really appear to focus on the challenge of accurately tracking the extent to which the disaster response meets the needs of the beneficiaries.

In a similar way Beamon and Balcik (2008) note that, due to the difficulties associated with measuring programme outcomes and impacts, most NGOs tend to measure performance related to inputs rather than outputs. As a result, they propose a measurement framework based on earlier work by Beamon (1999) that combines: Resources (where the costs of the evolution are measured in various ways); Outputs (relating to factors such as delivery volumes, fill rates, response times); and Flexibility (measures indicating the ability of the supply network to respond to a changing environment). Although the output element of this framework would not necessarily capture the perspective of the beneficiary, Beamon and Balcik (2008) make it clear that they believe the aim should be to quantify the amount of aid provided, and the extent to which it has reached the affected population. However, as in the case of the IFRC supply network, this approach does not specifically focus on ensuring that the needs of the beneficiaries are met. Nevertheless, Beamon and Balcik's work has been expanded by Westveer (2008) who proposed metrics relating to the quality of the output, such as the life expectancy of specific products (eg a tent). However, despite briefly alluding to the need for metrics that capture the views of the beneficiaries, Westveer does not pursue this issue in any detail.

In summary, although a number of academic researchers have attempted to develop metrics that capture the beneficiary's perspective, its operationalization remains elusive. This is clearly an important issue because, as Thomas and Ramalingam (2005: 8) note: 'Small changes in the type of aid administered and the process by which it is administered can potentially have a significant influence on the dignity and satisfaction of the aid recipients.'

Practitioner perspectives

It is clear from the above discussion that the development of appropriate metrics to support the management of a not-for-profit organization presents a significant cultural challenge. However, as Davidson (2006) observes, the capture of data requires time and money, and it can often be seen by those operating in the field as a distraction from their primary role of saving lives and enhancing the circumstances of the surviving beneficiaries. That said, NGOs as a whole do recognize that funding appeals are likely to reach a wider audience if supported by data rather than simply relying on emotional advertising. In this respect, the development of appropriate metrics is in line with the increasing desire on the part of both NGOs and their donors to improve the level of transparency (Walker and Russ, 2010), and this should lead to a greater level of accountability (Zimmerman and Stevens, 2006). This point was recognized in the recent UN Humanitarian Response Review (OCHA, 2005: 12), although the wording: 'The establishment of appropriate mechanisms to measure results, on which a consensus can be built between humanitarian organizations, donors and recipient countries' is notable for the absence of any mention of beneficiaries!

It could be argued that the existence of the Sphere Standards (Sphere Project, 2004) could provide the necessary policy lead for NGOs in this area. These standards lay down the minimum requirements for activities in disaster response and have been signed by over 400 organizations in 80 countries – although Hilhorst (2002) notes that there is an ongoing debate over the status of these standards. Should they be seen as absolute, as aspirational, or simply as a common language that can be used to debate challenging issues? Potentially the first step in 'value add' within this debate would be an agreement on a common language; however, emphasis on this aspect alone may result in the debate being sidetracked and the focus never moving on to the development of a series of appropriate, useable and measurable metrics that are aimed at capturing the needs and wants of the beneficiaries.

More broadly, however, a number of cases considering the issue of how best to measure the effectiveness of an NGO's supply network can be found within the academic literature. One example is the work of Sawhill and Williamson (2001) who proposed a framework for the US Nature Conservancy that clearly indicated the need for a measurement of the impact of this organization's work. In theory, given the organization's role of supporting habitats that cannot articulate their concerns, this case study is not dissimilar to the situation in which NGOs must make decisions on behalf of a group of beneficiaries. Unfortunately, however, the metrics chosen by the agency ('bio-diversity health' and 'threat abatement') are not directly transferable to the humanitarian logistic field. More importantly, these authors tested their measurement framework on 30 other not-for-profit organizations and reported that none of these groups had solved the general question of measuring success either.

Separately, Zimmerman and Stevens (2006) conducted a survey of 149 not-for-profit organizations in South Carolina. Among a wider set of questions, these researchers asked if the NGO concerned was making use of 'performance or outcome measures' (p 318), and although 65 per cent responded affirmatively to this question, it should be noted that its terms were not defined. In any event, and as discussed above, the research conflated two distinct concepts (ie 'performance' and 'outcome') and so no firm conclusions can be drawn from this work.

In an interesting reverse slant to the discussion, Brooks (2002) asked whether the approaches adopted in 'not for profit' organizations could be used to assist in the management of public sector (as distinct from 'for profit') entities. In this research the requirement for an outcome measure was underlined, and Brooks drew on the model of Kushner and Poole (1996) who include 'client satisfaction' as a key metric. Unfortunately, Brooks went on to suggest that this can be measured through customer interviews and repeat business ratios – neither of which is applicable to the underpinning scenario of this chapter.

Within the humanitarian logistics field itself, de Brito *et al* (2007) reported a case study of Médecins San Frontières – Holland (MSF-H) that assessed the extent to which this organization embraced what they perceived to be the key aspects of a humanitarian performance measurement system. These researchers concluded that:

- There is evidence that the strategic importance of logistics is recognized.

- MSF-H does not currently have accurate data to support performance measurement.

- Performance measurement is perceived to be important and there is organizational commitment to put it in place, but achieving this was considered to be rather difficult for the logistics division of this organization.

A second practitioner source is from the Logistic Resources and Mobilization Department (LRMD) of the IFRC, which has overall control of their supply network. According to Schulz and Heigh (2009: 1038), the LRMD's strategic goal is: 'To support the National Societies in ensuring that there is sufficient logistics capacity in terms of personnel and resources to deliver services in support of disaster preparedness activities. To achieve a response level of delivering an agreed set of standard relief items for a maximum of 5,000 families in 48 hours and a further 15,000 families in 14 days anywhere globally.' Clearly the 'agreed set' of relief items depends on the nature and location of the disaster but, typically, it includes: food items; hygiene kits; clothing; tents; blankets; and tarpaulins (ICRC, 2004). The list of requirements is normally generated in the aftermath of a disaster by the IFRC Field Assessment and Coordination Teams (FACTs) in consultation with members of the relevant Red Cross/Red Crescent National Society

(Heigh and Jahre, 2007). This has led the IFRC to develop a balanced scorecard-based performance management framework to manage their Regional Logistic Units (RLUs) in which the quadrants are Customer Service; Financial Control; Process Adherence; and Innovation and Learning.

Of these, the first quadrant (ie Customer Service) is the most relevant to the discussion in this chapter, but the detailed metrics very much reflect the RLU's role as a warehouse and inventory management centre that supplies 'front line' field workers. As a result, the metrics in use relate, once again, to the outputs of one element of the supply network (in this case the RLU), rather than to the outcomes of a given response operation and, as in other examples, do not capture the perspective of the aid recipients.

A further source of practitioner data is a web-forum hosted by the Humanitarian Logistics Association where the question of identifying humanitarian logistic Key Performance Indicators (KPIs) and their associated quality was raised (HLA, 2008). In response, the Emergency Logistics Manager for UNICEF gave an overview of a recent survey commissioned by that organization. Those surveyed indicated that their metrics were primarily focused on the areas of inventory quality and accuracy, service levels and finance. Furthermore, even within the area of service level metrics, the focus was on output (for example, the 'percentage of orders delivered' to the final consignee on or before the agreed date), rather than on outcomes or impacts. However, of greater relevance was the suggestion that survey respondents were also interested in monitoring positive and negative feedback from the final consignee. Unfortunately, the identity of this 'final consignee' (which could be either the individuals or organization(s) responsible for the 'last mile' of the supply network, or the beneficiaries themselves) was not specified.

At least in part, this apparent disregard for logistic metrics that focus on the end-beneficiary may, of course, reflect an organizational construct within aid agencies that differentiates between those responsible for 'programmes' and their supporting cast such as the logisticians – with the former element typically having greater organizational muscle. Thus, the programme staff may well be focusing on outcomes or impacts, leaving logistic metrics to be more process-orientated. Such a construct would reflect the concerns raised over half a decade ago by Thomas and Kopczac (2005) in which these authors severely criticized the lack of recognition for the importance of the logistics function. It also runs counter to the prevailing wisdom within the commercial field. The essence of supply network management is a recognition of the need for those managing the network to attempt to ensure that it operates seamlessly with a unitary focus not on, for example maximizing profit or benefit to the individual components, but on the effect of the network as a whole in meeting the end-customer's requirements. Under such an approach, there should be a much clearer line of sight from impact back to inputs (Figure 4.1B) than appears to be the case in many humanitarian agencies. Development of suitable metrics to provide this overview will do much to help ensure the coherence and focus of the network, to highlight optimal (and, indeed, sub-optimal practices) and, ultimately, to raise awareness of the requirements of the aid recipients.

On the other hand, there is some evidence of an increasing recognition of the importance of the beneficiary's perspective as noted by Apte (2010) who reports that CARE-USA are measuring performance in terms of 'timeliness of response', 'competence in core sectors' and 'quality and accountability'. Clearly, the last of these has the potential to allow an improved focus on the impact of an NGO's response from the perspective of an aid recipient, but this would appear to be the exception rather than the rule.

In summary, it is clear that performance measurement remains a difficult area for NGOs with numerous challenges, which include:

- Development of an appropriate suite of metrics for use in the field.
- The ability of fieldworkers to gather accurate information while working under significant time pressure and (often) in extreme circumstances.
- A system for ensuring that the captured information is available for use by the appropriate NGO decision maker in both a current disaster situation, and to guide future aid activities.
- Recognizing the key role of the logistic community as an integral part of the NGO's operations, which, in view of its massive impact on an organization's costs must actually become the prime focus of managerial attention rather than, as in many cases, perceived as a 'back office function' of little importance.

The recipient's perspective

As will be seen from the above discussion, there is a paucity of logistic-related metrics that satisfactorily meet the challenge of measuring the benefit of the humanitarian interventions from the perspective of the recipient of the post-disaster assistance – and this is all the more surprising in view of the final clause of the Thomas and Mizushima definition of humanitarian logistics quoted above: 'for the purpose of meeting the end beneficiary's requirements'. One approach suggested by the Fritz Institute for helping improve humanitarian logistics is the 'effective use of voice' (Thomas, 2003: 12), and this can be readily applied to improving and focusing the response on the needs of the recipient. The Fritz Institute's effort to give effect to this approach is demonstrated though a series of articles on 'recipient reflections' or 'perceptions of the affected' (Fritz Institute, 2005; 2006a; 2006b; 2007a; 2007b) all of which take the generic view that 'aid must not be donor-driven, but incorporate in a significant way the needs of the beneficiaries, which may be different across contexts' (Fritz Institute, 2005: 8).

In a similar way the International Council for Science (ICSU) has suggested that the decision-making process for disaster risk, response and humanitarian aid would improve if the needs of the beneficiaries are incorporated in the process: 'To be effective, communication of risk information and recommendations must be seen as a social process, reflecting the interests of the recipients' (ICSU, 2008: 24). Clearly, the first step in such an approach is to identify what is required and needed by recipients in the broadest sense of disaster response and, in this regard, NGOs are usually able to identify the 'requirements' for survival after disasters with some speed and accuracy especially based on past experience with these types of event. Indeed, for the most part, they do exceptionally well in the procurement, provision and supply of the essential goods and services required after an event. But we argue that NGOs should be aiming to extend this to include more than just *efficient* relief after a disaster, and drive further towards the provision of a more *effective* response that is tailored to the context of the requirements, needs (and, to a certain extent, the wants) of recipients. At the most fundamental level this includes the consideration of cultural and religious sensitivities and other 'soft' or intangible aspects that impact the perception by the recipient of the quality of the aid they receive. The overall aim being to select metrics that will foster an increase in 'the dignity of those who receive[d] it' (Thomas, 2005: 1) and improve 'the levels of satisfaction' with the aid process (Thomas, 2005: 4).

Perhaps unsurprisingly, the performance measures used in the reports for donors frequently focus on financial metrics in order to link activities in the field back to the donor communities or relevant stakeholder groups whose role is to ensure transparency and correct stewardship of funds. Although this is an important aspect of the overall process, efficiently supplying the wrong items is clearly a false economy. That said, a number of aid agencies do make a serious effort to gather feedback and information about their performance from their field staff and even from some recipients – although with this type of process it will be readily appreciated that there is a danger that the respondents will supply information about what is 'expected' rather than what is 'wanted'. However, this has been partially overcome in the micro-credit arena that uses 'a community-based approach, where recipients would interview each other about their experiences' (Kori and Onneshan, 2007: 1). Unfortunately, most evaluations are not consolidated across NGOs or events – except in the aftermath of major events such as the work of the Tsunami Evaluation Coalition (TEC). In short, the creation of relevant and widely accepted metrics encapsulating the viewpoint of the recipient remains in an embryonic form.

Nevertheless, one approach that has potential is the use of measures of human well-being that have moved beyond the comparatively simple metrics such as 'per capita Gross Domestic Product (GDP)'. Rather, they have been combined with other factors such as 'longevity', 'level of education' and appropriate measures of a 'standard of living'. Thus, as Tokuyama and Pillarisetti (2009: 45) note: 'Human wellbeing is increasingly being treated as a multidimensional measure... [with]... a number of composite indexes combining distinct dimensions.' Unfortunately, the resultant measures that are adopted are not directly applicable to situations in which the normal livelihood, social networks, physical infrastructure and communities of individuals have been severely disrupted. In such situations there is a need for more immediate metrics measuring well-being from a social-perceptual perspective. This observation follows on from the work of Quarantelli and Dynes (1977) whose discussion on modelling disasters and aid response emphasizes the importance and impact of socio-cultural conditions on individuals, families and communities.

One parallel area of research is that of quantifying 'the impact of natural disasters' for 'appropriate recovery measures and planning future mitigation strategies' (Gardoni and Murphy, 2010). To this end, the Disaster Impact Index (DII) has been proposed as a means of assessing the impact of an event on a society in terms of changes of capabilities. This index is based on the United Nations' Human Development Index (HDI) developed by the Pakistani economist Mabub Haq (1995) that incorporates life expectancy, education and per capita GDP at a national level to identify the development of societies. Other similar approaches to assessing 'well-being' in this way include the Life Quality Index (LQI), which uses similar factors to the UN's HDI, as it incorporates the expectancy of a healthy life at birth and the GDP per person (Nathwani et al, 1997; Pandey and Nathwani, 2004). However, the focus of the DII differs in two ways to our proposed metrics for identifying requirements of end-beneficiaries as discussed in this chapter. First, the emphasis of the DII is on the group/community rather than on individuals, and second, the use of the Index is for policy-making priorities for disaster recovery rather than identifying and assessing the requirements of beneficiaries *during* the disaster response effort. Similarly, the LQI is excellent for risk assessment and risk acceptability (Rackwitz, 2002 and 2006), but still does not address the end-beneficiaries' needs in the context of the aftermath of a disaster.

In order to help overcome this challenge, it is suggested that one potential source for 'borrowing' a measurement system is from the medical field where 'a number of models that provide a conceptualization of health and disability [exist]' (Pallant et al, 2006: 2). These frameworks emphasize the 'social model' of patient care where a disability is viewed as a socially induced problem, rather than as a characteristic of the individual. This area of research has developed out of the stream of publications focusing on a measure termed the 'quality of life' related to the medical model (see, for example, Renwick and Friefeld (1996) and Manns and Chad (2001)). The resulting 'patient-generated outcomes' focus on addressing the core problem(s) and empowering the individual by providing the means for self-assessment of the areas of their life that are impacted by their health issues. Although the value of using a patient's perspective has been debated for over a decade within the medical profession, it is argued that it may have some promise in providing a means by which the impact of post-disaster humanitarian logistic activities might be measured.

One example of the 'quality of life' metrics is the International Classification of Functioning, Disability and Health (ICF), as developed by the World Health Organization (WHO, 2005), which has been widely adopted in the medical field and includes identification of both health conditions and contextual factors such as the environmental and personal contribution to the situation. The ICF enables patients to self-report the perceived importance of the impact that their illness, disability or impairment has on their life. An alternative approach is that of the Perceived Impact of Problem Profile (PIPP) that includes a number of sub-scales such as self-care, mobility, participation, relationships and psychological well-being through which patients are able to assess the level of impact and distress of their situation (Pallant *et al*, 2006). Both these forms of the bio-psycho-social model seem to be ripe for adaptation into the humanitarian aid system at the stage following the immediate emergency response to disasters, and – in a similar way that Patel *et al* (2003) suggest for the health system – could be used as part of a consultative process to develop more appropriate long-term aid in a region.

Conclusion

Those affected by a disaster can, from a logistic perspective, be seen as the 'final customer' situated at the end of a complex supply network that is frequently created in haste and under extreme situations. Thus, although aid recipients are, self-evidently, the focus of NGOs' activities they are, at the same time, often the 'silent stakeholder' in the process. This is evidenced by the fact that the vast majority of the metrics used to monitor the operation of the supply network are financially (ie efficiency) based – although, in some cases, supplemented by metrics to capture the effectiveness of the NGO's response. It is argued therefore, that in order to improve the latter dimension of the delivery of service and goods to aid recipients, there is a need to include appropriate metrics capturing the recipient's viewpoint.

Although it is accepted that the basic survival needs of the beneficiaries are being met through the traditional response mechanisms, one result of the increasing pressure for transparency is the demand that NGOs provide aid in a manner that maintains and supports the dignity of the recipient. Clearly, however, the recipients of such aid cannot be seen in the same light as customers of commercial supply networks and, thus, there is a need to develop a suite of additional metrics to reflect the needs of the former and to measure not just the outcomes, but also the impact of all organizations that are responding to a disaster. It is suggested that, although progress is being made to meet the challenges outlined in this chapter, the next stage is to achieve an improved understanding of the beneficiaries' requirements. This is often obtained at a later date through interviews with survivors of disasters, but it would appear that this data is frequently not linked back to aid provision activities.

It is, of course, fully accepted that this is a complex area and, as demonstrated in the review of the approaches that have been considered, no particular method appears to be gaining favour. Against this background in which the principle of developing measures of effectiveness is unlikely to command serious challenge, it is argued that incorporating suitably adjusted 'quality of life' or 'well-being' metrics drawn from the healthcare sector may be a potentially valuable approach.

References

Apte, A (2010) Humanitarian logistics: a new field of research and action, *Foundations and Trends in Technology, Information and Operations Management*, **3**(1), pp 1–100

Beamon, BM (1999) Measuring supply chain performance, *International Journal of Operations and Production Management*, **19**(3), pp 275–92

Beamon, BM and Balcik, B (2008) Performance measurement in humanitarian relief chains, *International Journal of Public Sector Management*, **21**(1), pp 4–15

Blansjaar, M (2009) Private communication from the head of supply chain for Oxfam GB to the authors

Brooks, AC (2002) Can non profit management help answer public management's 'Big Questions?', *Public Administration Review*, **62**(3), pp 259–66

Buckmaster, N (1999) Associations between outcome measurement, accountability and learning for non-profit organisations, *The International Journal of Public Sector Management*, **12**(2), pp 186–97

Christopher, MC and Mangan, DJ (2005) Management development and the supply chain of the future, *The International Journal of Logistics Management*, **16**(2), pp 178–91

Davidson, AL (2006) Key Performance Indicators in humanitarian logistics, unpublished MEng thesis from the Massachusetts Institute of Technology (MIT)

de Brito, MP, van der Laan, E and Vergunst, D (2007) Humanitarian organisations and performance measurement, *Proceedings of the 1st International Symposium of Humanitarian Logistics*, Farringdon, UK, 19–20 November

Dyson, ME (2006) *Come hell or high water: Hurricane Katrina and the color of disaster*, Perseus Books Group, New York

EM-DAT Emergency Events Database (2008) Established by the Université Catholique de Louvain (Belgium); available at: www.emdat.be/Database/Trends/trends.html [accessed 29 June 2009]

Fritz Institute (2005) *Recipient perceptions of aid effectiveness: Rescue, relief and rehabilitation in tsunami affected Indonesia, India and Sri Lanka*; available at: http://www.fritzinstitute.org/PDFs/findings/NineMonthReport.pdf [accessed 15 Mar 2010]

Fritz Institute (2006a) *Hurricane Katrina: Perceptions of the affected*; available at: http://www.fritzinstitute.org/PDFs/findings/HurricaneKatrina_Perceptions.pdf [accessed 15 Mar 2010]

Fritz Institute (2006b) *Surviving the Pakistan earthquake: Perceptions of the affected one year later*; available at: http://www.fritzinstitute.org/PDFs/findings/PakistanEarthquake_Perceptions.pdf [accessed 15 Mar 2010]

Fritz Institute (2007a) *Recovery from the Java earthquake: Perceptions of the affected*; available at: http://www.fritzinstitute.org/PDFs/findings/JavaEarthquake_Perceptions.pdf [accessed 15 Mar 2010]

Fritz Institute (2007b) *The immediate response to the Java tsunami: Perceptions of the affected*; available at: http://www.fritzinstitute.org/PDFs/findings/Javatsunami_Perceptions.pdf [accessed 15 Mar 2010]

Gardoni, P and Murphy, C (2010) Gauging the societal impacts of natural disasters using a capability approach, *Disasters*, **43**(3), pp 619–36

Gattorna, J (2009) *Dynamic supply chain alignment: A new business model for peak performance in enterprise supply chains across all geographies*, Gower Press, Farnham, Surrey

Gunasekaran, A and Kobu, B (2007) Performance measures and metrics in logistics and supply chain management: a review of recent literature (1995–2004) for research and applications, *International Journal of Production Research*, **45**(12), pp 2819–40

Halldórsson, Á, Larson, PD and Poist, RF (2008) Supply chain management: a comparison of Scandinavian and American perspectives, *International Journal of Physical Distribution and Logistics Management*, **38**(2), pp 126–42

Haq, M (1995) *Reflections on Human Development*, Oxford University Press, New York, NY

Heigh, I and Jahre, M (2007) Improving the most important logistics – Changing the supply chain of International Federation of Red Cross and Red Crescent Societies (IFRC); teaching case prepared for BI School of Management, Department of Strategy and Logistics, Oslo, Norway

Hilhorst, D (2002) Being good at doing good? Quality and accountability of humanitarian NGOs, *Disasters*, **26**(3), pp 193–212

HLA (Humanitarian Logistics Association) (2008) Key Performance Indicators (KPI), discussion on HLA website; available at: http://www.humanitarianlogistics.org/log-forum/certification/821010198#855224852 [accessed 24 Jun 2009]

Hofman, D (2004) The hierarchy of supply chain metrics, *Supply Chain Management Review*, **8**(6) pp 28–37

Hofmann, C-A, Roberts, L, Shoham, J and Harvey, P (2004) Measuring the impact of humanitarian aid: a review of current practice, *Humanitarian Policy Group (HPG) Research Report*, Report 17, June, Overseas Development Institute, London, UK

ICRC (International Committee of the Red Cross) (2004) *Emergency items catalogue*; available at: http://www.icrc.org/emergency-items/ [accessed 24 Jun 2009]

ICSU (International Council for Science) (2008) *A science plan for integrated research on disaster risk: Addressing the challenge of natural and human-induced environmental hazards*, Report of ICSU Planning Group on Natural and Human-induced Environmental Hazards and Disasters

Kori, N and Onneshan, U (2007) *Improving microcredit programs. Listening to recipients: A summary of the pilot phase*, Golden Institute, May–August; available at: http://www.goldininstitute.org/_includes/File/GI_Summer_Report.pdf

Kovács, G and Tatham, PH (2009) Humanitarian performance in the light of gender, *International Journal of Productivity and Performance Management*, 58(2), pp 174–87

Kushner, RJ and Poole, PP (1996) Exploring structure-effectiveness relationships in nonprofit arts organizations, *Nonprofit Management & Leadership*, 7(2), pp 119–36

Lambert, D and Pohlen, T (2001) Supply chain metrics, *International Journal of Logistics Management*,12(1) pp 1–19

Larson, PD and Halldórsson, Á (2004) Logistics versus supply chain management: an international survey, *International Journal of Logistics: Research and Applications*, 7(1), pp 17–31

Larson, PD, Poist, RF and Halldórsson, Á (2007) Perspectives on logistics vs SCM: a survey of SCM professionals, *Journal of Business Logistics*, 28(1), pp 1–24

Manns, PJ and Chad, KE (2001) Components of life for persons with quadriplegic and paraplegic spinal cord injury, *Qualitative Health Research*, 11(6), pp 795–811

Micheli, P and Kennedy, M (2005) Performance measurement frameworks in public and non-profit sectors, *Production Planning and Control*, 16(2), pp 125–34

Morgan, C (2004) Structure, speed and salience: performance measurement in the supply chain, *Business Process Management Journal*, 10(5), pp 522–36

Moxham, C (2009) Performance measurement: examining the applicability of the existing body of knowledge to non profit organisations, *International Journal of Operations and Production Management*, 29(7), pp 740–63

Moxham, C and Boaden, R (2007) The impact of performance measurement in the voluntary sector, *International Journal of Operations and Production Management*, 27(8), pp 826–45

Nathwani, JS, Lind, NC and Pandey, MD (1997) *Affordable safety by choice: The life quality method*, Waterloo, Ontario: Institute for Risk Research, University of Waterloo, Ontario; available at: http://www.irr-neram.ca/pdf_files/LQI_Summary.pdf [accessed 18 Jun 2010]

Neely, A (1999) The performance measurement revolution: why now and what next? *International Journal of Operations and Production Management*, 19(2), pp 205–28

Neely, A, Bourne, M and Kennerley, M (2000) Performance measurement system design: developing and testing a process-based approach, *International Journal of Operations and Management*, 20(10), pp 1119–45

OCHA (UN Office for the Coordination of Humanitarian Affairs) (2005) *Humanitarian response review*; available at: www.reliefweb.int/rw/RWFiles2005.nsf/FilesByRWDocUNIDFileName/EVOD-6FUDDK-ocha-gen-02sep.pdf/$File/ocha-gen-02sep.pdf [accessed 26 May 2010]

OCHA (UN Office for the Coordination of Humanitarian Affairs) (2010) *Haiti earthquake situation report #23*;available at: http://www.reliefweb.int/rw/rwb.nsf/db900SID/MYAI-82X8LA?OpenDocumentandrc=2&emid=EQ-2010-000009-HTI [accessed 23 Feb 2010]

Okongwu, U (2007) An innovative supply chain management programme structure: Broadening the SCM skill set, *International Journal of Learning and Change*, 2(2), pp 192–212

Osborne, SP, Bovaird, T, Martin, S, Tricker, M and Waterson, P (1995) Performance management and accountability in complex public programmes, *Financial Accounting and Management*, **11**(1), pp 19–37

Pallant, JF, Misajon, RA, Bennett, E and Manderson, L (2006) Measuring the impact and distress of health problems from the individual's perspective: development of the Perceived Impact of Problem Profile (PIPP), *Health and Quality of Life Outcomes*, **4**, pp 36–49

Pandey, MD and Nathwani, JS (2004) Life Quality Index for the estimation of societal willingness to pay for safety, *Structural Safety: An International Journal on Integrated Risk Assessment for Constructed Facilities*, **26**, pp 181–99

Patel, KK, Veenstra, DL and Patrick, DL (2003) A review of selected patient-generated outcome measures and their application in clinical trials, *Value in Health*, **6**(5), pp 595–603

Quarantelli, EL and Dynes, RR (1977) Response to social crisis and disaster, *Annual Review of Sociology*, **3**, pp 23–49

Rackwitz, R (2002) Optimization and risk acceptability based on the Life Quality Index, *Structural Safety*, **24**(2–4), pp 297–331

Rackwitz, R (2006) The effect of discounting, different mortality reduction schemes and predictive cohort life tables on risk acceptability criteria, *Reliability Engineering and Systems Safety*, **91**, pp 469–84

Renwick, R and Friefeld, S (1996) Quality of life and rehabilitation, In *Quality of Life in Health Promotion and Rehabilitation: Conceptual Approaches, Issue and Applications*, eds R Renwick, I Brown and M Nagler, pp 26–38, Sage Publications, Thousand Oaks, CA

Sawhill, JC and Williamson, D (2001) Mission impossible? Measuring success in nonprofit organizations, *Nonprofit Management and Leadership*, **11**(3), pp 371–86

Schulz, S and Heigh, I (2009) Logistics performance measurement in action within a humanitarian organization, *Management Research News*, **32**(11), pp 1038–49

Sphere Project (2004) *Humanitarian charter and minimum standards in disaster response*; available at: www.sphereproject.org [accessed 23 Jun 2009]

Tatham, PH and Kovács, G (2007) The humanitarian supply network in rapid onset disasters, *Proceedings of the Nordic Logistic Research Conference (NOFOMA)*, Reykjavik, Iceland, 7–8 June

Thomas, A (2003) *Humanitarian logistics: Enabling disaster response*, Fritz Institute; available at: http://www.fritzinstitute.org/PDFs/WhitePaper/EnablingDisasterResponse.pdf [accessed 15 Apr 2010]

Thomas, A (2005) Improving aid effectiveness: Two studies suggested solutions, *UN Chronicle Online Edition*; available at: http://www.un.org/Pubs/chronicle/2005/issue4/0405p61.html [accessed 20 Apr 2010]

Thomas, A and Kopczac, L (2005) *From logistics to supply chain management: The path forward in the humanitarian sector*; available at: www.fritzinstitute.org/PDFs/WhitePaper/FromLogisticsto.pdf [accessed 22 Jun 2009]

Thomas, A and Mizushima, M (2005) Logistics training: necessity or luxury? *Forced Migration Review*, **22**(Jan), pp 60–61

Thomas, A and Ramalingam, V (2005) *Recipient perceptions of aid effectiveness*, Fritz Institute; available at: www.fritzinstitute.org/PDFs/findings/NineMonthReport.pdf [accessed 22 Jun 2009]

Tokuyama, C and Pillarisetti, JR (2009) Measuring and monitoring human welfare: how credible are the data in the UNDP's human development reports?, *Journal of Economic and Social Measurement*, 34(1), pp 35–50

Van Wassenhove, LN (2006) Humanitarian aid logistics: supply chain management in high gear, *Journal of the Operational Research Society*, 57(5), pp 475–589

Walker, P and Russ, C (2010) Professionalising the Humanitarian Sector, *ELRHA [Enhanced Learning & Research for Humanitarian Assistance]*; available at: http://www.elrha.org/professionalisation [accessed 3 Jun 2010]

Westveer, M (2008) Measuring performance during the immediate response of a sudden natural disaster, unpublished MBA thesis from Vrije Universiteit, Amsterdam, The Netherlands

WHO (World Health Organization) (2005) *International Classification of Functioning, Disability and Health*, World Health Organization, Geneva

Zimmerman, JAM and Stevens, BW (2006) The use of performance measurement in South Carolina nonprofits, *Nonprofit Management and Leadership*, 16(3), pp 315–27

Notes

1   It is accepted that the concept of a 'supply chain' is widely understood by academics and practitioners, but the authors would argue that the use of this phrase gives a false sense of a relatively straightforward linear arrangement of exchange. The reality is frequently much more complex and, thus, the term supply network has been adopted within this chapter as a means of reinforcing this point.

2   In practice there are clear distinctions between United Nations (UN) agencies such as the World Food Programme (WFP) or the UN Children's Fund (UNICEF), the International Federation of Red Cross and Red Crescent Societies (IFRC), and non-governmental organizations (NGOs) such as Oxfam or CARE. However, for simplicity, these are grouped together within this chapter under the generic heading of 'NGOs' except when the context dictates otherwise.

05
Humanitarian logistics and the cluster approach
global shifts and the US perspective

NEZIH ALTAY AND MELISSA LABONTE

"Since disaster relief is about 80% logistics it would follow then that the only way to achieve [results-oriented programmes and accountability] is through slick, efficient and effective logistics operations and more precisely, supply chain management. **LUK VAN WASSENHOVE**

Abstract

There is growing recognition among key humanitarian organizations that logistics plays an essential role in achieving greater synergies across and within the myriad of actors and institutions that currently constitute the humanitarian industry. In this chapter we examine the implications resulting from the establishment of the United Nations' Cluster Approach strategy in responding to complex humanitarian emergencies. Specifically, we analyse the evolution of the Logistics Cluster with respect to key factors such as preparedness, coordination, accountability, and information and knowledge management. In the five years and 36 country roll-outs since its establishment, the Logistics Cluster gets high marks operationally for improving coordination between and among other Clusters; information and knowledge sharing; building systematic emergency response capacity; and clarifying leadership roles and accountability between Cluster actors. Given its prominence as the global leader in foreign assistance and emergency relief, we also consider the role of US perceptions of and attitudes toward the Logistics Cluster and the overall Cluster Approach. We find that in spite of lingering challenges (eg civil–military coordination on logistics and global funding arrangements for the Clusters), the US government is positively disposed toward the Logistics Cluster. We conclude that the Logistics Cluster has met if not exceeded expectations as a key component of the Cluster Approach, and in a very short period of time has elevated the effectiveness of it as a global humanitarian response strategy.

Introduction

Whether it be in response to natural disasters like the 2005 Asian tsunami, man-made disasters like the ongoing conflict in the Democratic Republic of Congo, or the now common 'embedded' or 'hybrid' disasters involving both natural and man-made causes, such as the 2010 Haiti earthquake, adopting a supply chain management approach to humanitarian logistics (HL) holds great potential to enhance the future of humanitarian response and relief. HL stands as a key practical issue surrounding the systematic improvement of humanitarian action.

Analysing HL effectively involves a number of challenges for researchers. Altay (2008) has detailed the myriad issues affecting the study of HL, most of which are soft, ill-defined or mathematically difficult to code problems. Even though recent reviews of emergency management and the disaster relief literature provide a growing list of Operations Research/Management Science research, oddly enough many of the OR/MS models or applications developed so far fail to recognize this point (Altay and Green, 2006; Natarajarathinam *et al*, 2009; Simpson and Hancock, 2009). Moreover, the range and roles of actors involved in humanitarian action are both sizeable and complex, making it difficult to draw correlations, much less establish causality among factors and outcomes.

However, the importance of HL as a central component of humanitarian response has become increasingly recognized in recent years (Chaikin, 2003; Gustavsson, 2003). Logistics links nearly all stakeholders in humanitarian relief operations, including donor governments, intergovernmental organizations (IGOs), international nongovernmental organizations (INGOs), local NGOs, the military, the private sector, and local communities (Oloruntoba and Gray, 2006). Operationally, the constraints facing many of these actors are multiple and overlapping. They include donor demand/pressure for accountability and transparency, competition for scarce funding resources, marketization of the INGO sector, high levels of staff turnover and low levels of institutional memory, and a lack of effective evaluation mechanisms. Enhancing humanitarian logistics capacity and operational effectiveness has thus formed a critical element of global humanitarian reform undertaken by the international community and the structural manifestation of that process, the United Nations (UN) Cluster Approach (CA).

In this chapter we utilize this humanitarian supply chain management framework and its associated elements to examine more closely the implications carried by the establishment of the CA, broadly, and the Logistics Cluster (LC), specifically. Many of the norms undergirding this relatively new approach to humanitarian response reflect key elements constituting effective humanitarian logistics and supply chain frameworks. They include preparedness, coordination, leadership, accountability, and information and knowledge management. Given its prominence as the global leader in foreign assistance and emergency relief,[1] we also explore shifts in US perspectives on the CA and the LC, and offer conclusions about the future of humanitarian response under the CA and the role the LC is likely to play in this area. It is important to note, however, that much of the analysis in this chapter derives from examining the 'donor' side of humanitarian logistics. The impetuses for global humanitarian reform and evolving perspectives regarding the role of logistics that are constitutive of that effort have typically been driven by developed countries. While we feel that this inherent constraint necessarily limits the kinds of conclusions we can reasonably draw, it is, for the present time at least, a reality of the politics of humanitarianism with which we must grapple.

Background

Prior to the roll-out of the CA, very little natural or planned 'alignment' occurred among humanitarian actors to meet the challenges of enhancing HL. This had been the case both at the international level and even at the national level in some countries (eg the US response to Hurricane Katrina). Effective alignment requires, among other strategies, a 'standardization of tasks and products and a well designed infrastructure which consequently will promote coordination through assessment, management and dissemination of information' (Altay, 2008: 163). In part, this has been due to the nature of the actors operating within and across the humanitarian sector, donor funding priorities, a lack of common operational standards, and a scepticism among many humanitarian actors regarding centralization and coordination from above.

Some scholars argue that HL currently resembles the corporate world's logistics environment of 20 years ago, characterized as it was by underinvestment, lack of recognition, and no real training opportunities/ standards across the industry (Thomas and Kopczak, 2005; Beamon and Kotleba, 2006). This was largely the norm both at the international and donor country levels. It has also been claimed that because the humanitarian sector operates without the market forces of demand and supply regulated through price, there are few incentives to coordinate efforts or to use lessons learned to improve over time in any area, including humanitarian logistics (Van Wassenhove, 2006). Furthermore, it has been pointed out that the supply network of HL differs from corporate logistics in that there are no clear or stated linkages among the actors in HL (Kovács and Spens, 2007).

HL has also historically taken a back seat in emergency response planning, budgetary processes, and decision making in part because of the lack of consensus about its function and importance. According to some, the 'basic mentality' of logisticians in such situations has tended to be 'led by project managers' (Rickard, 2003: 9). The sub-optimal potential of this mindset has been compounded when humanitarian actors working in the same crisis zone failed to collaborate and instead maintained stove-pipe arrangements that perpetuated ad hoc arrangements, inefficient procurement strategies, and duplicate efforts across organizations working in the same or related sectors (or parts of a disaster-affected country).

Recent evidence suggests however, that there is growing recognition at the global and national levels among key humanitarian actors, including the UN system, IFRC, INGOs and the private sector, of both the importance of and need for preparedness (hence also indirectly logistics) in response to disasters (Van Wassenhove, 2006). An example of regional cooperation on HL involving developing countries has been the creation, by UN Office for the Coordination of Humanitarian Affairs (OCHA), of the Emergency Preparedness and Response Working Group (EPRWG). The EPRWG is constituted by 17 countries from the Great Lakes region and East Africa. It aims to improve practical collaboration and develop regionally informed solutions to common humanitarian response problems, develops initiatives to share procurement services and organizes resource sharing for logistics components of relief operations such as charter flights and contingency stocks. The EPRWG also trains staff for joint emergency preparedness; attempts to discover and apply to humanitarian operations appropriate corporate-derived logistics systems, and encourages common standards for relief resources and equipment so more agencies can use the same kinds of materials but still keep their individual logos and markings on them for use on the ground (Fenton, 2003).

Another example is the UN Joint Logistics Center (UNJLC). From a coordination standpoint, management of uncertainty during a humanitarian response, particularly through information sharing and cooperation between agencies, is critical to effective response (Altay, 2008). The need for an inter-agency coordination mechanism to deal specifically with logistics issues led to the creation of the UNJLC (Kaatrud *et al*, 2003). The UNJLC falls under the auspices of the World Food Programme (WFP) and, when triggered, is integrated into UN response coordination structures to support inter-agency logistics coordination and asset management. The UNJLC attempts to alleviate procurement and supply bottlenecks; tries to eliminate duplication and competition; serves as a liaison/broker to pool purchasing power among actors; arranges storage space and local transportation; establishes satellite offices to assist with logistics and supply chain management among various actors; and serves as an information clearing house and disseminator to humanitarian and other actors on the ground.

Despite these advances, more effective mechanisms for coordination and collaboration in HL as well as the field of humanitarian assistance and response were needed (OCHA, 2005). The inadequacy of the initial international response to the Asian tsunami in late 2004/early 2005, for example, was a wake-up call for many humanitarian actors. The 2005 Humanitarian Response Review (HRR) process and the subsequent establishment of the CA are the results of this recognition. The HRR recommended a new humanitarian response strategy premised on a range of factors, including predictability, timeliness and effectiveness via: 1) ensuring predictable funding; 2) strengthening the Humanitarian Coordinator system; and 3) strengthening the overall humanitarian response capacity (OCHA, 2006a). The Central Emergency Response Fund (CERF) fulfills 1 above; 2 is being addressed by developing mechanisms to improve training and qualification systems for HCs; and 3 is being fulfilled via the CA.

Collectively, the HRR and the CA represent one of the most significant innovation attempts in the coordination and capacity building of humanitarian response and disaster management undertaken by the international community. From the perspective of HL, the CA reflects the potential value-added of investing in and integrating how to get the 'right goods to the right people in the right time frame' into a more holistic and centralized effort to make humanitarian response more effective.

Change afoot – the cluster approach and implications for humanitarian logistics

The cluster approach stands as the prevailing organizational meta-strategy for humanitarian emergencies response. It emanated from the 2005 HRR, which identified gaps in and offered far-reaching recommendations for humanitarian coordination, preparedness and response to both natural disasters and complex emergencies. The review was thorough and comprehensive. We do not attempt to cover all areas of it in this chapter, but rather focus on areas of the review that tackled issues most closely related to HL. This overview also helps inform our analysis in the remaining sections of the chapter.

In the broadest terms, the HRR found that efforts designed to ensure logistical capabilities have been inconsistent and were closely linked to deficiencies in organizational coordination and capacity (OCHA, 2005). These factors, in turn, affected preparedness and response, both constituting vital dimensions of the disaster management cycle (Tomasini and Van Wassenhove, 2009). For example, although radio and telecommunications capabilities varied widely across organizations, most humanitarian agencies either did not know how to use their telecom technology or had difficulties accessing them when they were most needed. This was especially true in fluid response situations and/or where military presence on the ground complicated obtaining technology-use clearance. Moreover, efforts designed to ensure adequate stockpiling of emergency relief supplies were inconsistent and performance was almost always linked to organizational capacity. Smaller humanitarian organizations, for example, retained limited stockpiles designed for short-term use. Larger organizations, by contrast, stockpiled a wider range of goods, using them across different emergency phases.

The HRR also revealed that organizational reliance on individual solutions rather than coordinated, collective action constituted a major constraint to improved logistics and the supply chain across the humanitarian spectrum. For example, very few INGOs indicated that they utilized common sources of humanitarian supplies (eg through the UNJLC), whereas nearly all UN agencies made some use of pooled resources (OCHA, 2005). In addition, the review noted that procurement processes among agencies were carried out independent of one another; 80 per cent of the organizations surveyed indicated that they did not utilize any coordinated procurement policy (OCHA, 2005). Some 75 per cent of humanitarian spending is handled by fewer than 15 large transnational organizations (Feinstein International Famine Center, 2004). From a logistics standpoint, the purchasing power of this cadre should not be overlooked. Coordination among these mega-INGOs could dramatically lower costs of procurement and warehousing, and result in more efficient outlay of resources that does not compromise flexibility and speed in response. It could also render investment in technology much more cost-efficient and financially feasible, reduce information processing costs and increase the value of shared information and data among humanitarian actors at all levels.

The CA was thus born out of a widely recognized need for building systemic capacity for coordinated humanitarian response. The HRR recommended developing clusters constituted by organizations and other stakeholders with a designated lead agency, in gap areas such as service provision (emergency telecommunications, logistics); traditional relief and assistance sectors (water/sanitation, nutrition, health, emergency shelter); and cross-cutting issues (camp coordination/management, early recovery, protection).

Key HRR recommendations concerning humanitarian logistics included:

- Create consistent measurement standards for all humanitarian actors regarding surge capacity via stockpiles.
- Engage in global mapping of relief stocks and establish regularized transmission procedures for updated information through various humanitarian networks to the Inter-Agency Standing Committee (IASC) and Emergency Relief Coordinator (ERC).
- Generate increased awareness of the logistics planning and implementation benefits of using the UNJLC and the Humanitarian Common Services (HCS).
- Establish more predictable and sufficient donor support for the UNJLC.

Enthusiasm for the development of the CA was not shared by all major humanitarian donors. The USA although an interested party, was not a driver of the process. The UK and several northern European countries were among the most active and supportive actors in the process. According to at least one professional closely involved in the CA's establishment,[2] the US role was in keeping with its prevailing scepticism regarding whether centralized UN coordination constitutes the 'silver bullet' to achieve meaningful reform or that coordination is the single most important factor to improve humanitarian response effectiveness. As the world's largest provider of foreign assistance and emergency relief, the USA may also have been sanguine about committing to new arrangements that might, in turn, necessitate the commitment of new resources. After the IASC agreed on the CA, the US was an active participant in the Geneva-based donor group that worked with the IASC agencies and clusters in funding the CA's initial implementation.

Among the humanitarian donors polled by HRR, however, more than two-thirds cited coordination to be among the top three most important elements for improving global humanitarian performance. Sound needs assessment; effective management; greater accountability; and reducing the number of actors operating in humanitarian settings were also ranked as high-priority reform issues. Interestingly, donors ranked higher levels of preparedness and faster reaction as being less important for improving contemporary humanitarian response (OCHA, 2005).

Most scholars and practitioners agree that the CA represents a major change in the way humanitarian assistance is implemented at both the global, regional and national levels and creates complementarities among the actors involved. The CA is innovative because it generates clear lines of accountability and reporting; addresses capacity-building through unconventional approaches; and should lead to partnerships for common planning and implementation of humanitarian relief (OCHA, 2006a; Jury and DeMaio, 2007).

Global clusters were developed in 11 sectors – in the 'service provision' area, Logistics is chaired by the WFP, and Emergency Telecommunications is chaired by OCHA (process owner), while UNICEF serves as the common data communications service provider, and WFP as common security telecommunications provider (OCHA, 2006a).

In the field, Logistics Cluster operations are expected to:

- fill logistics gaps and alleviate bottlenecks;
- prioritize logistics interventions and investments;
- collect/share information and assets;
- coordinate port and corridor movements to reduce congestion;
- provide details of transporters and rough indication of market rates;
- provide guidance on customs issues;
- provide information on equipment and/or relief items suppliers.

In terms of resources, the cost of implementing the CA in its first year was approximately US $40 million. Of this, nearly one-quarter (the largest apportionment) of the budget was designated for LC operations. On the one hand, this may be interpreted as recognition by the international community of the importance of logistics in humanitarian operations. Alternatively, it may be an indicator of the decades of neglect that logistics has experienced in the humanitarian realm.

Business as usual or... ?

As noted above, the gaps identified by the HRR in logistics relate mainly to coordination and capacity deficiencies, both of which are important dimensions in facilitating effective disaster management. The gaps included a lack of inter-agency contingency planning; the absence of a global network of warehouse facilities for use in rapid response to emergencies; lack of supply chain information exchange (no coordinating body exists) or communications platforms for such exchanges between IGOs, NGOs, donors, suppliers; no global mapping of inventory of relief stocks; lack of inter-agency logistics response teams (LRTs) to carry out comprehensive and timely needs assessments; a strong need for improved information exchange on use of military and civil defence assets (MCDA) as part of emergency/humanitarian response; and a lack of coordination of airfield traffic and congestion during emergencies and especially natural disasters (OCHA, 2006a).

As the LC lead, WFP has demonstrated consistent and strong leadership and coordination. For example, it dedicates staff to focus on information and mapping logistics data as part of the inter-agency contingency planning process. WFP maintains its capacity to provide sufficient, high-quality supplies for preparedness and response and coordination with other actors of pre-positioning of relief inventories and warehousing arrangements (eg via its five Humanitarian Response Depots). It also identifies urgently needed relief items and attempts to ensure an 'under 48-hour- organizational response time, thereby reducing warehousing and freight costs and advancing coordinated procurement. WFP has also developed a register of emergency stockpiles, managed against its baseline data gathering. Information on the most commonly needed non-food items as well as most frequently stocked items are pooled and made available to humanitarian agencies that touch on each of the other traditional and relief sectors (eg sanitation, health, food).

The field-level rollout of the CA was not without challenges. First implemented in 2006 in the Democratic Republic of Congo (DRC), an interim review revealed high levels of confusion among humanitarian actors regarding the roles each agency should play. Many of the concepts embedded within the CA were not well understood by implementing agencies or INGOs (eg organizational and operational concepts such as provider of last resort, accountability, and cluster versus sector leads). The review also noted that, in spite of OCHA efforts there was a general lack of understanding among field staff regarding what cluster leads were expected to do and how they would carry out their mandates (OCHA, 2006b). In Chad, the CA received initial praise and appeared to have enhanced stakeholder buy-in as participating organizations were required to affiliate with a cluster, take part in overall strategy design for that cluster, and then implement the agreed-upon cluster strategy. According to some INGOs on the ground (eg CARE), this approach also enhanced cooperation between technical coordination within and across clusters by identifying which humanitarian organizations were best-equipped to provide particular services and reaching consensus on adapting international standards for implementation (IRIN, 2008).

The two most recent evaluations of the CA yield further insights into its impact of HL and supply network management on the effectiveness of humanitarian response.[3] The first review, finalized in 2007, focused on CA processes at the global level. The second evaluation concentrates on the results and effects of the CA at the country and field level. The combined findings of both undertakings reveal the CA as a maturing institutional arrangement that enjoys continued strong commitment from important stakeholders. Its roll-out has not been without difficulties, but with continued and careful monitoring and analysis, the CA is well positioned to facilitate higher levels of humanitarian response effectiveness in the medium- and long-term.

It should be noted that all clusters are being held to achieving a single overarching standard, with other operational standards flowing from it. The IASC Working Group baseline capacity parameters and preparedness standards are that all clusters should be able to respond to three major new emergencies per year, affecting 500,000 beneficiaries each, with two of the annual emergencies occurring simultaneously. At the time of writing, only one of the 11 clusters has met this baseline as of 2007 – the Logistics Cluster.

In terms of operational standards, the 2007 review showed that early challenges to the CA, which included confusion among cluster leads and implementing partners, some 'lingering ill-will', and uneven performance across case settings, did not overshadow what was an overall 'systematic improvement in coordinated humanitarian response'. Clusters in the field appeared to produce many improvements on their own, as the global clusters worked to complete capacity projects in the initial phase of the rollout (Stoddard *et al*, 2007: 1). From the standpoint of disaster cycle management, the LC (along with the Emergency Telecommunications Cluster) has excelled in the area of coordination, including sharing material stockpile lists, personnel rosters and deployable staff lists. Where individual clusters underperformed, the attributable cause was nearly always a lack of leadership – either by the cluster lead organization or by coordination actors. 'It goes without saying that agencies with the best funding, the best-quality and largest number of staff, the best in-depth field presence and the best NGO network are also the best cluster leads' (Stoddard *et al*, 2007: 9).

One important finding of the 2010 review is that the institutional learning has continued to improve within all clusters, including the LC. In addition, the report found that leadership has become more 'predictable' and leadership roles are now better clarified. Overall coordination levels are also higher among cluster organizations, and this provides focal points for other actors on the ground (local and governmental actors, including local NGOs). The 2010 review also noted that clusters are engaging in peer accountability, sharing information, developing lessons-learned exercises among clusters and dialoguing with one another on strategic, operational and technical issues (Streets *et al*, 2010). A lingering challenge however, involves inter-cluster coordination, which remains weak and ineffective. As was the case in 2007, leadership by cluster coordinators still has a direct impact on cluster effectiveness.

All of the reviews and critiques of the CA convey the message that it is an evolving and innovative concept and it is not business as usual for the humanitarian sector any more. For example, WFP continues to strive to improve the operations of the LC. WFP enlists field experts specializing in the appropriate use of MCDAs and to manage their implementation in humanitarian response. It maintains established procedures for managing and mitigating airfield congestion by entering into agreements with local authorities and experts to identify strategic air hubs and negotiate with local authorities. And, WFP continues to sustain supply chain management capacity via the LC web interface (http://www.logcluster.org/), which consolidates resources on every crisis setting where the LC has been activated. The site provides up-to-the minute information on stockpiles, road conditions, cargo tracking, customs information, offers logistics capacity assessments, information management kits, accurate maps and logistics operational guides. It is, literally, a one-stop shop for humanitarian logistics.

US perspectives on humanitarian logistics, the CA and the LC

Humanitarian assistance and relief have long constituted key foreign assistance undertakings of the US government, USAID, its Office of Foreign Disaster Assistance (OFDA) and the Federal Emergency Management Agency (FEMA). This does not mean that the US and international-level strategies have naturally aligned with one another, but in the area of logistics there are several trends worth noting, particularly where they align with the CA and the LC.

First, and in spite of the CA being a 'centralized' institutional arrangement, both it and US disaster-response reforms are guided by the principle of subsidiarity in relation to strategic thinking and operational response parameters. Subsidiarity focuses operational authority and implementation at the most effective level – in the field of emergency management and response, this means favouring smaller, decentralized approaches to mitigate crises. In the US governance framework, local governments are considered to be first responders, with state government intervening when local capacities are overwhelmed or when more 'complex' solutions need to be carried out by higher level authorities. Much like the CA, US federal authorities assist in emergency response by providing critical and emergency funding, access to resources, and orchestrating coordination during the response phase. Moreover, all CA roll-outs are carefully tailored to meet the needs of specific crises. Not all clusters are activated where national capacity in a particular sector is deemed to be sufficient, and even within sectors (eg logistics) there is a preference for utilizing national-level resources wherever possible.[4] And, in the CA, cluster leads provide last resort, filling gaps where other organizations within a particular cluster are unable to do so.

Second, organizational alignment exists between the CA and the US Disaster Assistance framework (see Table 5.1). Like the LC, USAID/OFDA's Logistics Sector focuses on preparedness, coordination and capacity enhancement. It pre-positions and stocks relief items at regional hubs around the world, including Florida, Italy and the United Arab Emirates. Like WFP's Augmented Logistics Intervention Team for Emergencies, the Sector also fields a full-time logistics team that can be augmented with additional US-based logisticians from other agencies who specialize in areas such as search and rescue. Coordination is also key to the Logistics Sector's work. Logistics experts at USAID/OFDA headquarters coordinate relief supply transportation and delivery (USAID, 2010), much like the LC lead agency, WFP, coordinates relief supply delivery in tandem with the UN Humanitarian Air Service, its own ocean transportation and surface transport services, and the UNJLC.

Third and perhaps most importantly, at both the international and national levels, logistics appears to be enjoying a renewed importance as a key element in effective disaster response. In 2007, for example, FEMA

TABLE 5.1 Organization of disaster assistance/response

US AID/OFDA	UN Cluster Approach/OCHA
Agriculture and Food Security	Agriculture
Economic Recovery and Market Systems	Early Recovery
–	Education
–	Emergency Telecommunications
Health	Health
IDPs and Protection	Protection
Logistics and Relief Commodities	Logistics
Nutrition	Nutrition
Risk Reduction	–
Shelter and Settlements	Emergency Shelter Camp Coordination and Camp Management
Water, Sanitation and Hygiene	Water, Sanitation and Hygiene

elevated Logistics from a branch to a directorate, signifying a positive change in mindset about its importance in emergency response. The recent reorganization of FEMA also mirrors the CA's structural framework of assigning 'lead' institutional actors for each cluster, including Logistics. FEMA has also established a National Logistics Coordinator, whose principal responsibilities include strategic capability, coordination, preparedness and creating more streamlined and effective accounting, procurement and tracking systems. This role is similar to that played by Cluster Leads in various sectors at the international level.

Logistics also feature prominently in each of OFDA's three central divisions.[5] Within DRM, for example, logistics management is central to its ability to coordinate and operationalize the use of technology for both natural and man-made crisis prevention and preparedness. Within OPS, all logistical, technical and operational facets of emergency response are offered, including search and rescue, and response teams to coordinate and operate both in the field and from Washington, DC. USAID/OFDA deploys Disaster Assessment Response Teams (DARTs) to crises around the world to conduct immediate damage and needs assessments for USAID partners on the ground. It also attempts to strengthen disaster planning, early warning and preparedness capacities in crisis-afflicted nations (USAID,

2006). And, within the PS division, administrative, financial and programmatic support is provided in areas such as procurement, budget planning and tracking, and support for communications in the field and in Washington, DC.

Among USAID's operating principles are several that align closely with the LC's fundamentals of supply chain management in emergency response and humanitarian crisis management (Tomasini and Van Wassenhove, 2009). They include resource allocation based on country analysis and capacities, transparency in operations and information-sharing; coordination within the organization and among its implementing partners and other stakeholders; sustaining collaborative efforts with inter-agency partners to more effectively integrate and coordinate foreign assistance; and professionalizing staff at both headquarters and in the field (USAID, 2006). Related to this is the demonstrated 'value-added' of logistics to emergency response and disaster management. According to a senior WFP representative, US government agencies recognize the desirability and benefit of the LC and have been highly supportive of its work, in large part because measurements of effectiveness are relatively easy to identify and measure. This has not been the case with other global clusters.[6]

There are at least two areas where alignment continues to pose challenges. The first is logistics coordination with military actors – Haiti being the most recent example of this. USAID/OFDA logisticians worked closely with the Air Forces Special Operations Command to manage and coordinate relief flights and search and rescue equipment arriving into the airport at Port-au-Prince (USAID, 2010). In contrast and while the UN Logistics Cluster does partner with military actors and utilize military assets for its supply chain management and emergency response, it does so in close consultation with the Oslo Guidelines on the Use of Military and Civil Defence Assets in Disaster Relief. These standards were established to help IGO and NGO actors preserve the humanitarian principles of independence and neutrality in relief operations. The logistics sector of US government emergency response is not held to these standards – and in many cases, the military constitute a central and key actor with clearly delegated domestic humanitarian response responsibilities. There is, however, evidence that the military is becoming more concerned with the civilian–military dimension of HL. For example, WFP and other LC partners have been approached by individual military commands from different countries, including the USA, to learn more about the CA and work more effectively in the area of logistics with non-military actors.[6]

Another key issue for the USA is funding for humanitarian response through the CA. As the global leader in foreign assistance and disaster relief (see Note 1) a natural concern of the US government with regards to the CA is its funding mechanism. US support has been very good for the service-oriented clusters and, in particular, for the LC. The USA remains wary of pooled global funds and has not been a strong supporter of the CERF. It has also increasingly signalled its preference for moving away from extra-budgetary funding for the LC (the USA typically is among the first donors approached for these needs). It favours a more sustainable arrangement involving the funding mainstreaming within the core operating budgets of the cluster lead, or through some share of country operations that the US presently supports.[6]

Conclusion

The intention in the adoption of the CA as part of the global humanitarian reform was to strengthen predictability, response capacity, coordination and accountability in emergency and disaster relief by strengthening partnerships in key sectors of humanitarian response, and by formalizing the lead role of particular agencies/organizations in each of these sectors (Stoddard *et al*, 2007). As of late 2009, the CA had been rolled out in 36 countries – and OCHA's goal is to extend the roll-out to every country that has a Humanitarian Coordinator.[7] At the international level, the CA can help ensure predictable leadership and accountability, as well as strengthening system-wide preparedness and coordination of the technical capacity to respond to humanitarian emergencies. At the country level, it creates high standards of predictability, accountability and partnership in all areas of humanitarian response (Jury and DeMaio, 2007). There are, on the other hand, at least two issues that remain unaddressed.

It should be noted that not all humanitarian actors found the establishing of the CA, including the LC, to be praiseworthy. Among the most common complaints registered was that the CA process has been top-down and UN-driven (IRIN, 2008). Others expressed the view that the CA appeared to be more about money and politics rather than creating positive outcomes for aid beneficiaries. From a bureaucratic standpoint, some emphasized that one of the CA's most serious drawbacks was that it increased humanitarian agency workload by creating new layers of administration and consultation without providing additional resources to perform these added responsibilities.

Many humanitarian actors outside the UN system feel that the current structures related to humanitarian response are very much 'UN driven' and do not always meet INGO expectations (OCHA, 2005: 46). Here, the lead organization concept was encouraged to be implemented system-wide – to increase efficiency by encouraging effective use of expertise and technical know-how of a variety of organizations and especially a designated lead organization (OCHA, 2005).

The USA has been a bit less enamoured of the CA stemming from its general scepticism of centralized UN coordination as a solution to global humanitarian problems. The USA supports the coordination agenda of the UN – its position on a variety of coordination mechanisms (not all) has been positive. It remains less convinced that centralized coordination is the silver bullet to achieve meaningful humanitarian reform or that coordination is the single most important factor to improve disaster response effectiveness. In contrast, the USA favours the kind of demonstrated effectiveness that perhaps is more measurable in some clusters, such as the LC.

Our analysis in this chapter hints that the CA is a step in the right direction in humanitarian response. Moreover, there are important areas of alignment with US foreign assistance and disaster management frameworks. Clearly the model is a work in progress and needs further refinement. However, it does improve the collection, processing and dissemination of information through generating clear lines of accountability and reporting, and pooling resources. The fact that there is a LC alone shows that the humanitarian aid industry is starting to recognize the critical role logistics plays in coordinating an effective response – by extension and in theory, the value of information in humanitarian response should also be enhanced.

References

ActionAid International (2007) *The Evolving UN Cluster Approach in the Aftermath of the Pakistan Earthquake: an NGO perspective*, London and Bangalore: ActionAid International and Books for Change

Altay, N (2008) Issues in disaster-relief logistics, in *Large-scale Disasters: Prediction, control and mitigation*, ed M Gad-el-Hak, Cambridge University Press, Cambridge

Altay, N and Green, WG (2006) OR/MS research in disaster operations management, *European Journal of Operational Research*, 175, pp 475–93

Beamon, BM and Kotleba, SA (2006) Inventory modelling for complex emergencies in humanitarian relief operations, *International Journal of Logistics: Research & Applications*, 9(1), pp 1–18

Chaikin, D (2003) Towards improved logistics: challenges and questions for logisticians and managers, *Forced Migration Review*, 18, pp 10

Feinstein International Famine Center (2004) *Ambiguity and Change: Humanitarian NGOs prepare for the future*. A report prepared for World Vision, CARE, Save US, MercyCorps, Oxfam USA, Oxfam GB and Catholic Relief Services. Medford: Tufts University. Available from: http://nutrition.tufts.edu/docs/pdf/famine/ambiguity_and_change.pdf [accessed 29 October 2009]

Fenton, G (2003) Coordination in the Great Lakes, *Forced Migration Review*, 18, pp 23–24

Gustavsson, L (2003) Humanitarian logistics: context and challenges, *Forced Migration Review*, 18, pp 18–21

Houghton, R (2008) *Education Cluster: Country-level lessons learned review*, Report prepared on behalf of Save the Children and the Global Education Cluster; available at: http://oneresponse.info/GlobalClusters/Education/publicdocuments/Education%20Cluster%20Lessons%20Learned%20Report%20October%202008.pdf

IRIN (2008) Chad: mixed verdicts on coordination of massive relief effort, *IRIN Humanitarian News and Analysis*, 23 January 2008; available from: http://www.irinnews.org/ Report.aspx?ReportId=76386 [accessed 14 March 2008]

Jury, A and DeMaio, G (2007) Cluster approach – a vital operational tool, *Forced Migration Review*, 29 pp 37–38

Kaatrud, DB, Samii, R and Van Wassenhove, LN (2003) UN Joint Logistics Centre: a coordinated response to common humanitarian logistics concerns, *Forced Migration Review*, 18 pp 11–14

Kovács, G and Spens, KM (2007) Humanitarian logistics in disaster relief operations, *International Journal of Physical Distribution & Logistics Management*, 37(2), 99–114

Natarajarathinam, M, Capar, I and Narayanan, A (2009) Managing supply chains in times of crisis: a review of literature and insights, *International Journal of Physical Distribution & Logistics Management*, 39(7), pp 535–73

OCHA (United Nations Office for the Coordination of Humanitarian Affairs) (2005) *Humanitarian Response Review*, an Independent Report commissioned by the UN Emergency Relief Coordinator and Under-Secretary-General for Humanitarian Affairs, New York and Geneva: United Nations

OCHA (2006a) *Appeal for Improving Humanitarian Response Capacity: Cluster 2006 Consolidated Appeals Process (CAP)*, United Nations, New York and Geneva

OCHA (2006b) *Guidance Note on Using the Cluster Approach to Strengthen Humanitarian Response*, United Nations, New York

OCHA (2006c) *IASC Interim Self-assessment of Implementation of the Cluster Approach in the Field*, 15–17 November, United Nations, New York

OCHA (2007) *Report on Implementation of Global Cluster Capacity-building (1 April 2006–31 March 2007)*, United Nations, New York and Geneva

Oloruntoba, R and Gray, R (2006) Humanitarian aid: an agile supply chain?, *Supply Chain Management: An International Journal*, 11(2), pp 115–20

Rickard, J (2003) A logistician's plea, *Forced Migration Review*, 18, p 9

Simpson, NC and Hancock, PG (2009) Fifty years of operational research and emergency response, *Journal of the Operational Research Society*, 60, pp S126–S139

Stoddard, A, Harmer, A, Haver, K, Salomons, D and Wheeler, V (2007) *Cluster Approach Evaluation, Final*, OCHA Evaluation and Studies Section, New York

Streets, J, Grünewald, F, Binder, A, de Geoffroy, V, Kauffmann, D, Krüger, S, Meier, C and Sokpoh, B (2010) *Cluster Approach Evaluation 2: Synthesis report*, Plaisians, Berlin

Thomas, M (2006) *The Roll-out of the Cluster Approach in the Democratic Republic of the Congo (DRC)*, UN Office for the Coordination of Humanitarian Affairs (OCHA)/International Council for Volunteer Agencies (ICVA) Mission to DRC; available from: http://www.icva.ch/ doc00001846.html [accessed 10 March 2008]

Thomas, AS and Kopczak, LR (2005) *From Logistics to Supply Chain Management: The path forward in the humanitarian sector*; available at: http://www.fritzinstitute.org/PDFs/WhitePaper/FromLogisticsto.pdf [accessed 29 October 2009]

Tomasini, R and Van Wassenhove, LN (2009) *Humanitarian Logistics*, Palgrave-Macmillan and INSEAD, London

USAID (US Agency for International Development) (2006) *USAID Primer: Who we are and how we do it*, US Agency for International Development, Washington, DC

USAID (2010) *Logistics and Relief Commodities Sector Update – June 2010*; available at: http://www.usaid.gov/our_work/humanitarian_assistance/disaster_ assistance/sectors/files/fy2010/logs_sector_update_06-2010.pdf [accessed 22 June 2010]

Van Wassenhove, LN (2006) Humanitarian aid logistics: supply chain management in high gear, *Journal of the Operational Research Society*, 57, pp 475–89

Notes

1   Between 2002 and 2004, for example, US contributions to humanitarian assistance constituted 39 per cent, 44 per cent and 22 per cent, respectively, of the global total (OCHA, 2005: 102). As of June 2010, the USA had contributed 24 per cent of the global total of both Consolidated and Flash Appeals. See UN OCHA Financial Tracking Service, available at: http://www. reliefweb.int/fts or http://ocha.unog.ch/fts/reports/daily/ocha_R6_ Y2010___1006260211.pdf (accessed 26 June 2010).

2   Author telephone interview with senior staff member of the World Food Programme, 24 June 2010.

3   In addition to several independent evaluations that have dealt with specific clusters or emergencies (ActionAid International, 2007; Houghton, 2008; Thomas, 2006), two other evaluations have also been carried out by OCHA; an interim self-assessment (OCHA, 2006c) and an assessment of global cluster capacity building (OCHA, 2007).

4   Operationally, this has been difficult to implement in some settings. Many CA clusters do not make adequate 'capacity' assessments and instead focus on 'needs' assessments – which may mean missing out on or ignoring local capacity and partnership opportunities. See Streets *et al* (2010).

5   Disaster Response and Mitigation (DRM), Operations Support (OPS) and Program Support (PS).

6   Author telephone interview with senior staff member of the World Food Programme, 24 June 2010.

7   For the complete list of countries, see: http://www.humanitarianreform.org/ humanitarianreform/Portals/1/cluster%20approach%20page/clusters%20pages/ WASH/CA_with_implementation_dates-Nov.2009.pdf.

06
The 2004 Thailand tsunami reviewed
lessons learned

STEPHEN PETTIT, ANTHONY BERESFORD, MICHAEL WHITING AND RUTH BANOMYONG

Abstract

This chapter reviews the events leading up to, and immediately following, the December 2004 tsunami that occurred in South East Asia; and the lessons that were learned from a logistical perspective are highlighted. It is clear that countries in the region lacked the communication infrastructure and logistics capacity and capability to deal with the aftermath of such an event. Logistics is central to the delivery of relief aid. In the context of the tsunami, the effectiveness and speed of response, the significance of the cost element and the fragility of emergency supply chains in extreme conditions are highlighted. The tsunami raised many issues relating to large-scale humanitarian disasters, including the level of preparedness for such events and how best to manage logistics and supply chain activities in volatile conditions such as those that immediately followed the tsunami strikes. Subsequently, many organizations, especially in Thailand, began to give more attention to the issues related to large-scale emergencies including preparedness and implementation of appropriate plans during emergency relief operations. The lessons learned from the response to the tsunami, especially the dissemination of information, should enable countries and organizations to better prepare for, and respond to, such emergencies in the future.

Introduction

The purpose of this chapter is to review the events leading up to and immediately following the tsunami disaster that occurred in December 2004 in South East Asia, and to highlight the lessons that were learned from a logistical perspective. The event made it tragically clear that the countries in the region completely lacked the communication infrastructure to provide the knowledge, capacity and capability to deal with the aftermath of such an event.

Although it is often the forgotten dimension of any humanitarian crisis, logistics is central to the delivery of relief aid for several reasons. First, logistics is crucial to the effectiveness and speed of response for major humanitarian programmes. Without the logistics support to deliver aid to the right place at the right time and in the right conditions, humanitarian aid provision will fail, or will be perceived to fail, irrespective of how good the programme is. Second, logistics is one of the most expensive parts of disaster response. If the broad definition of logistics is extended to include procurement and transport, logistics forms a very significant cost element of any aid operation. Third, the fragility of emergency supply chains in extreme conditions itself emphasizes the dependence of humanitarian aid distribution on reliable supply. The severing of physical links such as roads and railways is made much worse if communication mechanisms are also fractured, or if the area affected is so large that communities are unable to link their experiences to one common cause, for hours or even days. Coordination of the relief effort in these circumstances thus becomes almost impossible (see, for example, Brown, 1979; Long and Wood, 1995; Kovacs and Spens, 2007).

The tsunami highlighted many issues relating to large-scale humanitarian disasters, including how best to manage logistics and supply chain activities. Consequently, many organizations, especially in Thailand, began to give more attention to the issues related to large-scale emergencies including prevention, planning and emergency relief operations. The lessons learned from the response to the tsunami should enable countries and organizations to better respond to such emergencies in the future.

What happened on 26 December 2004?

The Asian tsunami disaster occurred on 26 December 2004. The waves severely affected the coastal fringe of most of the countries fronting the Indian Ocean including those in East Africa, the west Indonesian Archipelago and the Malaysian peninsula. Indonesia suffered most with more than 130,000 confirmed deaths (USGS, 2006) and almost total destruction of Banda Aceh and other coastal communities. In Thailand, according to Chanditthawong (2005), the tsunami was considered to be the most serious natural disaster the country has ever experienced. Table 6.1 shows the extent and scale of the disaster as gauged by the number of casualties listed by country.

TABLE 6.1 The Asian tsunami disaster, December 2004: casualties by country

Country	Deaths		Injured
	Confirmed	Estimated	
Indonesia	130,736	167,736	N/A
Sri Lanka	35,322	35,322	21,411
India	12,405	18,045	N/A
Thailand	5,395	8,212	8,457
Somalia	78	289	N/A
Myanmar (Burma)	61	400–600	45
Maldives	82	108	N/A
Malaysia	68	75	299
Tanzania	10	13	N/A
Seychelles	3	3	57
Bangladesh	2	2	N/A
South Africa	2	2	N/A
Yemen	2	2	N/A
Kenya	1	1	2
Total	184,167	~230,210	~125,000

SOURCE: USGS (2006)

The wave inflicted enormous damage on the six southern Thai provinces on the Andaman Sea coastline, namely: Ranong, Phang-Nga, Phuket, Krabi, Trang and Satun with Phang-Nga being the province that suffered the most damage. The tsunami was responsible for at least 5,395 deaths, over 8,000 people were injured and more than 2,200 persons were unaccounted for. The financial costs associated with the tsunami were estimated at over US $ 500 million in Thailand alone, and this figure does not include the loss of private dwellings (Rangsit University, 2005; BBC, 2005a).

The tsunami waves that hit the south west coast of Thailand, destroyed villages, roads and large swathes of urban coastal development. Specific problems included: communication systems failures due to the destruction of the telecommunication network; a lack of demolition and clearance equipment to remove the destroyed buildings and accumulated debris; very limited road access, and extensive flooding. This resulted in a situation where the delivery of basic humanitarian aid was often out of balance with requirements. In the immediate aftermath of the tsunami, aid was scarce, but as the crisis continued, the lack of coordination meant that there was often oversupply of certain items, or supply of items inappropriate to conditions on the ground (Pettit and Beresford, 2005; BBC, 2005b).

Further, local officials and relief volunteers were either poorly trained or ill-equipped to cope with a disaster on such a scale. There was also little inter-agency cooperation stemming from the fact that individual agencies were not fully aware of how their own role fitted into the complex nature of the relief operation or how their actions could affect other agencies. Thus agencies 'competed' against each other leading to territorial rivalry and 'turf' issues (Salam, 2006). The chaos that followed the tsunami led to numerous questions being asked; notably, how, if such an event were to occur again, the Thai authorities could better respond with their new warning and response systems so that the impact of a similar catastrophic event could be minimized (DPM, 2005a).

Immediately following the tsunami, aid provision across the region had to be coordinated on an unprecedented scale among a number of governments and a wide range of NGOs, United Nations (UN) bodies, the International Committee of the Red Cross (ICRC) and the military. The scale of the disaster was so large that in the early stages of the crisis it was only possible to get aid to a few of the worst-affected areas with the use of military resources. In Thailand, however, the government initially stated that they did not wish to receive help from external sources, particularly in the immediate aftermath of the tsunami.

In the region around Banda Aceh, in contrast, it was reported that around 400 separate organizations were working, providing a broad range of humanitarian assistance after the tsunami. The Indonesian government worked very closely with implementing partners and, as the situation on the ground began to stabilize, so only those organizations that were deemed to be performing effectively were permitted to stay. Such organizations included UN relief agencies, NGOs, government agencies, the military (both international and national) and private companies. Hindering all of them was the common problem of a lack of preparedness. Secondary serious problems were the widely diverging needs from region to region and the mismatch between requirements and goods supplied. The main need in Sri Lanka, India, Thailand, the Maldives and Malaysia was for clean water, food and medical supplies. The initial surge of donations, however, was often of the wrong materials. For example, in Thailand some of the clothing donated by garment export firms consisted of winter clothes, which was inappropriate for the location. Overall, the amount of unsolicited and inappropriate aid presented a real logistical problem in all areas (Beresford and Pettit, 2007).

Hazard event response in Thailand

The Department of Disaster Prevention and Mitigation at the Ministry of Interior (DDPMMI)

There were a number of problems associated with the need for the Thai government to respond quickly to the after-effects of the tsunami. In part this related to the need to have some form of plan to deal with such a crisis and such a plan did not exist. Before the occurrence of the tsunami, the Thai government had developed an emergency response plan that was under the remit of the DDPMMI. In this Master Plan for Flood, Windstorm and Mudslide Hazards Prevention, published in 2005 (but compiled prior to the tsunami) there was no mention of, and therefore no strategy for, tsunami contingency planning or response (DPM, 2005b). The underlying reason for this was the general belief that a tsunami would never affect Thailand. Emphasis throughout the document was on hazard evaluation processes relating to the other major forms of environmental disaster: floods, windstorms and mudslides. Historically these have regularly affected the country, especially in specific seasons, and it was therefore logical to have response plans for such events. The risk level for each area of Thailand was categorized as low, moderate or high for each of these perceived risks. Statistics for windstorms, for instance, indicate that there were 12,623 events from 1997 to 2003 (averaging 1,803 per annum), causing 283 deaths during that period. The windstorm-prone areas are well documented, with the main tropical cyclone paths reasonably predictable. Similarly, accurate statistics for floods are also maintained. From 1997 to 2004 there were 84 separate flood events resulting in 811 deaths. Mapping of Thailand's flood-prone areas is very detailed, providing a good level of overall awareness and preparedness for local communities.

The DDPMMI undertook a survey in 2004 prior to the tsunami and ascertained that the key organizations involved in disaster planning should have integrated short- and long-term prevention plans. This proposed that disaster warning systems should be installed, with the entire data system linked together. Additionally, there should also be detailed mapping of both disaster-prone areas and evacuation areas. Several specific problems were identified, relating to central organizations and associations. These included lack of knowledge and experience in large-scale disaster management, duplicated work among agencies, inadequate information technology systems and unclear communication and decision-making systems. At a more local level, problems included telecommunication inadequacies including cell-phone network coverage, shortage of rescue equipment, and disaster warning systems not covering all areas. Although there was a clear theoretical structure for disaster response, in these reports there was a complete absence of reference to the tsunami hazard and, by implication, there was thus a complete lack of preparedness for a tsunami-type event (DPM, 2005b).

Tsunami warning and evacuation

Following the December 2004 tsunami, there was a clear need to revisit disaster planning with regard to this type of event. A major review of preparation plans, evacuation procedures and future planning contingency measures was therefore conducted. A Master Plan for Tsunami Evacuation (DPM, 2005a) was developed, falling within the remit of two government Acts (the Civil Defense Act and the Building Control Act) and two government plans (the Civil Defense Plan and the National Preparedness Plan). The areas that were identified as being vulnerable to the tsunami hazard consist of mainland Thailand fronting the Andaman Sea, and all islands and island groups in the six southern provinces of Ranong, Phang-Nga, Phuket, Krabi, Trang and Satun. The vulnerable areas are split into sub-districts and villages as shown in Table 6.2.

TABLE 6.2 Tsunami-susceptible areas in Thailand

Province	Total	Sub-district	Villages
Ranong	2 Districts 1 Branch District	10	47
Phang-Nga	6 Districts	19	69
Phuket	3 Districts	14	63
Krabi	5 Districts	22	112
Trang	3 Districts 1 Branch District	13	51
Sutan	4 Districts	17	70
6 Provinces	23 Districts 2 Branch Districts	95	412

SOURCE: DPM, 2005a

The Master Plan tasks the Regional Civil Defence Directing Center (RCDDC) to direct, control, administer and provide recommendations about tsunami prevention and mitigation. The emphasis in this document is primarily on evacuation, communications and victim support; and reference to the distribution of aid materials to disaster victims mainly focuses on supplies, temporary shelter and health/welfare materials. Thus, within its remit, transport and logistics support are implicit rather than explicit.

Consistent with other approaches, eg that of Carter (1999), the Master Plan for Tsunami Evacuation highlights three main phases: Pre-disaster; During disaster; and Post-disaster. The pre-disaster phase highlighted all communities at risk in order to heighten individuals' awareness of the procedures that need to be adopted in the event of a tsunami strike. Specifically, the preparations involve identifying safe areas for evacuation, main and alternative evacuation routes, signage and maps showing these routes, emergency support units and the provision of vehicles, as well as tools and obstruction clearance equipment. Several models have demonstrated that 15 metres above sea level is generally safe; and 20 metres above is safe in virtually every tsunami case. The dissemination of tsunami warnings is in the first instance from two types of warning towers activated from a central location near Bangkok. The first type is manned at the time of an emergency, and is maintained and monitored by the Royal Thai Navy. The second type takes the form of automatic unmanned warning towers, which have been installed along the beaches in the six provinces bordering the Andaman Sea. Both types emit a warning either as a siren or as an amplified verbal alarm. Immediately backing up these initial warnings is an Amateur Radio Network that disseminates warning information from 76 Control Stations (one in each province) via an Echolink System and normal frequencies in the amateur radio network to provincial users of these networks.

As an example, during August 2009 a drill was conducted by Thai authorities in the provinces affected by the 2004 tsunami, to test the readiness of the existing relief protocol. The drill began at 10.20 am when the authorities simulated an earthquake in the Andaman Sea. After being notified of the tremor by the Thai Meteorological Department, the National Disaster Warning Centre then sent short messages to department executives, to the governors of the six provinces and to a variety of officials to monitor the earthquake situation. The disaster warning proceeded both in Thai and in English, instructing local residents, as well as Thai and international holidaymakers, to evacuate from shoreline areas to safer places on higher ground. From this drill several 'dead spots' were identified where sirens were insufficiently loud to be heard by the local community.

This was the second tsunami drill to occur within a month. A seabed earthquake in the Indian Ocean led to an unplanned tsunami practice in the early hours of 11 August 2009. Residents of the Phang-Nga village of Nam Khem, where more than 800 people perished in 2004, evacuated their homes for higher ground. Elsewhere along the coast, most people continued sleeping unaware that an earthquake had taken place (level one alert) or that those officials were on standby to begin evacuation (level two alert). The order to move people out (level three) never came because the earthquake did not generate a big enough wave. Thus, while drills are relatively easy to practice, there is little sign of any genuine preparedness for a tsunami as this involves both 'being prepared' *and* controlling the response.

The emphasis of the Thai government's approach is on clarity of responsibility and communications networks. Regarding the evacuation of people, there is a priority order and all villages must have arrangements for evacuation to safe areas. Areas designated as 'safe' are either outside the zone affected by the December 2004 tsunami or on land higher than 15 metres above sea level. These safe areas are, as far as possible, identified, advertised and signed. Similarly, primary and alternative evacuation routes are identified so that all communities have at least two routes to safety. Learning from the experience of the December 2004 event the Thai government has recognized the importance of an effective telecommunications network that can support both the evacuation procedures and any post-tsunami provision of aid and effective logistics operations (DPM, 2005a).

Once a tsunami alert has been given, assuming it is then cancelled, the resident population will be able to return to their properties, the return being managed by nominated community leaders in cooperation with evacuation officials. Where appropriate, the RCDDC coordinates with military units, government agencies, private companies (such as transport companies) and other organizations according to need. Overseeing the three phases is the National Disaster Warning Centre, which is operational 24 hours a day regardless of whether or not there is an emergency.

Logistics, transport and information gathering

A lesson learned from previous emergency responses is that people, rather than flee, tend to remain in the area of danger (Whittow, 1980) putting additional stress on transport resources that may be required for purposes other than forced evacuation. Concerning information and emergency telecommunications, of major importance is the provision of timely and relevant information about relief operations to local, national and international audiences. Communications with those affected by the disaster are often neglected. Two main objectives are: first, to establish communications networks to facilitate and coordinate relief operations, ensuring that there is system connectivity to support the humanitarian effort; and second, to harmonize activities between the humanitarian community and government counterparts to ensure effective communications and the maximum utilization of resources (United Nations, 2006). Although there is little specific reference in the Master Plan for Tsunami Evacuation to logistics requirements, effective transport of people away from danger, of supplies to displaced people and overall mobility to respond to rapidly changing circumstances is an implicit imperative. Clearly this implies that effective logistics systems are at the centre of any emergency contingency plan. Specifically, maintenance of key transport routes, vehicle fuel supplies and communication equipment were cited as key requirements.

In this context, examples of specific bodies that have on-the-ground experience are the World Food Programme (WFP) (although they were not active in Thailand at the time of the tsunami) and the International Organisation for Migration (IOM). In Indonesia, following the tsunami, they provided transportation, storage, communication and coordination support for the distribution of aid to affected areas. WFP and IOM provided these services because they were there in the region and able to respond quickly and WFP acted as a lead agency for logistics within the National Disaster Managing Board Secretariat. Activities included organizing the land fleet departing from Jakarta (one convoy – 20 trucks) and five convoys departing from Medan (20 trucks), storage of relief goods, and relief item procurement and application (United Nations, 2006). Subsequent to the tsunami, a review of how humanitarian response is carried out following major disasters (HRR, Aug 2005) was carried out and a new approach was developed known as the cluster system. Within this system WFP are now the lead agency for the logistics cluster, the first logistics cluster being formed following the Yogyakarta earthquake in May 2006. The most recent example of the effective use of the cluster system was seen following the Haiti earthquake of January 2010 (Whiting, 2010; Heraty, 2010a; 2010b).

Further, the degree of disruption, coupled with the surprise element and the sheer scale of the tsunami, generated a very high level of information inaccuracy. Getting an accurate picture of the tsunami impact and needs on the ground was a key priority in the hours after the tsunami waves struck. This encouraged responsible agencies to engage in various triangulation techniques (a widely used information and data verification method) in order to iron out as much uncertainty and information conflict as possible. Subsequently, for this purpose, Banomyong et al (2009) proposed using two triangulation techniques known as data triangulation and investigator triangulation (Denzin, 1989; Denzin and Lincoln, 1998) to reflect as accurately as possible the 'real' situation on the ground.

Data triangulation largely employs the use of published and unpublished papers, media coverage and on-the-ground reporting. Observations are backed up by data collected from several different secondary data sources such as websites, published and unpublished research work, contemporary media coverage and tsunami inquiry reports. The purpose of the data triangulation technique is to provide a broad coverage of the literature that relates to the incident and to reconcile it with observations on the ground.

Investigator triangulation, meanwhile, makes use of different respondents involved in the same event at the same location. During and immediately following the tsunami strike, there were thousands of innocent victims who became active participants in the information collection process and who played a key role in trying to alleviate the disaster. This technique was utilized to gain the best possible understanding of the situation from multiple perspectives, ie how relief operations were conducted and how they could be improved. Having accurate data on the nature of the disaster, its extent, the number of affected persons and the volume and type of goods needed are clearly a prerequisite for successful relief operations. Lessons to be learned can be derived from these two methodological approaches.

Reflections and lessons to be learned

In spite of the findings of a large number of 'After Action Reports' since the Asian tsunami, all too often the focus has been on high-level 'policy' rather than on addressing the underlying problem. Humanitarian aid, as has been shown, is largely about logistics, which in essence is 'End-to-End Humanitarian Supply Chain Management' – everything from procurement, through purchasing, to delivery to the beneficiaries. Without robust logistic solutions the best 'programmes' in the world will consistently fail to deliver aid quickly to the right people, at the right time, in the right condition and for the right price. In an emergency, logistics can account for as much as 70 to 80 per cent of the overall cost of aid depending on the location of the crisis and circumstances; this is up to twice as high as figures often quoted for commercial supply chains in stable conditions. It follows that, if organizations are to improve their ability to respond quickly, the logistics processes – and the professional training of those responsible for delivering them – must be the best that can be provided.

In 2005, following the Asian tsunami, under pressure from donor countries to improve the effectiveness of emergency response, the then UN Emergency Relief Coordinator (ERC) commissioned an independent Humanitarian Response Review (HRR) of the global humanitarian system (United Nations, 2005). The HRR was tasked with identifying those factors that have frequently hindered the speed and effectiveness of humanitarian response in the past, and to propose appropriate steps towards improving both the *timeliness* and *impact* of future humanitarian interventions. Four independent consultants undertook the review and, through adoption of customized questionnaires, face-to-face interviews, seminar discussions and reviews of background documents, they assessed the humanitarian capacities of the major international organizations.

The draft HRR report concluded that:

> It is imperative that agencies learn to look beyond individual capacities in order to achieve greater and more effective response capacity.

This is apparent, for example, in the development of stockpile capacity where the responses to the consultation show a picture of very uneven capacity. The draft HRR was believed by some to be flawed, since it focused on international response only and overlooked local *and* national responses, which in the immediate aftermath of the tsunami (and also seen more recently in the response to emergencies such as the Wenchuan earthquake (Beresford *et al*, 2009)) are extremely important. A number of observations and recommendations were made on covering the need for change and improvement. As a result of this debate, however, it was resolved that the priority for improving the humanitarian system should be the development of what is now known as the cluster system. In this system lead responsibility is taken by a particular organization, which, in the case of the 'logistics cluster', is the World Food Programme.

The HRR issued its Final Report in August 2005. The review encompassed several critical areas, including:

- an assessment of existing humanitarian response and identification of gaps;
- recommendations for mapping the response capacities of national, regional and international parties;
- strengthening response capacities, particularly human resources;
- application of benchmarks to measure and control performance;
- improvement of coordination; and
- the disparity between desired and current capabilities in the provision of emergency water and sanitation, shelter and camp management, and protection.

The HRR recommended assigning responsibilities by sector to lead organizations and the development of cluster models. The UN agencies all *apparently* agreed with the ERC's preferred solution to the problem of an unpredictable and varied humanitarian response, which was to assign certain specific and particular agencies to be cluster leads. However, others within the Inter Agency Standing Committee (IASC) questioned whether or not this cluster approach was the best way to improve humanitarian response. The peculiarities of tsunamis, such as the ribbon pattern of affected coastal zones, arguably mitigate against the application of conventional cluster response models. Nevertheless, in September 2005 the IASC agreed to designate global 'cluster leads' – specifically for humanitarian emergencies – in nine sectors or areas of activity (see Table 6.3).

The IASC Principals state that the cluster approach should be applied, albeit with some flexibility, at the country level. The cluster concept is seen by the UN as a genuine means of improving the way that the humanitarian response system works, and of ensuring more effective accountability. The intention is that cluster leads will provide a means of supporting the Resident and Humanitarian Coordinators in ensuring an integrated and coordinated response.

TABLE 6.3 Cluster responsibilities and lead organizations in humanitarian emergencies

Cluster	Lead
Camp Coordination & Management	UNHCR (for conflict-generated IDPs)
Emergency Telecommunications	OCHA for overall process ownership
	UNICEF for data collection
	WFP for common security telecommunications service.
Early Recovery (formerly called Reintegration and Recovery)	UNDP
Emergency Shelter	UNHCR (for conflict-generated IDPs)
Health	WHO
Logistics	WFP
Nutrition	UNICEF
Protection	UNHCR (for conflict-generated IDPs)
Water & Sanitation	UNICEF

SOURCE: authors

There is a general acknowledgement that there are three types of clusters, which are respectively concerned with:

- provision of assistance to beneficiaries (health, water and sanitation, camp coordination and management, emergency shelter and nutrition);
- provision of services (telecommunications and logistics);
- cross-cutting issues (protection and early recovery phase, which requires close coordination with other clusters).

It is important to appreciate that the Cluster Concept was developed by the IASC and it is thus seen by some as a creature of the UN and, until the last quarter of 2005, NGO involvement was limited.[1] It is also important to appreciate that non-governmental humanitarian action is, by its very nature, voluntary and NGOs do not easily lend themselves to top-down coordination by the UN system, not least because their structures are often highly decentralized. It is precisely for these reasons that the HRR failed to assess the NGO capacity satisfactorily. The sheer number of NGOs operating in Indonesia immediately post-tsunami was a case in point. Meaningful capacity and capability estimation was virtually impossible.

The designated lead organization for logistics was the WFP. Between August and December 2005, WFP established a Logistics Cluster Working Group[2] (Logistics Cluster WG) and engaged in discussions with other UN agencies and NGO partners. The Logistics Cluster WG aims to improve surge capacity, speed and effectiveness of humanitarian response, thus ensuring better logistics preparedness and response, and facilitating improved inter-agency inter-operability through the pooling of resources.

There can be no doubt that, in principle, surge capacity management was at the heart of the logistics response in the aftermath of the Asian tsunami, so in the event of a similar emergency in the future, response should better fit needs. On 6 March 2006, the Logistics Cluster WG presented the logistics gaps, and activities to fill these gaps, with detailed funding requirements, as part of the 'Inter-Agency Appeal for Improving Humanitarian Response Capacity, Clusters 2006'. This submission was built on the September 2005 Logistics Cluster Progress Report and further discussions and recommendations coming out of the Logistics Cluster. A phased implementation plan was provided by the Logistics Cluster WG to the IASC Principals Meeting of 12 December 2005;[3] however, since the establishment of the Cluster Approach in September 2005, the reality of world events has overtaken the phased approach for implementing the Logistics Cluster that was planned as part of emergency response at both the global and country level. The Logistics Cluster operates under the following precepts:

- Logistics: The Fritz Institute defined *humanitarian* logistics as 'the process of planning, implementing and controlling the efficient, cost-effective flow and storage of goods and materials, as well as related information, from the point of origin to the point of consumption for the purpose of alleviating the suffering of vulnerable people. The function encompasses a range of activities, including preparedness, planning, procurement, transport, warehousing, tracking and tracing and customs clearance.'[4]

- Logistics Cluster:[5] group of humanitarian organizations and other stakeholders (Participants) committed to commonly address logistics needs during humanitarian crises (global and field).

- Logistics Cluster Participants: Individual organizations with recognized institutional logistics capacity that are involved in the logistics cluster approach and can provide dedicated staff (global and field).

- Logistics Cluster Lead: Organization appointed by the Inter-Agency Standing Committee (IASC) to:
  - take the lead in the implementation of the logistics cluster approach;
  - be accountable to the Logistics Cluster Participants and the Emergency Response Coordinator (ERC) or Humanitarian Coordinator (HC);
  - be the provider of last resort (global and field).

The Logistics Cluster participants agreed on the following criteria:

- Accountability of Cluster Lead Agency: Cluster Leads are accountable to the ERC/HC for ensuring adequate preparedness and effective responses in the sectors or areas of activity.
- Provider of Last Resort: commitment of cluster leads to do the utmost to ensure an adequate and appropriate response.
- Option 1: a critical gap is identified and the lead agency requests a Logistics Cluster Participant to fill the gap.
- Option 2: a critical gap is identified and no other agency is capable or willing to fill this gap. The lead agency will use its capacity to address the gap on the condition that funding becomes available.

Conclusions

The earthquake and the resulting tsunami on 26 December 2004 claimed approximately 230,000 lives and displaced 1.7 million people. The damage to infrastructure was huge. The world responded by donating more than US $13 billion initiating the largest relief operation in history. The plethora of assessments and after-action reports showed beyond reasonable doubt that there was a compelling need to improve humanitarian response, and the best way of achieving this in the future is to be better prepared, to have robust response structures in place and to act appropriately after emergency triggers.

In the case of the Indian Ocean tsunami, the vast majority of people with logistics responsibilities did not have training in logistics. Large multinational corporations acknowledge that one of the biggest challenges in logistics is the identification, recruitment, training and retention of quality staff. The trend towards the 'professionalization' of logistics has been slow to take hold in the humanitarian world, as field experience is considered much more valuable than formal training in logistics.

Needs Assessment is a vital process in planning for relief activities. Simply put, a good assessment template provides the data which enables organizations to ensure that the right product reaches the right beneficiaries at the right time. Although 72 per cent of the humanitarian organizations who responded to the Indian Ocean tsunami had an assessment process that enabled them to plan for relief in the tsunami region, 62 per cent of them stated that their plans failed to meet needs. Eighty-eight per cent of the assessment team members were internationals and 38 per cent of organizations had assessment teams from the affected areas. Only 58 per cent of organizations used logisticians in their assessment teams – a fact that undoubtedly contributed to the failure to anticipate some of the logistics bottlenecks that were experienced.

Comparing data from the 2004 Indian Ocean tsunami to data from the 2006 Jakarta earthquake and tsunami, supply chain set-up times are said to have decreased from 18 days to three days, while the cost to deliver aid per family reduced from US $800 to US $142. Whether these numbers are accurate or not, since the tsunami the implementation of the findings of the Humanitarian Response Review (HRR) in August 2005 and the introduction of the cluster concept, collaboration and coordination has improved. The very introduction of the clusters has brought about closer coordination and collaboration between UN agencies themselves, between UN agencies and NGOs, and between NGOs.

One of the starkest messages the tsunami provided was the fact that the effectiveness of humanitarian aid response hinges on logistics efficiency. It is imperative that, for humanitarian logistics to adequately serve the purpose of successful delivery of aid, the humanitarian aid organizations at large must recognize the role that logistics plays in the delivery of programmes large and small, and the need for humanitarian logistics to be adequately resourced in terms of trained and capable staff, adequate information management systems, and logistics infrastructure.

Much has been achieved in the intervening five years, particularly in the South East Asian region where disaster planning and preparedness has been embraced and acted upon very effectively. In general terms much still remains to be done. The basic premise behind the HRR 2005 was 'the perception that humanitarian response does not always meet the basic requirements of affected populations in a timely fashion and the response provided can vary considerably from crisis to crisis'. This is generally still the case as the response to both the Haiti earthquake of 2010 and the Pakistani floods of 2010 testify.

In many areas the lessons identified as a result of the Indian Ocean tsunami 2004 remain just that – lessons identified – they cannot qualify as lessons learned. Only in specific areas such as disaster planning and preparedness in Indonesia and Thailand have lessons been learned. The key factor is that, with the greater incidence of concurrent sudden-onset natural disasters affecting the lives and livelihoods of more and more people, focus needs to be on building national and regional capacity and developing robust national and regional disaster and response plans – the success of this approach in Indonesia and Thailand is clear. The need for humanitarian logistics to embrace commerce, academia and the military and to share experience and assets is also obvious. More than ever, logistics needs to show the way by advocating a dynamic alignment of concepts and ideas that will deliver consistently – the right products, to the right place at the right time and in the right condition for a price that is transparent and measurable.

References

Banomyong, R, Beresford, AKC and Pettit, S (2009) Logistics relief response model: the case of Thailand's tsunami affected area, *International Journal of Services Technology and Management*, **12**(4), pp 414–29

BBC (2005a) *Asia's tsunami death toll soars*; available at: <http://news.bbc.co.uk/1/hi/world/asia-pacific/4189883.stm>

BBC (2005b) *Asia quake relief effort – logistics delivering the aid*; available at: <http://news.bbc.co.uk/1/shared/spl/hi/world/04/asia_quake/relief_effort/html/1.stm>

Beresford, AKC and Pettit, SJ (2007) *Disaster Management and Risk Mitigation in Thailand following the Asian Tsunami*, Proceedings of the International Conference on Supply Chain Management, Bangkok, July

Beresford, AKC, Shan, H and Pettit, S (2009) *Humanitarian Aid Logistics following the Wenchuan Earthquake*, 2nd Cardiff–Cranfield Humanitarian Logistics Initiative Conference, Shrivenham, March

Brown, BJ (1979) *Disaster Preparedness and the United Nations – Advance Planning for Disaster Relief*, Pergamon Press, Oxford

Carter, WN (1999) *Disaster Management: A disaster management handbook*, Asian Development Bank, Manila

Chanditthawong, T (2005) *Damages and Assistance Rendering to Tsunami Tidal Wave Victims in the 6 Southern Provinces on the Coastal Line of Andaman Sea*, Thai Ministry of Interior: Bangkok, Thailand (in Thai)

Denzin, NK (1989) *The Research Act: A theoretical introduction to sociological methods*, Prentice Hall: Englewood Cliffs, NJ

Denzin, NK and Lincoln, SY (eds) (1998),*The Landscape of Qualitative Research*, Sage Publications, Thousand Oaks, CA

DPM (2005a) *Master Plan for Tsunami Evacuation*, Office of Civil Defense Committee Secretariat, Department of Disaster Prevention and Mitigation, Ministry of Interior, Bangkok

DPM (2005b) *Master Plan for Flood, Windstorm and Mudslide Hazards Prevention, Mitigation and Recovery Services in Emergency Period (5-Year Master Plan)*, Office of Civil Defense Committee Secretariat, Department of Disaster Prevention and Mitigation, Ministry of Interior, Bangkok

Heraty, M (2010a) Logistics response and needs in Haiti field perspective, *Logistics and Transport Focus*, **12**(5), pp 35–38

Heraty, M (2010b) Haiti: the logistics response and challenges, *Logistics and Transport Focus*, **12**(6), pp 42–45

Kovacs, G and Spens, KM (2007) Humanitarian logistics in disaster relief operations, *International Journal of Physical Distribution and Logistics Management*, **37**(2), pp 99–114

Long, DC and Wood, DF (1995) The logistics of famine relief, *Journal of Business Logistics*, **16**(1), pp 213–29

Pettit, S and Beresford, AKC (2005) Emergency relief logistics: an evaluation of military, non-military and composite response models, *International Journal of Logistics: Research and Applications*, 8(4), pp 313–31

Rangsit University (2005) *Tsunami: what remains after*, Nation Multimedia Group Public Company limited, Bangkok

Salam, MA (2006) *Disaster Logistics Management – A Case Study of the Thai Tsunami*, Proceedings of the Logistics Research Network Conference, CILT, Newcastle, Sept, pp 373–78

United Nations (2005) *Humanitarian Response Review – Commissioned by the UN Emergency Relief Coordinator and USG for Humanitarian Affairs*; available at: http://www.reliefweb.int/rw/lib.nsf/db900sid/EVOD-6FUDKN?OpenDocument

United Nations (2006) *Indonesia Earthquake 2006: Response plan*, OCHA Situation Report No 5, United Nations Office Coordination of Humanitarian Affairs, New York/Geneva

USGS (United States Geological Service) (2006) *Magnitude 9.1 – off the west coast of Sumatra*, available at: http://earthquake.usgs.gov/earthquakes/eqinthenews/2004/usslav/#summary/

Whiting, M (2010) The Haiti earthquake January 2010, *Logistics and Transport Focus*, 12(4), pp 26–29

Whittow, J (1980) *Disaster – The anatomy of environmental hazards*, Penguin Books, London

Notes

1   International Council of Voluntary Agencies (ICVA) Report – What is all the cluster talk?

2   The Logistics Cluster Working Group is led by WFP and participants at the global level include IOM, WHO, UNHCR, UNICEF, OCHA, the United Nations Joint Logistic Centre.

3   See Annex of IASC Principal's Meeting 12 Dec 2005: *Cluster Working Group on Logistics, Progress Report* (38 pages), circulated 08 Dec.

4   See: Thomas, AS and Kopczak, LR (2005) *From Logistics to Supply Chain Management. The path forward in the humanitarian sector*, Fritz Institute. Available at: http://www.fritzinstitute.org/PDFs/WhitePaper/FromLogisticsto.pdf

5   An introduction to the Cluster Leadership Approach is available in the *Guidance Note on Using the Cluster Approach to Strengthen Humanitarian Response, 24 November, 2006*; available at: http://www.humanitarianreform.org/humanitarianreform/Portals/1/Resources%20&%20tools/IASCGUIDANCENOTECLUSTERAPPROACH.pdf

07
The journey to humanitarian supply network management
an African perspective

PAUL SN BUATSI

Abstract

This chapter discusses the growing importance of humanitarian logistics and supply chain management in Africa, noting the multiplicity of actors and processes involved. Given the diversity of disasters that pose obstacles to sustainable development in Africa, public institutions are collaborating with international development and relief agencies, provincial, state, district and metropolitan authorities in disaster management activities. Stakeholders at the national, continental and international levels are addressing the key challenges regarding the development of institutional frameworks and policies, standards and indicators, poor service infrastructure, technology and communication information flow and information sharing as well as the lack of coordination, collaboration, needs assessment, appreciation of logistics and supply chain management, logistical expertise, and inadequate training. It is therefore argued that stakeholders in humanitarian logistics and supply chain management have to focus on the key success factors required for efficient and effective humanitarian interventions.

Introduction

This chapter acknowledges the growing importance of humanitarian logistics and supply chain management in the African context. This discussion is within the context of the multiplicity of actors and processes involved in the delivery of development aid and relief during disasters and emergencies, a reflection of the complexity of humanitarian supply networks. The advances made towards the application of theoretical concepts in business logistics and supply chain management provide a background to the discussion of the African experience. The emphasis here is that the context within which humanitarian interventions occur in Africa is complex and therefore poses serious management and leadership challenges: the types of disaster, the conditions of the victims, marked political and cultural diversity, the limited and poor state of infrastructure and other resource constraints required to support and manage humanitarian interventions. In addition, the role of continental, regional, international organizations, global humanitarian agencies, civil society organizations and opinion leaders influence the efficiency, effectiveness and therefore success of interventions and moderate the degree of cooperation and collaboration. The complexity of the humanitarian supply networks in Africa, like elsewhere, with a multiplicity of actors raises serious logistical management and leadership challenges.

Types of disaster

Definition of disaster

The general area of humanitarian supply networks is predicated on the fact that the world is increasingly plagued by disasters, thus calling for the adoption and adaptation of business supply network principles and practices in the face of humanitarian interventions. As such:

> The event becomes a disaster when the community's capacity to cope is overwhelmed and the status quo becomes untenable. Disasters happen when hazards meet exposure due to vulnerability. Russell, 2005

Theoretically, disasters have been categorized as man-made or natural disasters. According to Barbarosoglu et al (2002), sudden-onset disasters have a strong negative impact on the physical infrastructure of the region, destroying transport infrastructure such as bridges and air fields, electricity networks and communication infrastructure. Due to their nature, responding to a sudden-onset disaster calls for agile supply chains, thus focusing on response times, while the planning horizon for slow-onset disasters enables logisticians to focus on cost efficiencies (Oloruntoba and Gray, 2006).

The nature and incidence of disasters in Africa

In recent years, the world has witnessed a succession of disasters – floods, wildfires, storms, earthquakes, volcanic eruptions and landslides. These claimed many thousands of lives, caused material losses in the billions of dollars, and inflicted a terrible toll on developing countries in particular, where disasters divert attention and resources from development needed desperately to escape poverty. Today's disasters are often generated by, or at least extended by, human activities. Inadequate land-use planning, poor environmental management and a lack of appropriate institutional and legislative arrangements increase the risk and multiply the effects of disasters. Africa is the only continent where the regional share of reported disasters in the world has increased over the past decade (Africa Union, 2004). According to Chatora (2005, 2007), disasters in Africa range from civil strife, population movement (refugees and internally displaced people), earthquakes, cyclones, flooding, droughts and epidemics with countries exhibiting varying degrees of exposure. On an individual hazard basis, epidemics are leading disasters. In particular, the effects of the HIV/AIDS pandemic and the malaria and tuberculosis epidemics place downward pressure on sustainable development, particularly in sub-Saharan Africa.

Disasters and sustainable development in Africa

The African Ministerial Statement to the World Summit on Sustainable Development stressed that the increased incidence of natural disasters in Africa poses a major obstacle to the African continent's efforts to achieve sustainable development. This is aggravated by Africa's insufficient capacities to predict, monitor, handle and mitigate natural disasters. The continent's state of disaster preparedness is therefore of much concern (Marjanovic and Nimpuno (2010)). In 2000–01, about 35 million people, equivalent to 13 per cent of the total population in Africa, were affected by disasters. Disasters significantly derailed development in affected countries. For example, in the year 2000 floods in Mozambique lowered the country's Gross Domestic Product (GDP) by about 12 per cent, and the 1992 drought reduced Zimbabwe's and Zambia's GDPs by about 9 per cent (African Union, 2004). Further examples can be found in the Algeria floods in October 2008, which killed 93 people, left many more injured and thousands of homeless in several provinces of Algeria (IFRCRC Annual Report, 2009). In the same month and year, torrential rains, a cold wave and snowfalls affected several provinces of Morocco, claiming the lives of 70 people and leaving homeless families having to be accommodated in temporary shelters due to considerable damage (destruction of houses, roads, bridges, electrical networks, etc). In September 2008, rockslides in Cairo (in the impoverished Manshiyet Nasser shantytown) left 98 people dead, 72 injured and forced 166,731 families to move as their houses were partially affected (ibid).

Thousands of families had to relocate as their houses were partially destroyed due to the rockslides in Manshiyet Nasser shantytown in September 2008 (ibid).

The scope and role of humanitarian logistics

With the challenges posed by diverse forms of disaster in Africa there is a growing awareness of the significance of humanitarian logistics and supply chain management. With the increase in the number and impact of recent disasters, the shortcomings in planning for disasters have become more apparent and the critical role of humanitarian logistics in effective disaster relief delivery has been recognized. Humanitarian logistics is defined by Fritz Institute as:

> the process of planning, implementing and controlling the efficient, cost-effective flow and storage of goods and materials, as well as related information, from the point of origin to the point of consumption for the purpose of alleviating the suffering of vulnerable people. The function encompasses a range of activities, including preparedness, planning, procurement, transport, warehousing, tracking and tracing, and customs clearance. (Thomas and Kopczak, 2005: 2)

Also, Aruna Apte (2009) defines

> humanitarian logistics as that special branch of logistics which manages response supply chain of critical supplies and services with challenges such as demand surges, uncertain supplies, critical time-windows in face of infrastructure vulnerabilities and vast scope and size of the operations.

The understanding that logistics efforts account for 80 per cent of disaster relief operations affirms its critical role in saving lives and improving living conditions (Van Wassenhove, 2006; Trunick, 2005; Scholten et al, 2009). Activities take place along the whole supply chain from the point of origin to the point of consumption with the aim to improve conditions for people affected. Without doubt, logistics must always be an important factor in humanitarian aid operations in Africa. The level of demonstrated professional involvement has been low. As with other contexts, despite the importance of supply chain management in fulfilling most of the critical tasks in humanitarian relief operations, logistics may still be seen in Africa as a support function in many humanitarian organizations (Thomas, 2003).

Unpredictable demand and supply

Disaster relief operations often have to be carried out in environments with destabilized infrastructure ranging from a lack of electricity supplies to limited transport infrastructure (Cassidy, 2003). Moreover, since most natural disasters are unpredictable, the demand for goods in these disasters is also unpredictable (Cassidy, 2003; Murray, 2005). The speed of humanitarian aid after a disaster depends 'on the ability of logisticians to procure, transport and receive supplies at the site of a humanitarian relief effort' (Thomas, 2003, p 4). Managing humanitarian supply chain holds unique challenges, as unlike commercial supply chains, demand cannot be anticipated (Long and Wood, 1995). Existing poor infrastructure and weak political systems in Africa, like other undeveloped regions, make it difficult to assess demand and supply requirements and pose serious challenges to the high need of flexibility as distribution networks have to be set up quickly (Van Wassenhove, 2006; Scholten et al, 2009; Buatsi, Oduro, Annan, Asamoahand Boso, 2009; Buatsi, Oduro, Annan, Asamoah and Lartey, 2009).

Efficiency of disaster response

Ertem et al (2010) raise the question of how the world community responds to the challenges posed by natural disasters (eg floods, hurricanes, earthquakes, etc). They observed that:

> non-governmental organizations (NGOs), local governments and the United Nations do not perform disaster relief operations in an efficient and standard way that can overcome all of the consequences of a disaster. In the aftermath of natural disasters, vital resources (eg food, water, tents, clothing, medicine, etc) are usually not readily available to the victims of the natural disasters.

Ertem et al (2010) argue that this inability to deliver the resources to the disaster location in the right quantity and at the right time can be addressed by effective resource allocation, 'the principal objective of disaster-relief organizations and NGOs during disaster-relief operations' (Medina-Borja et al, 2007). Acquiring the right amount of disaster supplies and allocating the available resources at the right time and in the right quantity are key elements of humanitarian supply chain management essential for proper disaster response that decreases fatalities and preserves perishable food and medical supplies (Beamon, 2004; Van Wassenhove, 2006; Kovács and Spens, 2007; Ertem et al, 2010). The speed with which emergencies are declared, the speed of response to appeals, the quality of assessments by national and international relief organizations, inefficiencies in procurement and transportation, and the degree of political interference are issues of concern. These were experiences during the 2007 floods in Northern Ghana

(Buatsi, Oduro, Annan, Asamoah and Boso, 2009; Buatsi, Oduro, Annan, Asamoah, and Lartey, 2009).

Critical success factors in the context of humanitarian aid supply chains

In the light of the challenges outlined above, it would be necessary for humanitarian logisticians to focus attention on the key success factors required for efficient and effective interventions to meet the needs of clients in humanitarian situations. In their review of the literature on critical success factors in business logistics and their application to humanitarian logistics, Pettit and Beresford (2009) identified the following: inventory management, transport and capacity planning, information management and technology utilization, human resource management, continuous improvement and collaboration and supply chain strategy.

To enhance our understanding and operational efficiency of humanitarian supply networks, due consideration should be given to the recommendations of Richey (2009) that supply chain disaster and crisis preparedness and recovery be 'theoretically supported in combination of four mature theoretical perspectives': the RBV of the firm, communication theory, competing values theory, and relationship management theory. This is predicated on the common thread in recent discussions in supply chain disaster and crisis management (and related supply chain strategy and logistics operations). Emphasis is on what will enable supply chain managers and researchers to develop plans to get people out of harm's way and get aid into the impacted areas: agility (Oloruntoba and Gray, 2006); risk management/insurance issues (Kleidt *et al*, 2009); humanitarian issues (Gibbons and Samaddar, 2009; Kovacs and Spens, 2007); inventory management (Beamon and Kotleba, 2006); facility location (Balcik and Beamon, 2008); collaboration/networks (Gibbons and Samaddar, 2009); and multi-level partner/non-partner integration (Perry, 2007; Rathbun, 2007). According to Ertem *et al* (2010):

> Although nothing can be done to stop the natural disasters, the means to serve millions of people affected from natural disasters can be improved. A key requirement is to utilize all available resources in locations other than the disaster location. Some potential methods that should be considered for improving resource allocations include: offering similar items that will work in place of the required item (eg substitution options) and supplying quantities that are less than the requested quantity (eg partial demand fulfilment options). Since timely response is critical, there should also be procedures to address the urgency of requirements (eg priority of items). Humanitarian organizations in disaster locations should also consider methods to acquire a minimum amount of items (eg require a minimum threshold level).

Disaster risk management and contingency planning in Africa

In response to the challenges posed by disasters on the African continent, various countries have established public institutions that are collaborating with international development and relief agencies to engage in disaster management activities. Institutional involvement spans national governments, regional, provincial, state, district and metropolitan authorities, depending on the country involved. In South Africa, for example, the Disaster Management Act: 57 of 2002 of the Ekurhuleni Metropolitan Council defines disaster management as a continuous and integrated multi-sectoral, multi-disciplinary process of planning and implementation of measures aimed at: a) Preventing or reducing the risk of disasters; b) Mitigating the severity or consequences of disasters; c) Emergency preparedness; d) A rapid and effective response to disasters; and e) Post-disaster recovery and rehabilitation. After the Nairobi consultative meeting on the establishment of National Platforms, Ghana has established a National Platform for Disaster Risk Reduction. The objectives of the programme are to achieve: Political Commitment from the Government including political figures in the Regions as well as the Districts; Making Disaster Management *everybody's* business through the establishment of focal points in the Ministries, Government Agencies and Private Institutions, etc; Incorporating Disaster Risk Reduction concepts into National Development Programmes; and Community Participation and Poverty Reduction.

Disaster Management in Africa has programmes and measures designed to *prevent, mitigate, prepare for, respond to* and *recover* from the effects of all disasters. However, disaster response is often hindered by the inadequate state of disaster preparedness through well-developed contingency plans, as well as limited response capability within governments and humanitarian organizations in the region. According to Chatora (2005) some of the gaps identified in disaster management include inadequate preparedness plans and insufficient contingency planning. In order to effectively respond to any disaster it is essential that contingency plans are developed for each hazard or potential disaster (Buys, 2002). The role of contingency planning cannot be overstated in disaster management. The UNHCR handbook for emergencies (1996: 5) defines contingency planning as:

> A forward planning process, in a state of uncertainty, in which scenarios and objectives are agreed, managerial and technical actions defined, and potential response systems put in place in order to prevent, or better respond to, an emergency or critical situation.

> Contingency planning builds organizational capacity and should become a foundation for operation planning and emergency response. (UNHCR, 2003: 14)

Among other roles, contingency planning: 1) enhances an organization's capacity to prepare, reduce/mitigate, warn and respond to disasters timely, with appropriate materials (including HR); 2) facilitates moving from 'a culture of reaction when disasters have happened, to more of a preparedness culture'; 3) increases humanitarian accountability by preparing, mitigating and responding to disasters through agreed benchmarks; 4) promotes the development and testing of evacuation plans. Without adequate contingency planning, managing disasters is not systematic, can be costly, and may result in unnecessary loss of lives, as well as duplication of efforts and wastage of resources.

Contingency planning, as a continuous process, requires continuous monitoring of the plan as the situation evolves (UNHCR, 2003). In Southern Africa lessons learned from the 2000 Cyclone Eline revealed that there was lack of preparedness and insufficient contingency planning as compared to the 2007 floods and cyclone Favio, which struck Mozambique and some parts of Zimbabwe (IFRCRC, 2007). The 2007 floods were severe and cyclone Favio struck Mozambique's Inhambane province when there was already flooding in the province. As a result of contingency planning, provision of early warning and the increased preparedness capacity, the resulting impact was minimal compared to that of 2000 (IFRCRC, 2007).

Mozambique's Disaster Management Authority, in collaboration with other government ministries, United Nations agencies, the Red Cross, non-governmental organizations and international humanitarian organizations put into place contingency plans for floods and cholera that could be activated in time. This included pre-positioning of stocks, having clearly defined roles and responsibilities, shared information on available resources and gaps and pre-disaster deployment of human resources to support operations in accommodation areas where displaced people were housed. This resulted in swift coordinated disaster response through the cluster approach as reported in the situation report (OCHA, 2007).

Institutional frameworks and policies

African governments are making efforts to enhance the effectiveness and efficiency of institutional policies to deal with the multiplicity of challenges associated with disasters on the continent. As such, the African Union (AU) with its New Partnership for Africa's Development (NEPAD) has put in place an Africa Regional Strategy for Disaster Risk Reduction (African Union, 2004). In Africa, most of the factors associated with vulnerability to disasters are due to development pressures or outcomes of the development process. Disaster Management thus intends: 1) to reduce the impact of disasters; and 2) to promote development processes that help to reduce disaster risks. The study carried out prior to the development of the strategy revealed that development in Africa was at risk from disasters mainly because of gaps in: *institutional frameworks*; *risk identification*; *knowledge management*; *governance*; and *emergency response*. The implementation and monitoring of the strategy is the responsibility of key stakeholders with clear-cut institutional – AU/NEPAD, Regional Economic Communities (RECs), the Africa Working Group on Disaster Risk Reduction, national governments, major groups (mainly civil society bodies and the private sector) – and international development partners. The strategy was adopted by Heads of State at the 3rd Ordinary Session of the AU Assembly in Addis Ababa, Ethiopia, from 6–8 July 2004, with a call to develop a Programme of Action for its implementation (African Union, 2004).

The AU notes however that:

> disaster management is not yet integrated in national development frameworks in most of the African countries, even though few countries have explicitly included disaster reduction as specific thematic focus areas in their Poverty Reduction Strategy Papers (PRSPs). Disaster risk reduction practice in Africa has focused on attempting to reduce the impacts of disasters on development through emergency management. Substantial amounts of humanitarian assistance flow into Africa, partly to provide relief assistance in emergencies. But despite the relatively longer history of emergency response management relative to disaster risk reduction and significant humanitarian assistance, disaster response activities remain largely divorced from mainstream development activities in Africa. Relief agencies often focus on immediate emergency needs, with an emphasis on food aid distribution. They concentrate less on bridging the relief-rehabilitation gap or investing in developing people's capacities to cope with future disasters. (African Union, 2004)

Development partners and international relief and development agencies such as World Vision International, ActionAid, Care International, Oxfam and ADRA, among others, are collaborating to address the challenges through policy formulation and implementation through diverse interventions on the continent. However, the above initiatives at disaster risk reduction and the multiplicity of challenges associated with these efforts have implications for humanitarian logistics and supply chain management in Africa, especially because of uncertainties surrounding the determination of demand and supply for humanitarian relief, which leans towards emergencies.

Multiplicity of actors: the critical roles of inter-agency communication, collaboration and coordination

Noting that there are always multiple players in supply chain disaster and crisis situations, it is suggested that our understanding of collaboration in effective humanitarian logistics and supply chain management should benefit from relationship management theory (Min *et al*, 2005: 237). According to Pettit and Beresford (2005), the diversity of actors in any disaster situation includes governments, national non-governmental organizations (NGOs), foreign NGOs, military organizations and UN aid agencies. In this regard, both the 'structural' elements of supply chains and cultural elements are considered essential to the establishment of an effective supply chain. Our earlier discussions clearly depict some degree of collaboration by organizations involved in humanitarian relief activities in Africa. Since the key actors include organizations with a global network, cultural sensitization with an understanding of critical success factors in humanitarian relief delivery would have to complement current efforts being made on the African continent. The efforts of African regional and multilateral institutions in strategic planning and implementation as they impinge on disaster management are clear pointers to the realization of the need to focus on key success factors for effective humanitarian logistics and supply chain management.

Ford *et al* (2002) note that humanitarian emergencies such as those seen in Somalia, Kosovo and Afghanistan are characterized by multinational humanitarian and military efforts. These emergencies are complex and difficult to operate in because they contain political, military and humanitarian considerations. The various actors responding to a Complex Humanitarian Emergency (CHE) need each other to effectively respond to the crisis, thus communication, collaboration and coordination are critical. Technology can significantly facilitate information sharing between the various participants during complex humanitarian emergencies (Ford *et al*, 2002; see also Buatsi, Oduro, Annan, Asamoah and Nketia, 2009).

Similarly, there are many players in humanitarian relief operations in Africa such as governments and governmental agencies; the United Nations (UN); individuals; military and non-governmental organizations; corporations/businesses; religiously affiliated organizations; foundations; and universities and colleges (Scholten *et al*). These entities strive to improve the conditions of people in Africa by providing essentials such as water, food, clothing, shelter, medical supplies, medical treatment and basic human rights. Demand is assessed through aid agencies (Long and Wood, 1995), which can be viewed as the primary actors through which governments channel aid that is targeted at alleviating suffering caused by natural and man-made disasters. The largest agencies are global actors, but there are also many small regional and country-specific aid agencies (Thomas and Kopczak, 2005). Other actors include the military, host governments and neighbouring country governments, other non-governmental organizations (NGOs) and logistics service providers (Kaatrud *et al*, 2003). The benefits of an inter-agency contingency planning outweigh the individual organizational benefits and allow for information and resource sharing, while minimizing duplication and confusion among organizations.

Donors and international organizations also play an active role in forging policies to mitigate the impact of disasters in Africa and evolve effective humanitarian logistics and supply chain management systems. For example, various reports were presented by donors and international organizations at the Southern African Development Community Disaster Management Committee and Technical Seminar, 6–9 December 2000, Harare, Zimbabwe: USAID, Office of Foreign Disaster Assistance (OFDA), DFID, the Department for International Development, UK; UNDP Geneva – the Programme Advisor to UNDP Emergency Response Division in Geneva; US Army Corps of Engineers; USAID/FEWSNET; UNHCR – The United Nations High Commission for Refugees; United States European Command (USEUCOM); and United Nations Development Program (UNDP) (SADC, 2000).

The role of technology in humanitarian logistics in Africa

The essential role of communication theory in humanitarian relief and supply chain management is one of the four theoretical thrusts proposed by Richey (2009). The quality of communications technology, effective communication, information exchange and support are essential in supply chain disaster and crisis situations (Large, 2005; Buatsi, Oduro, Annan, Asamoah and Nketia, 2009). Communications and information systems are vital in controlling relief operations. Such systems 'can assist in crisis, disaster and emergency planning, response and management'. Current efforts to develop telecommunications infrastructure and information systems should enable African countries to avoid capacity difficulties (Fritz Institute, 2005) and facilitate the efficiency of humanitarian supply networks in Africa.

Humanitarian logistics information systems can improve the effectiveness of humanitarian supply chains by providing timely and accurate information regarding what supplies are required and have been delivered, enabling donors to be more responsive to the needs of beneficiaries (Fritz Institute, 2005). Moreover, because humanitarian logistics operates across the disaster management cycle, it can improve logistics activities in each of the phases and also help to provide continuity to humanitarian operations throughout the entire cycle. According to Scholten *et al*, supply chain technology for humanitarian aid organizations is only in the development stage. For humanitarian supply chains to be virtually integrated information technology is a necessity so that data can be shared between buyers and sellers. These researchers discovered that humanitarian organizations are only starting to deploy technology and are far from sharing data with suppliers. In Africa, the deployment of modern technology in the operations of humanitarian organizations is on the ascendancy, though at different levels of adoption. Apart from the national and international aid agencies (Red Cross, World Vision, WHO, etc) few to none of the local NGOs use Enterprise Resource Planning Systems.

A case in point of efforts to address the challenge of the technological gap is a project known as Advancing ICT for Disaster Risk Management in Africa – AÏDA (AIDA, 2009). The AÏDA project, sponsored by the EU 'aims to acquire and share knowledge about affordable ICT solutions to support disaster risk management (DRM) in Africa and disseminates this knowledge and best practices among all stakeholders across different communities at risk'. AÏDA is setting up a test case in South Africa, where the Forest Fire Association (FFA) in Nelspruit will use wildfire alarms from the South African Council for Scientific and Industrial Research (CSIR) in its operational activities to fight wildfires. Fire detection is based on the CSIR's Advanced Fire Information System, which ingests satellite-based products, such as the Meteosat Second Generation (MSG) and MODIS active fire products, and provides automated alerts to pre-defined areas. Also in South Africa, Umoya Networks specializes in the design, deployment and management of satellite networks specifically in response to the necessity for the establishment of technical supporting systems for disaster management, noting that the faster the authorities respond the lower will be the loss of life and property. In the Western Cape the Department of Local Government and Housing, Disaster Management and the Fire Brigade Services have deployed Africon's GEMC³ system together with a satellite communications solution provided by Umoya Networks which facilitates effective preparation for, and response to, disasters (Umoya Networks, 2007). The South African Disaster Management Act No. 57 of 2002 calls for 'significantly strengthened capacity to track, collate, monitor and disseminate information on phenomena and activities'. Furthermore, the Act states that 'A key to having good information systems is to invest in mechanisms and capacity for surveillance, monitoring and evaluation.' (Disaster Management Act 57: 2002). As such:

> the South African National Disaster Management Centre (NDMC) has entered into an agreement with the Satellite Application Centre (SAC) to procure their sensor portfolio to assist and enhance the National Disaster Management Information System (NDMIS). The system relates to various aspects concerning hazard analysis, vulnerability assessment, contingency planning, reporting systems as well as early warning systems. The Range of Sensors includes NOAA, LandSat 7, MODIS, and the SPOT Range amongst many including the new SPOT 5 Imagery that will provide a national coverage annually in a 2.5m resolution and be presented as a level three product (imagery is already orthorectified with ground control points and a DEM for terrain displacement corrections). *Disaster Management Southern Africa*

These investments do and will enhance the interventions of humanitarian logistician as they collaborate with other stakeholders in various African humanitarian supply networks.

Human capacity building for disaster risk management in Africa

Training and capacity building needs in humanitarian logistics in Africa are extensive, diverse and multidisciplinary. However, capacity is lacking and there are not enough training units/institutions. Marjanovic and Nimpuno (2009) propose that a cooperative network approach is essential to ensure that effective training and capacity building in disaster management can be developed and implemented in Africa. Africa needs to establish a stable and sustainable training and capacity-building programme to respond to the long-term needs of the region.

Formal training in disaster management, logistics and supply chain management

There is a combination of short courses to address short-term needs, focusing on fundamentals of disaster management from a practical point of view and formal training programmes in disaster management leading to undergraduate and postgraduate qualifications. In Ghana, for example, systematic training programmes have been developed for public sector officials (such as the National Disaster Management Organisation) who also benefit from overseas training. Officials of international relief agencies are constantly undergoing in-house training at home and abroad, while professional bodies such as the Chartered Institute of Logistics and Transport, who have incorporated courses in humanitarian logistics, run programmes for professional certification in collaboration with the Ghana Institute of Management and Public Administration (GIMPA). GIMPA also offers a course in Supply Chain Management on the MBA Programme. Ghanaian polytechnics have focused mainly on Higher National Diplomas in Purchasing and Supply Management while the KNUST School of Business at the Kwame Nkrumah University of Science and Technology offers Logistics and Supply Chain Management as a concentration at the undergraduate and postgraduate levels where faculty and students undertake research in humanitarian logistics. The Ghana Procurement Authority has developed comprehensive courses in logistics and supply chain management for undergraduate and diploma students in Ghanaian Polytechnics and Universities as a national effort at capacity building. In the Republic of South Africa, the Disaster Risk Management Training and Education Centre for Africa at the University of The Free State offers postgraduate education and training. Also, the Disaster Management Institute of South Africa offers disaster management training. In response to the Disaster Management Act (No 57 of 2002) and the Municipal Systems Act (No 32 of 2000) that stipulate the inclusion of a disaster management plan into the municipality's integrated development plan (IDP), the Provincial Disaster Management Centre (PDMC) of the Western Cape embarked on disaster management/ IDP training, which was targeted at municipal politicians and officials involved in the field of disaster management. This capacity-building programme is part of a provincial-wide strategy to ensure the implementation of the Disaster Management Act (Act 57 of 2002), as well as the National and draft Provincial Disaster Management Frameworks and the draft National Guidelines.

Library resources

It is reported that the United Nations International Strategy for Disaster Reduction (UN/ISDR) Unit for Africa donated an Inter-Agency Field Library for Disaster Reduction to the Disaster Management Institute of Southern Africa (DMISA) in July 2006. This initiative provides literature and practical, technical and educational information on disaster risk reduction and related subjects as support to hazard-prone countries. According to Styn (2007):

> The library consists of a metal trunk filled with material intended to stimulate the engagement of disaster reduction practitioners, researchers, national, provincial and local leaders, regional institutions, libraries, NGOs, UN and other international agencies. The library is a tool that encourages learning and develops skills in disaster reduction. It is targeted to support leaders, disaster management officers and key educational institutions. The content of the library is designed according to the hazard, vulnerability and disaster history of each country. Guidelines for the use of the library were also provided in order to promote a culture of disaster prevention worldwide.

Challenges of humanitarian logistics in Africa

The foregoing discussions have brought to the fore the challenges of humanitarian logistics in Africa. These are collaborated by the findings of the research preceding the development of the Africa Regional Strategy for Disaster Risk Reduction (African Union, 2004). Some of the challenges that are likely to confront the management of humanitarian supply networks are:

- **Poor service infrastructure:** Africa is plagued by poor service infrastructure in most parts of the continent. This hampers quick response to disasters.

- **Lack of investment in technology and communication:** Very little capital is invested in the development and implementation of modern management information systems (MIS), information technology (IT) or logistics systems (Gustavsson, 2003).

- **Information flow and information sharing:** During the early stages of any disaster, speed and accuracy in information flow are necessary factors. Poor communication infrastructure and lack of modern equipment are constraints in Africa (Buatsi, Oduro, Annan, Asamoah and Nketia, 2009).

- **Lack of strong institutional frameworks and policy:** Institutional frameworks and disaster risk-reduction policies do exist at various degrees of completeness in African countries, but their effectiveness is limited. Many African countries are at different stages in the development of institutional frameworks for comprehensive disaster risk reduction. Consequently, disaster risk-management mechanisms in Africa do not yet possess the capacity to adequately help reduce and manage disaster risks (African Union, 2004).

- **Lack of standards and indicators:** Africa is yet to achieve convergence in harmonizing national policies and efforts to facilitate regional and continental interventions.

- **Lack of coordination:** There is a serious lack of coordination in humanitarian efforts in Africa, though efforts are being made to enhance coordination (Kovács, Spens and Buatsi, 2007).

- **Lack of collaboration:** Lack of collaborative information sharing among stakeholders often results in the duplication of efforts and a waste of resources. Lack of collaboration affects the coordination of humanitarian efforts in Africa (Kovács, Spens and Buatsi, 2007).

- **Lack of needs assessment:** Needs assessment following a disaster is paramount for efficient and effective relief efforts. Unfortunately, because of the lack of expertise in humanitarian logistics and resources in Africa, international aid agencies usually conduct needs assessments of disasters occurring in Africa when they arrive on the scene. In both man-made and natural disaster relief, humanitarian logistics operations have been hampered by a lack of coordination between actors, which directly affects performance in terms of reactivity and reliability (Buatsi, Oduro, Annan, Asamoah and Lartey, 2009; Buatsi, Oduro, Annan, Asamoah and Boso, 2009).

- **Lack of appreciation of logistics and supply chain management:** by NGOs and humanitarian aid agencies.

- **Lack of logistical expertise:** Despite a willingness to embrace logistics and supply chain management in Africa, Africa has a shortage of logisticians. This greatly hampers efforts at leveraging humanitarian logistics and supply chain management principles to achieve operational effectiveness and cost efficiency in humanitarian relief.

- **Inadequate training:** There is an extreme lack of training in the area of humanitarian logistics in Africa, a major hindrance to the continent's state of disaster preparedness and management.

Conclusion

In order to provide an understanding of the context of African humanitarian supply networks, this chapter examined the nature and incidence of disasters in Africa and their impact on sustainable development. The scope and role of humanitarian logistics within the African context then becomes clear, given the unpredictability of disasters and their associated demand and supply. The degrees of efficiency and success of humanitarian response and recovery efforts by the multiplicity of actors that demonstrate different levels of collaboration and cooperation were shown to be important considerations. As such, the identification of key success factors and the grounding of humanitarian supply network management in sound management theory become important considerations within the African context as elsewhere.

The institutional developments in and adoption of disaster risk management, including policy development, strategic planning, inter-agency communication, collaboration and coordination, the adoption a diversity of technologies to facilitate hazard analysis, vulnerability assessment, contingency planning, reporting systems as well as early warning systems are indications of change that will increasingly enhance the efficiency of humanitarian supply networks and therefore the degree of success in humanitarian interventions. These efforts are being complemented by the development of human capital at all levels in all aspects of disaster management, including humanitarian logistics and supply chain management. The discussions on Africa highlight the enormity of the challenge but the progress being made in various areas at all levels should result in the evolution of greater efficiency and effectiveness in the management of humanitarian supply networks in Africa. Above all, the issues discussed should guide the development of models of humanitarian supply networks in Africa that would enhance the performance of humanitarian logisticians working for the various organizations on the continent.

References

African Union (2004) Africa Regional Strategy for Disaster Risk Reduction, July, African Union, Addis Ababa, Ethiopia

AÏDA (Advancing ICT for Disaster Risk Management in Africa) (2009) Fact Sheet FS.02, v.1, © EUMETSAT, April 2009, Am Kavalleriesand 31, 64295 Darmstadt, Germany, +49 6151 807 366/377, +49 6151 807 379; available at: www.eumetsat.int

Apte, Aruna (2009) Humanitarian logistics: A new field of research and action, *Foundations and Trends® in Technology, Information and OM*, 3 (1), pp 1–100; available at: http://dx.doi.org/10.1561/ 0200000014

Balcik, B and Beamon, BM (2008) Facility location in humanitarian relief, *International Journal of Logistics: Research & Applications*, 11(2), pp 101–21

Barbarosoglu, G, Ozdamar, L and Cevik, A (2002) An interactive approach for hierarchical analysis of helicopter logistics in disaster relief operations, *European Journal of Operational Research*, 140(1), pp 118–33

Beamon, BM (2004) *Humanitarian relief chains: issues and challenges*, Proceedings of the 34th International Conference on Computers & Industrial Engineering, San Francisco, CA

Beamon, BM and Kotleba, SA (2006) Inventory management support systems for emergency humanitarian relief operations in South Sudan, *International Journal of Logistics Management*, 17(2), pp 187–212

Buatsi, P, Oduro, FT, Annan, J, Asamoah, D and Boso, R (2009) *Needs assessment in the delivery of relief to the 2007 Ghana Flood Disaster Victims*, 2nd Cardiff/ Cranfield Humanitarian Logistics Initiative (CCHLI) International Humanitarian Logistic Symposium, Faringdon, Oxfordshire, UK

Buatsi, P, Oduro, FT, Annan, J, Asamoah, D and Lartey, G (2009) *Evaluation of the Needs Assessment use by the National Disaster Management Organization – A case study of the 2007 Northern Ghana floods*, 2nd Cardiff/Cranfield Humanitarian Logistics Initiative (CCHLI) International Humanitarian Logistic Symposium, Faringdon, Oxfordshire, UK

Buatsi, P, Oduro, FT, Annan, J, Asamoah, D and Nketia, P (2009) *Coordinating Humanitarian Logistics though ICT – A case study of NADMO Ghana*, 2nd Cardiff/Cranfield Humanitarian Logistics Initiative (CCHLI) International Humanitarian Logistic Symposium, Faringdon, Oxfordshire, UK

Buys LJ (2002) Disaster Management in South Africa. *Consultative conference on search and rescue*, 20–21 September, South African Search and Rescue Organisation, Government of South Africa, Department of Transport, Pretonia, www.sasar.gov.za/pubs/reports/confsept02/app10-12.pdf

Cassidy, W (2003) A logistics lifeline, *Traffic World*, October 27, p 1

Chatora, G (2005) *A Critical Evaluation of the Regional Disaster Response Training Programme of the International Federation of Red Cross and Red Crescent Societies in Southern Africa (2000–2004)*, Zimbabwe Open University, Harare

Chatora, G (2007) *An Analysis of the Contingency Planning Systems for Disaster Management Authorities in Southern Africa*, a thesis submitted to the University of The Free State in fulfilment of the requirements of the award for the Masters Degree in Disaster Risk Management, University of the Free State, Bloemfontein, Republic of South Africa

Disaster Management Act, 57 of 2002, Cape Town: Government Gazette

Disaster Management Bill (2001) Pretoria, South Africa: Government Printer

Disaster Management Southern Africa (2007) **14**(1), October/December

Ertem, Mustafa A, Buyurgan, Nebil and Rossetti, Manuel D (2010) Multiple-buyer procurement auctions framework for humanitarian supply chain management, *International Journal of Physical Distribution & Logistics Management*, **40**(3), pp 202–27

Ford, TD, Hogan, JL and Perry, MW (Sep 2002) Master's thesis, Naval Postgraduate School, Monterey, CA

Fritz Institute (2005) 'Humanitarian Logistics: getting the right relief to the right people at the right time', fact sheets available at: www.fritzinstitute.org/fact_sheets/f_s-Ws.html

Gibbons, DE and Samaddar, S (2009) Designing referral network structures and decision rules to streamline provision of urgent health and human services, *Decision Sciences*, **40**(2), pp 351–71

Gustavsson, L (2003) Humanitarian logistics: context and challenges, *Forced Migration Review*, 18, pp 6–8

Kaatrud, DB, Samii, R and Van Wassenhove, LN (2003) UN Joint Logistics Center: a coordinated response to common humanitarian logistics concerns, *Forced Migration Review*, 18, 11–14

Kleidt, B, Schiereck, D and Sigl-Grueb, C (2009) Rationality at the eve of destruction: insurance stocks and huge catastrophic events, *Journal of Business Valuation and Economic Loss Analysis*, 4(2), pp 1–25

Kovács, G and Spens, KM (2007) Humanitarian logistics in disaster relief operations, *International Journal of Physical Distribution & Logistics Management*, 37(2), pp 99–114

Kovács, G, Spens, K and Buatsi, S (2007) *Challenges of Humanitarian Logisticians in Africa,* 1st Cardiff/Cranfield Humanitarian Logistics Initiative (CCHLI) International Humanitarian Logistic Symposium, Faringdon, Oxfordshire, UK.

Large, RO (2005) Communication capability and attitudes toward external communication of purchasing managers in Germany, *International Journal of Physical Distribution & Logistics Management*, 35(6), pp 426–44

Long, DC and Wood, DF (1995) The logistics of famine relief, *Journal of Business Logistics*, **16**(1), pp 213–29

Marjanovic, P and Nimpuno, K (2010) *Living with Risk: Toward effective disaster management training in Africa*; available at www.bvsde.paho.org/bvsacd/cd46/cap14-living.pdf [accessed January 2011]

Medina-Borja, A, Pasupathy, KS, Triantis, K (2007) 'Large-scale data envelopment analysis (DEA) implementation: a strategic management approach', *Journal of the Operational Research Society*, Vol 58, pp 1,084–98

Min, S, Roath, AS, Daugherty, PJ, Genchev, SE, Chen, H, Arndt, AD and Richey, RG (2005) Supply chain collaboration: what's really happening, *International Journal of Logistic Management*, **16**(2), pp 237–56

Murray, S (2005) How to deliver on the promises: supply chain logistics – humanitarian agencies are learning lessons from business in bringing essential supplies to regions hit by the tsunami, *Financial Times*, 7 January, p 9

OCHA (2007) *Situation Report Number 8: Mozambique floods*, 23 February, Office for the Coordination of Humanitarian Affairs (OCHA), Palais des Nations, 8–14 Avenue de la Paix, Geneva

Oloruntoba, R and Gray, R (2006) Humanitarian aid: an agile supply chain?, *Supply Chain Management: An International Journal*, **11**(2), pp 115–20

Perry, M (2007) Natural disaster management planning: a study of logistics managers responding to the tsunami, *International Journal of Physical Distribution & Logistics Management*, **37**(5), pp 409–33

Pettit, SJ and Beresford, AKC (2005) Emergency relief logistics: an evaluation of military, non-military and composite response models, *International Journal of Logistics: Research and Applications*, **8**(4), pp 313–31

Pettit, S and Beresford, A (2009) Critical success factors in the context of humanitarian aid supply chains, *International Journal of Physical Distribution & Logistics Management*, **39**(6), pp 450–68

Rathbun, BC (2007) Hierarchy and community at home and abroad, *Journal of Conflict Resolution*, **51**(3), pp 379–407

Richey, R Glenn Jr (2009) The supply chain crisis and disaster pyramid: a theoretical framework for understanding preparedness and recovery, *International Journal of Physical Distribution & Logistics Management*, **39**(7), pp 619–28

Russell, TE (2005) *Analysing the 2004 South-East Asia earthquake and tsunami*, thesis for Master of Engineering in Logistics, Massachusetts Institute of Technology, Cambridge, MA

SADC (Southern African Development Community) (2000) *Southern African Development Community Disaster Management Committee and Technical Seminar, 6–9 December 2000*, Harare, Zimbabwe

Scholten, K, Sharkey-Scott P and Fynes, B (2009) Supply chain management concepts and humanitarian aid agencies – an exploratory study, 16th Annual EurOMA (European Operations Management Association Conference, Chalmers University of Technology, Göteborg, Sweden, June 2009, EurOMA Brussels, Belgium; www.euroma-online.org

Styn, Elmien (2007) The establishment of a Resource Centre for the Provincial Disaster Management Centre in the Western Cape, *Disaster Management Southern Africa*, **14**(1), October/December

Thomas, AS (2003) Why logistics? *Forced Migration*, **18**, p 4

Thomas, A (2003) *Humanitarian Logistics: Enabling disaster response*, San Francisco, CA: The Fritz Institute

Thomas, A (2005) Improving aid effectiveness: two studies suggest solutions, *UN Chronicle*, p 61; available at: www.un.org/chronicle [accessed August 2007]

Thomas, A and Fritz, L (2006) Disaster Relief, *Harvard Business Review*, **84**(11), pp 114–26

Thomas, A and Kopczak, L (2005) *From Logistics to Supply Chain Management: The path forward in the humanitarian sector*, San Francisco, CA: Fritz Institute, pp 1–15

Thompson, N (2003) *The end of Children's Aid Direct*, Humanitarian Exchange, Humanitarian Practice Network, London: Overseas Development Institute, p 32

Thompson, PM (2008) *Supply Chain Analytics for Humanitarian Logistics Transformation*, Rockefeller Foundation Conference – Humanitarian Logistics: Networks for Africa, Rockefeller Foundations Bellagio Center, Lake Como, Italy, 5–9 May 2008

Trunick, PA (2005) Special report: delivering relief to tsunami victims, *Logistics Today*, **46**(2), pp 1–3

Umoya Networks (2007) Satellite Communications for Disaster Management, *Disaster Management Southern Africa*, **14**(1) October/December 2007

UNHCR handbook for emergencies (1996), p 5

UNHCR 2003:2

UNHCR Global Report 2003, p 14

UNHCR Global Report 2005

Van Wassenhove, LN (2006) Blackett memorial lecture, humanitarian aid logistics: supply chain management at high gear, *Journal of the Operational Research Society*, 57, pp 475–89

08
Humanitarian logistics in the United States
supply chain systems for responding to domestic disasters

JARROD GOENTZEL AND KAREN SPENS

Abstract

The number of hurricanes and other weather-related disasters impacting the United States are increasing in both frequency and severity, not only in terms of lives lost but also financial impact. In addition, other major events such as terrorist attacks have forced governments on all levels from federal to local to analyse response efforts and many reports on improving domestic response in the US have been issued. However, few of these reports offer a systemic overview of the supply chain components and strategies. Therefore, this chapter analyses humanitarian logistics from the perspective of a domestic response to disasters in the United States. The case of Florida Division of Emergency Management is used to highlight the importance of developing and communicating a clear supply chain strategy in order to create a system capable of rapidly scaling up. The case also highlights several innovative supply chain approaches; for example the concept of vendor managed inventory (VMI). The innovations and practices discussed in this chapter should be particularly useful for government in structuring the supply chain for domestic emergencies but can also inform humanitarian logistics practices for other organizations in different contexts.

Introduction

The number of hurricanes and other weather-related disasters impacting the United States seems to be increasing in both frequency and severity, both in terms of lives lost as well as financial impact. Between the years of 1980 and 2003, the US sustained 58 weather-related disasters with overall losses exceeding $1 billion dollars at the time of the event (Ross and Lott, 2003). This number of '$1 billion disasters' between 1980 and 2009 had already increased to 96 (Lott, 2010). In addition, man-made disasters, such as terrorist attacks and oil spills, have resulted in casualties and/or serious economic and environmental damages.

In addition to the overall numbers, some major events such as the 11 September 2001 terrorist attack and Hurricane Katrina in 2005 have forced the government on all levels – federal, state and local – to analyse response efforts. Many reports have been issued with critiques and recommendations for improving domestic response in the USA. There has been an extensive debate on the responsibilities and roles that each actor in the response should, or should not, have played (see for example Daniels *et al*, 2006). Analysis and policy recommendations have also been proposed to improve various aspects of the response logistics. However, few offer a systemic overview of response supply chain components and strategies.

This chapter analyses humanitarian logistics from the perspective of a domestic response to disasters in the United States. The context is distinct from many events studied in the realm of humanitarian logistics since the USA will always position itself as being self-sufficient in times of disaster. So, although there can be international support, the USA relies primarily on its own resources and supply chains when disaster strikes. The innovations and practices discussed below should be particularly useful for government in structuring the supply chain for domestic emergencies but can also inform humanitarian logistics practices for other organizations in different contexts.

The chapter begins by providing an overview of the US emergency response structure. It starts with the leading role of government across various levels of jurisdiction and across functional agencies as well as the increasing role of the private sector in emergency response. Against this backdrop, we provide a detailed case study of the supply chain system for the Florida Department of Emergency Management. This case study is meant to present the emergency response supply chain as an integrated system of components: infrastructure, human resources, planning and coordination processes, information and communication technologies and supply chain strategies.

Overview of US emergency response

As in most countries, disaster response in the USA is managed at the lowest possible jurisdictional level with critical support from higher levels as called upon. Local government in the US is basically comprised of two levels: county and municipality township (for the cities/towns in the county). In some states the county is called a 'borough' or 'parish'. Local governement responds to emergencies on a regular basis using their own resources such as the fire department (which may be run by the county and/or city), ambulance/paramedic services (which may be contracted to private service providers), city police and county sheriff. Some cities that are large or that face higher risks may be more proactive in building disaster response operations. One example is New York City, where the Commissioner of Emergency Management, who is part of the mayor's office, leads the Office of Emergency Management (OEM). During an incident, the New York City OEM activates its Emergency Operations Center (EOC), which includes representatives of the police and fire departments, the public health and hospital communities, and utility and transportation companies (Kahn and Barondess, 2008). Representatives from several of these large cities convene annually at the Big City Emergency Managers conference.[1]

When severity or scale overwhelms local capacity, the local government officials ask the state for assistance. In cases where a significant event can be anticipated, such as a hurricane, the state government can take the lead from the start. States typically provide valuable training and preparedness support for the local government. States facing higher risks may have extensive staff and resources within the emergency management agency. In all states, effective emergency management relies on interoperability across state and local agencies and the National Guard.

The National Guard is the oldest component of the Armed Forces of the United States, tracing its history back to the militias in the colonies. It has a dual mission; providing states with first-line defence and emergency response while also providing reserve military force for the United States Department of Defense. The civilians in the National Guard have also been called up in response to international crises from Bosnia to Iraq to Haiti. In its largest response to a domestic disaster, the National Guard deployed more than 50,000 troops in support of the Gulf States following Hurricane Katrina in 2005 (National Guard, 2010).

In large-scale events, the governor may request assistance from other states through interstate mutual aid and assistance agreements such as the Emergency Management Assistance Compact (EMAC). The Federal Government also maintains a wide array of capabilities and resources that can assist state governments in responding to incidents. After being requested by the governor of the state, the President of the United States may sign a disaster declaration that includes both individual and public assistance programmes.

The US federal government's strategy for managing domestic emergencies has evolved in the past decade. Following the 11 September 2001 terrorist attack, Congress passed the Homeland Security Act of 2002, which consolidated many federal activities into a single new agency: the Department of Homeland Security (DHS). DHS includes the Federal Emergency Management Agency (FEMA), which is the principal federal agency responsible for responding to disasters, the US Customs Service and the US Coast Guard. In 2003, Homeland Security Presidential Directive 5 (HSPD-5) designated the Secretary of Homeland Security as the principal coordinator for all federal response operations in major disasters, both natural and man-made. The DHS was also tasked by the HSPD-5 to create an integrated National Response Plan (NRP) for all types of incidents.

The National Response Framework (NRF), which in 2008 replaced the NRP, provides the principles and mechanisms to prepare for and provide a unified emergency response. It describes how various levels of government – federal, state, and local – along with the private sector and non-governmental partners can apply the principles outlined and align efforts. The National Incident Management System (NIMS) complements the NRF by providing a management template that applies across jurisdictional levels and functional disciplines. By providing a common framework, terminology and standards, the template enables the various actors in a response to communicate and coordinate more easily.

In addition to the governmental capacity, non-governmental organizations (NGOs) have long been essential partners in responding to incidents. The American Red Cross stands out among these NGOs since it was given a specific charter by the US Congress in 1900 as the official US disaster relief organization to 'carry on a system of national and international relief in time of peace and to apply the same in mitigating the sufferings caused by pestilence, famine, fire, floods, and other great national calamities' (Kosar, 2006). Many of the NGOs are faith-based, such as the Salvation Army and various denominational organizations.

During Katrina, significant capacity came from the private sector, which had not traditionally been associated with disaster response. Several companies effectively made preparations for the impending disaster long before Katrina hit and were willing and able to bring resources to the disaster area before government agencies in many cases. Notable responses came from 'big box' retailers such as Wal-Mart and Home Depot, which were able to anticipate the hurricane and focus their large-scale supply chains to providing communities with critical commodities. As an example of the quick and sizeable response, Wal-Mart was able to recover 66 per cent of the 173 stores impacted by the hurricane within 48 hours; and 93 per cent had recovered within one week. Wal-Mart also supplied 2,498 trailers of merchandise, over 3 million gallons of drinking water, US $17 million in donations and US $3.5 million in merchandise to relief organizations (Sultemeier and Koon, 2008).

Formal relationships between the private sector and various levels of government have been increasing. Quotes from both sectors in a recent newspaper article illustrate these developments (Albright, 2009):

- Brian Koon, Director of Emergency Management at Wal-Mart: 'Since Katrina, there has been a sea change among government agencies to make what retailers do part of their overall emergency plan. Now we finally have a seat at the table. Retailers get merchandise to customers every day. It's only logical we're best at it in times of need.'

- Chuck Hagan, Chief of Logistics for the Florida Department of Emergency Management: 'Depending on the severity of the storm, we could not pull it off without the job done by the retailers.'

Budhiraj and de la Torre (2010) profile the efforts of several companies in developing emergency response capabilities, with brief case studies spanning manufacturing (Coca-Cola, GlaxoSmithKline), retail (Home Depot, Lowe's, Target, Wal-Mart) and transportation (Federal Express) sectors.

In summary, the US response structure and its strategies for responding to disasters have changed significantly during the last decade. It shifted command at a federal level with the creation of the DHS, while maintaining local and state governments as the primary responders. It has also added capacity with private companies playing a more significant role. The increased frequency and severity of events, coupled with increased scrutiny of the response activities, have pushed all actors to innovate and improve.

Florida division of emergency management

With over 18 million residents, Florida is the fourth most populous state in the United States. The state also has the longest coastline in the contiguous United States, over 1,300 miles, which happens to be located in the one of the world's most active hurricane regions. Though known for hurricane disasters, Florida also has frequent and strong thunderstorms, which can lead to tornadoes and floods.

With all of these factors, the scale of disaster response needs in Florida can be significant. For example, during 2004 the state was hit by one tropical storm and four hurricanes (Charley, Frances, Ivan and Jeanne) in a period of 43 days. This succession of storms impacted all 67 counties, destroyed 13 hospitals and 57 schools, left 368,000 people without shelter and 8.5 million people without power and created over 37 million cubic yards of debris – triggering the largest series of disaster relief operations in the United States prior to Katrina (Hagan and Nunn, 2008). The scale of Florida's supply chain and the level of expertise created to manage it offer a rich context for analysing the public sector role in emergency response.

State agency overview

The Florida Division of Emergency Management (FDEM) is the state agency responsible for emergency preparedness, response, recovery and mitigation programmes in Florida. FDEM works with partners at all levels, including local, state and federal agencies, the private sector and volunteer agencies. In terms of funding, FDEM ranks sixth nationally compared with other state emergency management agencies (Florida Division of Emergency Management, 2009).

FDEM summarizes its activities in four functional categories: preparedness – aligning efforts of various stakeholders in the community to reduce the impact of a disaster; response – delivering resources rapidly after a disaster; recovery – providing access to programmes that rebuild lives and communities that have been impacted by a disaster; and mitigation – reducing or eliminating long-term vulnerability to disasters. Our focus is on the response function, which is further organized into four sections: Operations, Logistics (eg vendor management, resource acquisition, deployment and tracking), Infrastructure (especially focused on hurricane shelters) and Domestic Security. FDEM is also organized geographically into seven DEM regions that provide onsite assistance and state liaison capabilities to all 67 counties (Florida Division of Emergency Management, 2009).

The FDEM established the State Emergency Response Team (SERT) to coordinate across functions from planning to execution and act as a liaison with federal and local agencies. SERT advises policy making, provides technical assistance for preparing emergency plans and procedures, runs training exercises and offers public education. The SERT is comprised of Emergency Coordination Officers who are selected to serve in an operational and advisory capacity (Florida Division of Emergency Management, 2009). While it sounds like a formal organization, in practice the SERT is a very inclusive group welcoming participation from individuals and organizations willing to contribute. According to Chuck Hagan, Unified States Logistics Chief, the only rule in joining the SERT team is 'leave your logo and your ego at the door' (Hagan, 2010).

The Division's number one strategic goal is: 'Develop the capability and capacity to shelter and meet the basic needs of 10,000 survivors with on hand resources – cots, blankets, pillows, food, water, emergency roofing supplies, etc – and be on scene within six hours from time of a no notice incident' (Florida Division of Emergency Management, 2009). This sets a clear target for logistics performance in terms of scale and timing.

The FDEM supply chain has been put to the test in recent years and the scale of operations has been impressive. In response to the series of hurricanes in 2004 mentioned above, the state shipped 4,715 truckloads carrying 9.6 million gallons of water, 78.5 million pounds of ice, 14 million meals-ready-to-eat (MREs), and 561,000 tarps. In addition to distributing commodities, the logistics group supported field operations by shipping 1,088 portable generators ranging from 25 kW to 3.2 GW, 189 portable light towers, 46 portable water pumps, 26 portable HVAC units and 327 forklifts. In total, over 26,000 truckload shipments were made to support the 2004 relief – a shipping volume during that brief period that rivalled Wal-Mart's supply chain. The next year, in 2005, the State of Florida shipped 3,744 truckloads of commodities to serve nearly 5 million people affected by Hurricane Wilma (Hagan and Nunn, 2008). Given these volumes of commodities, there is clearly a solid supply chain to support relief efforts.

Supply chain infrastructure

The FDEM supply chain leverages a mix of permanent facilities and designated locations that are transformed into flow-through facilities as needed for a response. **The State Emergency Operations Center (SEOC)** in the capital city of Tallahassee is the central information and communications hub for overall emergency operations, which goes beyond logistics and supply chain management. The hub of the supply chain, however, is the **State Logistics Response Center (SLRC)** situated at a nexus of transportation routes and modes in Orlando, Florida. In addition to logistical connections, the inland location for this key node in the physical and information supply chain flows also offers lower risk for hurricane damage than coastal locations. Immediately after an event, various types of temporary facilities are established in key areas to support affected citizens.

SLRC

Established in 2007, the SLRC is the only state-level facility of its type in the United States. It combines 187,196 square feet of climate-controlled warehouse space for pre-staged commodities with 19,196 square feet of office space for coordination and communication. The office space hosts employees and volunteers from various State of Florida agencies (eg Division of Emergency Management, Department of Agriculture, Department of Health, Department of Management Services, National Guard, Division of Forestry) as well as the US Federal Emergency Management Agency (FEMA), Army Corps of Engineers, Centers For Disease Control (CDC) and private contractors. During a round-the-clock emergency, the billeting and showers for 20+ people and dining facility for 80+ people come in handy. Below we discuss the critical roles this combined human resource pool tackles.

The warehouse area, serviced by 27 loading docks that can actively load/unload 24 trucks at one time, is stocked with the volume and variety of pre-staged commodities to respond to the '10,000 survivors' goal stated above. These commodities and equipment include:

- 300 truckloads of bottled water (1.4 million gallons);
- 54 truckloads of shelf-stable meals (1.6 million meals);
- 19 truckloads of tarps (45,047 tarps);
- 3 truckloads of roll plastic (1,896 rolls);

- 16 pallets of insect repellent;
- 1 Disaster Mortuary Team Package;
- 5,080 cots and bedding kits;
- 350,000 hygiene kits;
- 2 Disaster Medical Health Screening system packages;
- Emergency Deployable, Tactical Communications System (EDICS), Emergency Deployable, Wide Area Remote Data System (EDWARDS), and tactical satellite voice/data systems;
- 12 tactical generators with 4,800 feet of commercial generator cable.

The SLRC also has specialized areas such as a Class 1 Secure Vault (860 sq ft), a repair and maintenance shop and a certified pharmaceutical warehouse. The facility has built in redundancy and backup, including a Caterpillar 800 kW generator onsite (Hagan and Nunn, 2008; Hagan, 2010).

Temporary facilities

While the SLRC is the hub of prepositioned stock and activity coordination, the supply chain infrastructure is rapidly expanded after an event to provide a quick response. The flow of materials can become complicated as various facilities are established in a response. In a large-scale response, the flow of goods needs to be more direct and at a greater scale than a central warehouse such as the SLRC can support. Hence, the FDEM often establishes a **State Mobilization Area (SMA)** to pre-stage resources outside of potential impact areas. An SMA must be located near a major highway and ideally near an airport and have at least 50,000 square feet of covered area, with four loading docks, and 800,000 square feet of 'hard stand' area, which is ground that is paved or otherwise prepared for parking vehicles and storing material. An SMA is intended to act as a flow-thorough facility where goods are rapidly transshipped, although it can also accept a backlog of resources.

In closer proximity to the event, the **Logistics Staging Area (LSA)** is the key stocking location to provide resources as shortages arise in the impacted area. The LSA is activated within 24 hours of the event and remains in place until the private sector and government structures return to a self-sufficient state. It should also be located near a major highway and ideally near an airport. In total, 56 optional sites have been pre-qualified for locating an LSA across the state. In major events, the impacted area is divided with an LSA supporting each division.

An LSA can vary by size and scale and fall into three types (I, II and III). A Type I LSA should have at least 150,000 square feet of covered area with eight loading docks and 800,000 square feet of 'hard stand' area, including two helicopter landing zones. In addition to material flow, the LSA must support information flows with satellite voice and data communications (T-1 line), mobile office and automation equipment, personnel and life support systems. Also, an LSA requires at least 180 personnel and the billeting and food service requirements must be considered. The LSA must also have areas for check-in/check-out, driver support (eg food, shower) and fuelling.

At the end of the supply chain, the **County Point of Distribution (POD)** distributes bulk emergency relief supplies to beneficiaries, with the peak activity 24–96 hours after an event. The largest POD site requires 32 workers and can distribute commodities to 1,080–1,440 cars (or 3,240–4,320 persons) per day based on FDEM models. PODs operate 24 hours per day with public distribution during daylight hours when it is safe and truck arrival/offloading occurring primarily at night to avoid impact on distribution efforts. County PODs are typically active for three to seven days after the event; and in the case of a catastrophic event, PODs may not be established since it is difficult to immediately support more than 150 PODs (Hagan, 2010).

FDEM pushes water to each county pre-identified POD within the first 24 hours after the event. Commodities such as ice, food and tarps as well as equipment such as power generators, water pumps and heavy rescue equipment are then provided within 48–72 hours depending upon the assessed needs. FDEM also provides at least one forklift and two pallet jacks to each POD site, along with temporary staff such as National Guard for 72 hours. After 72 hours, each of the 67 counties must be able to assume management of its PODs. Counties can also elect to establish one or more **County Staging Areas (CSA)** as an intermediate stocking point between LSA and POD.

Cities and towns request resources through their County EOC. The County EOC reports needs, inventories and shipping/receiving activities to the SLRC twice per day. Certain commodities require three to four days' lead-time and counties must forecast their requirements four days in advance for these items. An important aspect of information flow is that backorders are not used. The balance of an order that is not filled by the FDEM is cancelled and not backordered. In this case, counties must place another order the next day for the next operational period.

Truck is the primary mode of transport; however, air and sealift may be used to replenish large stocking points as required to support operations. Vendors can ship to the SMA or SLRC, although FDEM prefers to send trucks directly from vendor to the LSA, CSA or POD whenever possible (Hagan and Nunn, 2008).

Human resources

As mentioned above, disaster response in Florida engages human resources across local, state and federal agencies, the private sector and volunteer agencies. The State Emergency Response Team (SERT), which coordinates the response, is a very inclusive group welcoming formal and informal participation from individuals and organizations willing to contribute. Emergency response depends on an effective combination of full-time employees and a large temporary workforce.

The SERT maintains a staff of around 20 in Tallahassee to handle planning, contracting and preparedness. When an emergency or disaster exceeds the response capabilities of the county, the FDEM Director will mobilize further resources of the State Emergency Response Team (SERT) to assist. The SERT may further obtain resources and capabilities from the 18 Emergency Support Functions (ESFs) led by various state agencies. Refer to Figure 8.1 for an overview of SERT Sections and ESFs.

The SLRC in Orlando maintains permanent office space for several state agencies; FEMA, the US Corps of Engineers, Centers for Disease Control and also for some of the companies working with FDEM as contractors. Two full-time SERT staff at the SLRC manage the facility, rotate stock and coordinate small-scale response activities that happen all the time. In addition, two Department of Health members are staffed at SLRC for pandemic response. The SLRC is used on a regular basis as a logistics laboratory for advance training involving state and county personnel (Hagan, 2010).

Response to large-scale events depends on rapid mobilization of the state employees who have been trained to serve on an Incident Management Team (IMT). The IMT is deployed to the SLRC to run the Logistic Operations Center (LOC) – which manages inventory, orders, communications, etc – and the Movement Coordination Center (MCC) – which manages multimodal transportation. The IMT can be in place as soon as one hour after activation – speed that is needed for quick response events like tornadoes. The LOC is ready 24/7 at the SLRC with pre-configured workstations with the appropriate technology and software for each role on the IMT (see Figure 8.2 for a picture). When activated there is a staff of 60–70 people at the SLRC plus up to 300 drivers. More than a dozen Incident Management Teams are trained to enable rotation, especially in severe years. For example, the IMT was activated for approximately 120 days in 2004 and approximately 60 days in 2007.

Training led by FDEM is critical in developing the strong human resource base required to extend the supply chain from source to beneficiary. The SLRC itself is a 'logistics laboratory' for training state and county personnel in topics such as logistics management, inventory, multi-modal transportation and certified training in heavy equipment operation. Training also includes hands-on exposure to the key information technology platforms including the State Resource Management Network (SRMN) and the National Incident Management System (NIMS) (Hagan and Nunn, 2008).

Planning and coordination

Planning and coordination encompass a broad set of processes and activities conducted prior to and during a response. We outline the planning process, coordination efforts and the role of partnerships both prior to an emergency (preparedness) and organizations during a response (operational).

FIGURE 8.1 Organization chart including the SERT sections and Emergency Support Functions (ESFs)

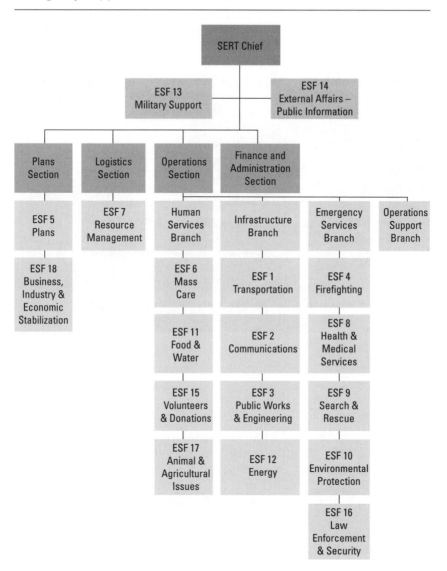

SOURCE: Florida Division of Emergency Management (2010)

FIGURE 8.2 The Logistics Operation Center is set up 24/7 at the SLRC and ready to make IMTs productive immediately upon arrival

PHOTO: Jarrod Goentzel

Preparedness

Florida law requires the FDEM to prepare a Comprehensive Emergency Management Plan (CEMP) for the state that aligns with the emergency management plans and programmes of the federal government, eg the National Response Framework (NRF) and the National Incident Management System (NIMS). The CEMP is the master operations document outlining the basic response plan for all emergencies and disasters and defining the roles and responsibilities of all levels of government as well as the companies and NGOs that comprise the SERT. The CEMP is always in effect, although certain plans and procedures are only engaged once the governor declares a state of emergency (Florida Division of Emergency Management, 2010). The body of the CEMP document defines the basic 'concept of operations' and annexes describe specific operational plans developed by the 18 Emergency Support Functions (ESFs) as well as incident-specific plans that address unique situations like a radiological emergency at a nuclear power plant or terrorist attack. The 2008–13 Strategic Plan is a complementary document that defines more specific goals and objectives (Florida Division of Emergency Management, 2009).

The State Unified Logistics Plan (Florida Division of Emergency Management Logistics Section, 2008), developed by the SERT and published by the FDEM Logistics Section, describes the supply chain plan for deploying resources in support of the agencies implementing the operational plans. It outlines specific roles and responsibilities in the logistics section and sets guidelines for operating the supply chain, from setting up Logistical Staging Areas and Points Of Distribution to the coordination and control mechanisms required. It also provides a basis for the municipal and county organizations to develop the County Emergency Management Plan, which establishes critical facilities such as shelters, County Staging Areas and County Points of Distribution, for example. SERT provides support and training for the counties to develop their planning process. It also conducts catastrophic planning efforts, such as the Hurricane Ono (Oh No!) scenario in which the hurricane has landfall in South Florida as a category 5, crosses the state hitting Tampa Bay as a category 2, and finally makes a second landfall in the panhandle as a category 2.

In addition to defining the roles and responsibilities, preparedness includes development of relationships and coordination mechanisms among the various actors. The foundation of effective coordination in a US emergency response is the relationships and mechanisms that connect the state, county and municipal levels of government within the state. If the governor declares a state of emergency, then coordination with the federal government and other states, through the Emergency Management Assistance Compact (EMAC), also becomes important. However, the federal government does not position itself as a source of significant stockpiles, and some states may be hesitant to deplete their own buffer stock, especially during hurricane season.

As a result, the private sector, especially the companies under contract with FDEM, is increasingly becoming a critical source of commodities. The State Unified Logistics Plan clearly outlines that the private sector can be used not only to provide commodities and equipment on a complementary and supplementary basis but also to provide overall logistical and management support to assist the state's efforts. This is especially important for local companies that have private fleets and available warehousing space that might be used as a Logistics Staging Area (LSA). For example, K-Mart's regional distribution center in Ocala, Florida was used as an LSA during the 2004 relief efforts (Hagan and Nunn, 2008). The private sector's involvement during relief efforts is coordinated through Memorandum of Understanding or Mutual Aid Agreements signed by the company and SERT. SERT has signed agreements with companies such as Home Depot, Lowes, Publix, Winn Dixie and Wal-Mart.

Operational

After a disaster hits, the FDEM conducts Preliminary Damage Assessment (PDA) to advise the governor on whether to declare an emergency and seek federal relief funds. As mentioned above, SLRC is equipped to push basic supplies, eg water, to impacted areas based on this initial assessment.

Resupply planning begins with resource needs estimated by ESF-5 Plans (led by FDEM), which uses HAZUS (a FEMA tool) or other computer models to predict the expected impacts of the event on the population. Once CSAs and CPODs are established, the county EOC sends resource requests through the EM Constellation system to the SEOC. The state verifies the request and routes it to the appropriate Emergency Support Function. If the ESF cannot provide the requested resources, then it is forwarded to the State Logistics Section (Florida Division of Emergency Management, 2010). For many commodities, the County EOC also reports to the SLRC directly the commodity burn rates, inventory levels, resources received and resources distributed at each of its sites as a basis for planning.

The fundamental approach for planning during a response is based on the Critical Path Method, which defines a sequence of dependent activities required to meet a goal. In a response, the CPM foundation helps to project response times, identify bottlenecks, prioritize activities and assess the need for additional resources. The implementation of the CPM approach within SERT is called the Time Phased, Force and Deployment Data List (TPFDDL). The TPFDDL should project all pre-event actions and post-event activities and resources through the first four to seven days. Starting with this base and working backwards, planners determine the start time and responsible party for each action. For example, in a hurricane event resources must be ordered from vendors at least 72 hours prior to landfall since they may be sourced from distant locations throughout North America. Additionally, truckload capacity may be tight and carriers need to be notified days in advance. SMAs require three days to set up while LSAs need at least 24 hours. Trigger events upon which an activity is dependent are also determined (Hagan and Nunn, 2008).

The TPFDDL can also be used as a basis for calculating resource requests for the SEOC – a process SERT calls Delta Planning. The difference between the total resource requirements in the TPFDDL and the resources available through local contracts or other sources is the county's Delta.

SERT is continually improving its planning and coordination processes. It also collaborates actively with FEMA in developing capabilities such as LCAT (assessment tool) and RAP (remedial action plan).

Information and communication

The primary hub of communication for reporting emergencies and coordinating state response activities is the State Emergency Operations Center (SEOC) in Tallahassee. The State Watch Office (SWO) is a 24-hour emergency communications center within the SEOC that provides situational monitoring during non-emergency periods as well as in times of emergencies and disasters. The SWO also provides the state with a single point to disseminate information and warnings, including the State Warning Point to provide official notifications for governmental programmes.

The SEOC has a permanent facility in Tallahassee with an Operations Room housing 87 workstations for SEOC staff and capacity to accommodate

FIGURE 8.3 Example of a Time Phased, Force and Deployment Data List (TPFDDL)

STATE OF FLORIDA
State Emergency Response Team
Unified Logistics Operations
Time Phased, Force and Deployment Data Listing (TPFDDL)

Date Revised:
By: C Van Treese, ESF 11

FOR OFFICIAL USE ONLY

PLANNING APPLIES TO THE FOLLOWING EVENTS

H	F	W	P	C	R	T	C	B	R	N	E	INITIATION TIME −/+ HRS	ACTION or RESOURCE	NIMS TYPING	PRIMARY ESF SUPPORT AGENCY	ASSET CLASS	ACTION ID	TRIGGER POINT	DTG COMPLETED
X	X											−80	Alert ESF 11 team members - Stand-by		ESF 11	State	DACS	Activation	
X												−72	Activate core Team members to EOC		ESF 11	State	DACS	Activation	
X		X										−72	Request food inventories from warehouses		ESF 11	1; State, vendor	DACS	Activation	
X	X											−72	Determine population affected/quantities needed (water & ice; commodities)		**ESF 5; ESF 11**	1; state	FDEM, DACS	Activation	
X												−72	Identify pre-mobe area for delivery of water and ice		**Logistics Section;** DOF	State	FDEM, DACS	Activation	
X	X											−72	Contact vendors; determine availability of water and ice; ETAs for truckloads needed		ESF 11	1; vendors	DACS	Activation	
X												−48	GO/No Go on FPOs for water and ice		ESF 11	1	DACS	Anticipated point of landfall	
X												−48	Prepare Field POs		ESF 11	1	DACS	Anticipated point of landfall	
X	X											−36	Place orders-water and ice for delivery to designated pre-mobe location; establish # trucks expected per day		ESF 11	1; vendors	DACS	Activation	
X	X											−36	Input food inventories into disaster inventory spreadsheet		**BFD staff;** ESF 11	1	DACS	Activation	
X	X											−36	Determine anticipated food needs; if sufficient quantities of commodities in state warehouses		**BFD staff;** ESF 11	1; state	DACS	Activation	
X	X											−24	Contact other (local) vendors; determine local availability of water and ice; maximum quantities available per day		ESF 11	1; vendors	DACS		
X												−24	Alert ESF 11 LSA team members - Stand-by; information on possible LSA location(s), if known		Logistics Section; ESF 11		DACS		
X												−24	Check/ready all LSA equipment, supplies, etc		ESF 11		DACS		
X	X											−24	Notify SFSAs-Authorize release of USDA commodities to disaster organizations for mass/congregate feeding		ESF 11; BFD staff	1	DACS	Evacuation; shelters opening	
X	X											−24	Notify USDA SERO - releasing commodities		ESF 11; BFD staff	1	DACS	Evacuation shelters opening	
X												−12	Identify anticipated needs for baby formula/food		ESF 11; DOH/WIC staff	1	DACS		

SOURCE: http://www.floridadisaster.org/Response/Logistics/2007/Documents/TPFDL%20-%20WaterIceFood%20-%202005.xls

up to 244 personnel. It offers functional space for Executive Rooms, 18 ESF Breakout Rooms, Conference Rooms, the State Watch Office and the Media Briefing Room (Florida Division of Emergency Management, 2010). The SLRC in Orlando, which has similar capabilities, pays a support role to the SEOC in managing the communications around logistics efforts.

To facilitate coordinated operations, the FDEM manages a secure, encrypted network of communication systems called the Florida Interoperability Network (FIN). Some of the systems incorporated in FIN include EDICS (Emergency Deployable Interoperable Communication System), EDWARDS (Emergency Deployable, Wide Area Remote Data System), MIL-WAVE (a wireless GSM communications network), MARC (Mutual Aid Radio Communications) and TAC-SAT (Tactical Satellite Communications). A list of other communications systems maintained by the state and federal agencies is provided in Figure 8.4.

As mentioned above in the Human Resources section, during a response the SLRC hosts the Logistic Operations Center and the Movement Coordination Center. The control room at the SLRC is set up with large number of computer terminals pre-configured with the appropriate software for the different roles in the LOC and MCC. In this way, the Incident Management Team (IMT) members can hit the ground running.

The SLRC also has a stockpile of totes with a preconfigured mix of voice and information communications systems that can be readily deployed to the LSAs and other temporary facilities. The communication pack includes satellite voice/data systems as well as the EDICS and EDWARDS components of the FIN. The information pack includes a 'cache' of laptop computers pre-configured with the appropriate software and labelled clearly as nodes in the network, power supplies, CAT-5 cables and mice (see Figure 8.5 for a photo).

To track the goods in transit, the SLRC has a stockpile of Numerix satellite transponders that are given to each driver to place on the dashboard of the truck. The drivers return the unit to the SLRC directly or via the FedEx envelope they are given along with the unit. The transponder sends a ping every 30 minutes when moving and once per day when parked. FDEM has an agreement with the hardware vendor to stock the units on consignment and then are charged $425 per unit once it is activated plus a service fee of $5/day and $0.25/ping. Some of the units that are owned by FDEM avoid the daily service fee. They also use the transponders to track expensive equipment such as forklifts, generators and pumps. In this case, they are attached in out-of-sight places with 'Super Velcro', which according to Chuck Hagan, 'you need a crowbar to get it off' (Hagan, 2010).

In addition to establishing a ready base of hardware, the FDEM Logistics Section has integrated software tools from five vendors to create the State Resource Management Network (SRMN). The two key components of SRMN are:

- ResourceVision. This is an asset catalogue and management system that enables any facility to track its equipment, supplies, vehicles and

FIGURE 8.4 Communications systems used by the state and federal government

STATE COMMUNICATIONS SYSTEMS	FEDERAL COMMUNICATIONS SYSTEMS
1. Commercial Telephone (tested daily)	1. National Oceanic and Atmospheric Administration (NOAA) Weather Wire System (NWWS)
2. Hot Ring Down for Nuclear Power Plants	2. National Warning System (NAWAS)
3. Amateur Radio Emergency System	3. Radio Amateur Civil Emergency Services (RACES)/Amateur Radio Emergency Services (ARES)
4. Wireless Devices	4. Shared Resources (Shares) High Frequency (HF) Radio Program
5. Emergency Satellite Communication System (ESATCOM)	
6. Terrestrial Based Satellite Telephone System (ESATPHONE)	
7. Emergency Alert System (EAS)	
8. Emergency Notification System	
9. Florida Crime Information Center (FCIC) Network	
10. State Law Enforcement Emergency Radio System (SLERS)	
11. Florida Interoperability Network (FIN)	
12. Florida Emergency Information Line (FEIL)	

SOURCE: Florida Division of Emergency Management (2010: 27)

even personnel. In essence, ResourceVision provides an effective inventory management system for any facility across the supply chain.

- GTVC. This situational awareness tool leverages a geographic information system to provide mapping and tracking of resources against a background of high-resolution satellite imagery. The system not only provides a map of facilities such as hospitals and fire departments but also real-time tracking and incident mapping. Layers of information such as flood plains and evacuation routes can be added.

The SRMN software is compliant with FEMA's National Incident Management System (NIMS) and is installed on all of the laptops that are sent out to the facilities during a response.

FIGURE 8.5 Laptop computer cache ready for deployment by the Florida Department of Emergency Management

PHOTO: Jarrod Goentzel

Supply chain strategies

The previous sections define various fundamental building blocks upon which supply chain strategies can be implemented. This section articulates some of these strategies for managing the supply chain.

One of the key strategic decisions is the prepositioned stock level. Recall that the strategic objective stated above was to serve 10,000 people immediately. Chuck Hagan articulated the Logistics Division philosophy: 'We would rather over-respond and pull back resources than to be short' (Hagan, 2010). As you can see in Table 8.1, the base stock level at the SLRC is prepared to serve many more people than the minimum strategic objective with key commodities such as water, food and shelter.

How does the state defend the millions of dollars of inventory prepositioned to serve food and water to 1 million people? The answer lies in another key strategy: Vendor Managed Inventory (VMI). The vendor, not the State of Florida, owns the inventory at the SLRC. The state only

TABLE 8.1 SLRC base stock levels and the derived rations of immediate response

Commodity	Truckloads	Quantity	Population Served First Day
Water	300	1.4 million gallons (4,750 gal/TL)	1.4 million people (1 gallon per person)
MREs (meals ready to eat)	54	1.8 million meals (34,560 Meals/TL)	900,000 people (2 MREs per person[1])
Tarps	19	45,000	45,000 people

SOURCE: Hagan and Nunn (2008)

1 MREs are high in calories and thus two meals per day is the guideline. The Florida SERT is considering a new design that contains three more appropriately sized meals in one package.

takes ownership once it leaves the dock during a response. The water vendor agrees to the VMI approach for a couple of key reasons. First, they can use the warehouse to store strategic buffer stock for their own supply chain. SLRC also provides office space for one water vendor employee and forklifts to manage this stock, since the water must be rotated annually to stay fresh. Second, the state pays the vendor a slight premium of $0.015 per litre above the base price of $0.69 per litre, approximately a 2 per cent markup (Hagan, 2010). Similar VMI strategies are in place for food and satellite transponders. Beyond the strategic vendors, FDEM does have multiple vendors under contract for key commodities. For example, there are seven alternate vendors for water. They obtain bids and set contracts approximately every three years.

For transportation, the FDEM also establishes creative contracts. Most shippers pay carriers a rate per mile, sometimes with a fixed charge according to the specific origin–destination, plus accessorial charges. Occasionally, shippers will contract for a 'dedicated fleet' over a period of time ranging from weeks to months. FDEM instead pays for a dedicated truck by the day, including fuel and driver time. This eliminates freight payment auditing processes that are difficult to establish and conduct during a response. It also provides FDEM flexibility and control over critical assets. The following rates are representative of the payment terms:

- $1200/day for dry van, etc;
- $1,500/day for drop trailer (moving heavy equipment);
- $1,800/day for refrigerated trailer;
- $900/day for standard, non-emergency moves.

(Hagan,2010)

The speed of flow through the supply chain is capped at three days from order to receipt for all vendors, regardless of distance. Many vendors have much shorter lead-times, of course. FDEM ships directly from vendor to LSAs or CSAs whenever possible.

One final strategy that is worthy of note is reverse logistics. Clearly the equipment deployed to LSAs and other temporary facilities must be returned. As mentioned above, drivers return transponders directly or by FedEx. Another critical reverse flow is for generator cables. These cables, which carry electricity from generators to users, are purchased by the spool and can be as expensive as $20 per linear foot. Cables are then cut before being distributed. When they are no longer required, remnants are 'piled on a pallet like snakes'. These pallets are then sent to a staging area where they stretch them out and measure them for further deployment, as needed. Through this process, FDEM is able to recover 85–90 per cent of cable after a response (Hagan, 2010).

Conclusions

Effective disaster response in the United States relies on supply chains spanning various public, private and NGO organizations. Some issues in responding to large-scale events in recent years have forced the public sector to reconsider its organizational structure, while some of the same events have demonstrated the important role private sector supply chains can play in scaling-up a response.

However, the backbone of the response supply chain remains with the local and state governments. In most areas of the country, except for large cities, the state emergency management agency takes the lead in designing and deploying the response system – including the supply chain. The case of the Florida Division of Emergency Management highlights the importance of developing and communicating a clear supply chain strategy in order to create a system capable of rapidly scaling up. The extensive training offered by the Florida SERT ensures that county and municipal plans are aligned with the state system. Furthermore, FDEM's active collaboration with FEMA in designing supply chain plans and technologies facilitates alignment not only with federal guidelines but also with other states following the federal lead. Florida's SERT also encourages active coordination between government and private sector disaster relief efforts.

The case also highlights several innovative supply chain approaches that might inform other humanitarian logistics organizations and contexts:

- Temporary capacity in the form of LSAs, PODs, etc, is critical in moving commodities from suppliers to beneficiaries. To be ready, FDEM pre-screens numerous locations across the state to determine where best to establish temporary capacity in rapidly scaling up the supply chain. Although it is difficult for international NGOs to map out potential supply chain sites around the world, they can work with government agencies to document some baseline logistics information. One example is the collection of Logistics Capacity Assessments developed by the United Nations Logistics Cluster.[2]

- FDEM stockpiles enough key commodities such as food and water to serve millions of daily rations. The key to financing this stockpile is establishing a Vendor Managed Inventory (VMI) relationship where the state only takes ownership upon use. The authors are aware that some international NGOs also set up blanket agreements and occasionally consignment inventory, and these mechanisms should be further explored. Integration up the chain can dramatically improve buffer capacity and response scalability.

- To facilitate the information flow, FDEM also stockpiles critical information and communication hardware. For some expensive equipment, such as satellite transponders, they also establish a VMI relationship to postpone capital expenditures. Other equipment such as laptops is pre-configured and pre-packaged to be ready to deploy and effectively work within hours of the event.

- Where off-the-shelf software is not available, FDEM was willing to take the lead in developing information systems. The State Resource Management Network (SRMN) integrates technology from several vendors to provide resource management and tracking capabilities across state and local teams. Information technology development efforts involving international NGOs in consortia[3] and open source efforts[4] have led to similar kinds of software innovations.

In summary, Chuck Hagan describes the FDEM logistics approach as '80 per cent military, 20 per cent Wal-Mart' (Hagan, 2010). This is one example of how effective humanitarian logistics approaches can come from various sectors: public, private, NGO and military. Response strategies in the United States increasingly look to combine these sectors more effectively, not only in the midst of the event but also in preparing their supply chains to respond.

References

Albright, M (2009) Stores prepare for gale of needs: big chains have precise plans for storm season, *St. Petersburg Times*, 7 June, p 1D

Budhiraj, K and de la Torre, G (2010) *Suggested Strategies and Best Practices in Private Supply Chain Disaster Response*. Master' thesis, Massachusetts Institute of Technology, June 2010

Daniels, R, Kettl, D and Kunreuther, K (2006) *On Risk and Disaster: Lessons from Hurricane Katrina*, University of Pennsylvania Press, Philadelphia, PA

Florida Division of Emergency Management (2010) *Florida Comprehensive Emergency Management Plan*; available at:http://floridadisaster.org/cemp.htm [accessed 29 August 2010]

Florida Division of Emergency Management (2009) *2008–2013 Strategic Plan*; available at: http://www.floridadisaster.org/documents/FDEM%202008-2013%20 Strategic%20Plan.pdf [accessed 29 August 2010]

Florida Division of Emergency Management Logistics Section (2008) *State of Florida Unified Logistics Plan*; available at: http://www.floridadisaster.org/ Response/Logistics/Index.htm [accessed 27 March 2010]

Hagan, C (2010, 29 March) Unified Logistics Chief, State of Florida Emergency Management [J Goentzel, interviewer]

Hagan, C and Nunn, C (2008) 2008 County Logistics Training Course, State of Florida Emergency Response Team; available at: http://www.floridadisaster.org/ Response/Logistics/2008/LOGISTICS_OPERATIONS_%20MANAGEMENT_ TRAINING_2DAY_2008_Revised.pdf [accessed 27 March 2010]

Kahn, L and Barondess, J (2008) Preparing for disaster: response matrices in the USA and UK, *Journal of Urban Health*, 85(6), pp 910–22

Kosar, K (2006) *The Congressional Charter of the American National Red Cross: Overview, history, and analysis*, Washington, DC: Congressional Research Service, The Library of Congress

Lott, NR (2010). *NCDC: Billion Dollar US Weather Disasters*; available at: http:// www.ncdc.noaa.gov/oa/reports/billionz.html [accessed 26 August 2010]

National Guard (2010) *About the National Guard*; available at: http://www.ng.mil/ About/default.aspx [accessed 3 May 2010]

Ross, T and Lott, N (2003) *A Climatology of 1980–2003 Extreme Weather and Climate Events*, Asheville, NC 28801-5001: National Climatic Data Center Technical Report No 2003-01

Sultemeier, C and Koon, B (2008) *Corporate Role in Disaster Response: Lessons from Katrina*, CSCMP 2008, Council of Supply Chain Management Professionals, Denver

Notes

1   Cities represented in 2010 include Boston, Chicago, Dallas, Denver, Houston, Jersey City/Newark, Los Angeles, Miami-Dade County, New York City, Philadelphia, San Diego County, San Francisco, Seattle and Washington.

2   http://www.logcluster.org/tools/lca

3   One example is NetHope (http://www.nethope.org)

4   Some examples include Sahana (http://sahanafoundation.org), Helios (http://www.helios-foundation.org) and OpenMRS (http://openmrs.org)

Acknowledgements

The authors would like to express their gratitude to Chuck Hagan from Florida Emergency Management for his helpfulness in collecting data as well as his input in terms of the chapter. Karen Spens would also like to express her gratitude to Liikesivistysrahasto and the Hanken and Wallenberg foundations who made her visit at MIT – and thus writing this chapter – possible.

09
The supply network's role as an enabler of development

DEBORAH ELLIS

Abstract

This chapter considers another application of logistics and supply chain principles in the humanitarian cause – but in this case, not in the sudden-onset disaster response situation, but the everyday 'disasters' of poverty and disadvantage in developing countries.

Supply networks are a critical, but often unrecognized, piece in the jigsaw of development. Where development aid is concerned there is a slowly dawning recognition that funds spent on direct aid such as supply of antiretrovirals for HIV/AIDS, anti-malaria drugs and vaccines may be wasted, and many fewer people may be assisted, if focus is not directed to improving the supply system through which these medicines are sourced and distributed. Similarly it is now becoming apparent that more effective procurement and distribution strategies could greatly improve the health outcomes that governments of developing countries can achieve with the scarce resources they have available.

From a different side of the development equation, the opportunity for rural communities to grow their incomes has always been tied to their ability to use land and labour resources to produce surpluses and find markets for them. The opportunities in this regard are changing, as sophisticated retailers (the *modern trade*) emerge in the cities of Asia and Africa and as the corporate social responsibility agendas of large corporates, such as the mining companies, remind them of their obligations for local engagement and sourcing in the countries and regions in which they operate. For small producers to supply the consistency and quality that these customers require, however, is challenging – and the barriers are mainly associated not with production itself, but with the physical and organizational aspects of the supply chain from farm to market. It appears that, just as in health, this is a high-leverage point and an opportunity for governments, donors and the private sector to facilitate new business and 'social business' models that help small producers link to the emerging opportunities.

The chapter uses four cases studies to explore these different situations in which the supply network can be a significant *barrier*, or can be leveraged to become an important *enabler* of development initiatives.

Introduction

Most discussion about humanitarian logistics and supply relate to disaster response situations, and the emerging discipline is mainly focused on applying commercial and military lessons to improve preparedness, response and effectiveness in these situations. There is also, however, another application of the supply chain and supply network discipline in the humanitarian cause: this relates to using our growing body of knowledge for improved outcomes in the slow-burn, 'everyday' disasters of poverty and disadvantage in developing nations.

This chapter considers some of the situations where building an effective supply network has provided, or can provide, a significant improvement in the lives of disadvantaged individuals. It looks at two situations: first, where focusing on supply chain factors can improve access to, and reduce the cost of, essential medicine in developing countries and the cases of HIV/AIDs and diabetes are discusses in this regard; and second, where provision of the physical and organizational linkages between supply and market can improve a community's income-earning capacity, and initiatives in Thailand and Papua New Guinea are discussed.

1 Improving access to essential medicine

Three of the eight UN Millennium Development Goals[1] relate directly to improved health outcomes (targets are set for dramatic improvements in child mortality and maternal health and halting the spread of HIV/AIDs). In association with this focused effort there have been substantial increases in donor funding for essential medicine across many developing countries. The application of this increase in funding, however, has encountered many of the same supply and distribution inefficiencies that local agencies working on a smaller scale and the country ministries of health have been encountering for many years. The two cases below discuss the state of play for two major diseases, HIV/AIDs and diabetes. They contrast the situation where supply chain barriers have been recognized and are being addressed as part of the equation (AIDS) and another where supply chain has not yet made it onto the agenda at either the global or local level (diabetes).

1.1 *Supply chain initiatives in the fight against HIV/AIDS*

The recognition of the devastating march of HIV/AIDS through the developing world led to a massive mobilization of resources from 2002. Major inputs came from the US government, when President George Bush committed US $15 billion in 2003 to provide antiretroviral drugs to assist 2 million HIV-infected people in Africa and the Caribbean. This, and several later substantial commitments from the President and his successor Barack Obama (totalling US $32 billion to date), have been administered through an organization known as PEPFAR.[2] The Global Fund was also established during this time to consolidate and increase international funding for AIDS, tuberculosis and malaria; the Bill and Melinda Gates Foundation (also supported by Warren Buffet) increased its commitments and support of AIDS programmes; and the World Bank's Multi-Country HIV/AIDS Program for Africa (MAP) and the Clinton HIV/AIDS Initiative (CHAI) were established. The majority of the funding and focus has been on Africa, as two-thirds of those living with AIDs are in sub-Sahara Africa (UNAIDS, 2008).

The new organizations entering the Global Health arena brought with them new, more commercial, mindsets. Whereas supply and distribution issues had rarely been a key focus in health or development initiatives in the past, supply chain received prominent attention in this new surge of projects – particularly in PEPFAR, the Global Fund and CHAI and through associated organizations such as USAID and John Snow International. These organizations recognized that their ability to use their financial resources effectively was severely restricted by the lack of infrastructure, procurement and logistics capability in the countries that required most support. They also identified that the supply dynamics could be changed if viewed from a more strategic and aggregated position.

As with all aid there has been criticism along the way about how and where funds are used, and the wider impact of intervention, but there has also been recognition that the enormous threat that HIV represented to the developing world has at the least been reduced and is possibly approaching a tipping point by the actions of the large donors.[3] Many of the successes that these organizations have had in the HIV/AIDS fight to date they attribute to changing the rules of the supply chain for the key antiretroviral drugs they fund.

Supply chain strategies that have been initiated are:

1 **Global forecasting and supply planning.** Supply professionals usually recognize that there is some disconnect between 'realized' demand (sales) and 'real' demand, but in the case of HIV/AIDS in the developing world this gap was massive. Those using antiretroviral medication (ARVs) represented the tip of the iceberg, and under the water were those who had not been diagnosed as yet, those who could not afford the medication and those who had no knowledge about, or access to, treatment. The early work by the Global Fund, CHAI and others to identify and quantify the real need and the ongoing use of more systematic methods of forecasting demand have been the starting point for many of the initiatives that followed.

2 **Economies of scale and pooled procurement.** When the 'true' demand started to be captured and tabled with suppliers the cost equation began to change – and with ongoing negotiations and aggregated volumes, the ARV marketplace started to shift from a 'low-volume, high-margin business' towards a 'high-volume, low-margin business'. One of the mechanisms employed for aggregating volumes is pooled procurement, which involves a single purchasing group negotiating and procuring for multiple purchasers to leverage economies of scale and drive the price down. PEPFAR uses a pooled procurement mechanism to leverage its volume and to work with manufacturers to stabilize supply and plan for capacity expansion (PEPFAR, 2010). In a similar vein, CHAI has become a third-party negotiator with generic ARV suppliers on behalf of countries, developing a 'cost-plus' pricing approach and providing technical support to manufacturers to improve efficiencies and bring costs down (the shift to generic suppliers has been possible because several of the originators have agreed to waive their rights to enforce patent rights in the least-developed countries).

3 **Strategic positioning of inventory.** A key principle of inventory is that the further back in the network it is held the less variability and thus less need for buffer stock – or the more demand that can be serviced with the same levels of stock. This principle has been used to make more effective use of stocks to serve wide regional demand, and SCMS,[4] the supply chain organization set up by PEPFAR, operates three sophisticated regional distribution centres to service sub-Sahara Africa. Countries do not need to tender and take delivery of 12 months of forecast requirements, as they had in the past (and still do for many other essential medicines). As these forecasts, and thus stock levels, were invariably wrong they either wasted resources or resulted in stock-outs before the next delivery. The more flexible access to supply is designed to improve availability level across the countries involved, and reduce the investment in inventory. They

provide regular scheduled shipments, and expedite emergency shipments to prevent stock-outs (SCMS, 2010).

4 **Building health logistics capability.** The initial approach of the major donors to distributing ARVs (and to provide health care to communities generally) was to build new distribution systems. In most of the developing countries involved, the procurement and logistics capability (usually largely public) was thought to be inadequate to absorb the rapid ramp-up that was needed to have an impact on the spread of AIDS. Over time, complex parallel systems developed, which although achieving the initial aims, have been criticized for not building capability for the country generally, and even of draining the best people from the Ministry of Health systems. This criticism is being recognized and there is an increasing emphasis on using the donor funding in ways that can leave behind sustainable capacity and capability. An example is the PEPFAR-funded SCMS, which has initiated programmes to strengthen Ministry of Health supply chains utilizing private sector third party logistics warehouse interventions as highlighted in the box below.

Leveraging the private sector to build logistics capability

Although there are sophisticated third-party logistics providers operating in Africa using modern technology, and winning commercial contracts with PowerPoint presentations, they would rarely be invited through the doors of a Ministry of Health (MOH) warehouse. Apart from a lack of funding to pay for their services, the paradigm is different – the management responsible for these facilities typically comes from a public administration or health-related background – rarely would they see themselves as being in the business of 'logistics'.

In the recent search for ways to use the HIV/AIDS funding to build in-country capability, PEPFAR has developed a programme that harnesses the skills of third-party Logistics Providers while integrating ARV distribution into the public health distribution system. PHD, a division of the Fuels Group, for example, who specialize in pharmaceutical distribution have been engaged in the five-year PEPFAR-funded **'plan to leave'** interventions with MOH warehouses. PHD provides technical assistance to enable strengthening of specific processes or oversees the management of the warehouse for a period, while retaining the ministry staff. They develop Standard Operating Procedures, train and mentor local staff, and install and commission equipment and systems. The strategy requires their involvement to gradually reduce as they move to **'hand-back'**, but with an ongoing mentoring role to provide support on an as-required basis.

1.2 *From AIDS to diabetes – can we learn anything?*

There are some striking similarities between AIDS and diabetes. The number of people globally that die prematurely from each is similar – about 3.8 million per year (International Diabetes Federation, 2002), or about 6 per cent of total global mortality; treatment for both usually involves a lifetime daily regimen of drugs; both diseases are a major concern in terms of their impact on the health systems of developing countries. There are, of course, also some key differences. Most importantly that HIV/AIDS is a communicable disease, ie it can be readily transferred between individuals, and is thus a threat at the epidemic level. This has rightly driven an urgent response from the international community.

Diabetes, however, is a true and growing problem for the health systems of many countries and the statistics clearly indicate that a large part of the burden of diabetes is falling on those that can least afford to respond. The International Diabetes Federation (IDF) estimates that '80 per cent of the 246 million people with diabetes today live in developing countries' and propose that:

> In many developing countries, the burden of diabetes care threatens to undermine the benefits of improving standards of living, education and economic growth. (IDF, 2005)

Very few developing countries have been able to adequately support the high reliability of insulin supply needed by Type 1 diabetes patients, who die without access to insulin for several days.[5] Type 2 patients, when diagnosed, typically only need oral medication, but without reliable supply and ongoing monitoring their needs quickly escalate as complications arise including stroke, kidney failure, heart and eye problems, and nerve damage (often resulting in foot ulceration leading to amputations).

Supply issues, of course, are only a part of the story, just as they are with AIDS. Medical care and education are critical elements in the management of diabetes. But, here also it is apparent that there are many issues that impede the effective procurement and distribution of supplies, and that impact the cost of medication. And, just as with AIDS, the available funding (whether domestically sourced or from donors) could be used more effectively if some or all of these could be addressed. Many of these issues are common in the supply and distribution of other essential medications in resource-poor settings, and as a point of focus diabetes is thought to be instructive more broadly Nolte *et al* (2006) for example, proposed diabetes as a '**tracer' condition** to assess and compare health system performance.

These supply issues include:

1 Knowing the 'true' level of demand. It is recognized by the IDF that in poorer countries many, if not most, people with diabetes go undiagnosed.[6] The supply parameters thus relate to a fraction of true need in these countries, and there has been limited opportunity to capture economies of scale. As diagnosis improves it is likely that the numbers involved will increase dramatically, accompanied by increasing needs for treatment. To apply the lessons from the AIDS initiatives, it will be important to capture the growing opportunities to reduce cost per patient and to lift availability levels. Even now, however, a better understanding of likely 'true' demand and dialogues with suppliers in terms of this perspective can potentially lead to better medium-term outcomes.

2 **Dispersed and fragmented demand.** The low levels of insulin availability are heavily impacted by the dispersed nature of demand. Unlike communicable diseases where clustering occurs, there is no pattern to the location of insulin-dependent patients, and many regional clinics will only have a few patients. Inventory levels to support fragmented demand are of course inefficient and problematic – an extra patient can quickly lead to stock-outs at the local level. Alternatively, to cover all contingencies requires high levels of safety stock throughout the health system. Complicating this situation further is product proliferation driven by the variations in insulin type and methods of dispensing (especially different syringe sizes and/ or insulin pens). Within countries there is minimal knowledge on inventory management, and considerable gains are likely from more structured inventory and location policies. In a few countries, such as Kyrgyzstan, diabetes medication has separate channels of distribution and thus there is some opportunity for holistic planning of stock locations. In most it is included in the public, or public/private health distribution system. The World Health Organisation (WHO) has been working with established supply chain planning companies to make available tools for central health planners to increase their strategic level planning in this regard (LLamasoft, 2010). There also appears, following the AIDS lessons, to be potential for aggregating demand across countries, and for using this volume to improve the effectiveness of procurement processes, and to allow strategic positioning of stocks.

3 **Visibility and control.** In most developing countries stock levels and deployment of medications are still largely controlled by manual, paper-based systems. There is minimal central visibility and control and little opportunity to optimize within the system – for example to shift over-stocks in one clinic or hospital to relieve stock shortfalls in another. While the thinking has been that this serious constraint to more effective supply would not be overcome until the MOH could fund computers in every clinic, the thinking is now shifting towards finding low-cost options based on the increasingly pervasive mobile phone.

4 **The *Last Mile*.** The problem of delivering supplies to the final point of need, whether it be to a clinic, a patient in a remote area, or a refugee camp is a universal issue cited by those working in development supply chains (Ellis, 2010). Although poor-quality road infrastructure is part of the issue, much of the problem relates to a lack of structured private distribution systems. Insulin supplies are more difficult than most products to distribute across this last mile because of the need to maintain a cold chain. As with many situations in the developing world the 'system' for insulin is very often about individuals: staff from clinics and even hospitals collecting supplies from the next level up in the network (usually many hours away) with cooler bags and ice bricks. This solution comes at a cost, withdrawing trained staff from their healthcare role while they perform high-cost distribution. In the various formats for encouraging entrepreneurial activity to support development, such as micro-financing and social business models, actions to develop local delivery networks associated with health appears to warrant further attention. The parallel systems that were mentioned earlier also need to be considered in this regard – many of the countries with inadequate cold chains for insulin have stand-alone cold chains operating for vaccines. Rationalization of resources and building of whole-of-system capability is obviously an important progression from the advances made in the last decade in health supply chains.

5 **Patient-centric perspectives.** Increasingly the commercial world is turning to more closely understanding the customer (for example, how they use a product, and what their underlying needs are) to identify the next round of innovation. Similarly, in health there is an increasing understanding that the picture, and thus the opportunity for improvement, can look very different if viewed from a patient perspective. In the case of Type 1 diabetes, from a procurement perspective the focus is on supplying insulin. From a patient perspective, however, that insulin may be of no benefit if, as in the case of Kyrgyzstan in 2009, there are no syringes available in many regional areas. Similarly, there is no benefit afforded by the thousands of glucometers donated to that country, and distributed by a grateful government to all hospitals, clinics and patients, without an ongoing supply of the strips that the monitors require to measure glucose levels. Health supply chains are not just *product* supply chains – they waste resources at all levels of the health system if they do not deliver effective *patient* solutions.

Diabetes and HIV/AIDS illustrate two versions of the supply chain for essential medicines in developing countries. In the desperate bid to reverse the march of AIDS, new approaches have emerged. It is apparent when we review the supply issues that diabetes faces – a disease recognized as representative of the health system more generally – and significant in itself because of the growing threat it presents – that there is much similarity with the underlying problems that HIV/AIDS donors have attempted to address. Although there have been massive sums applied to HIV/AIDS, there has also been a recognition that more effective procurement and supply approaches enable many more people to be treated for any given amount of funding. It appears likely, given the many parallel issues, that both MOH and donor funding of health systems in developing countries could also be leveraged more effectively by new approaches to demand planning, procurement and building distribution capability. Diabetes also signals a note of warning – that these solutions must always be developed in the context of the end recipient.

2 Reliable supply links and economic development

The economists seeking to understand the levers for economic development focus on those that build wealth and 'create value', especially trade; those that grow capability, particularly education; and on the underpinning elements of good economic governance that allow individuals and businesses to make decisions and plan in a stable and predictable environment.

Within the context of the first two of these sit the following cases studies, which relate to situations where enhancing local production capability, and proactively developing a modern supply chain, can enable groups of small producers to access larger and more sophisticated markets beyond their local community.

2.1 From poppies to herbs in northern Thailand

In north-west Thailand crop substitution programmes have been under way over several years aimed at shifting hill tribe communities from producing opium poppies to alternative commercial crops. One of these communities was assisted to convert to growing coriander and other herbs, ostensibly for the growing modern trade in Bangkok. The transition started with much promise, but had failed to create the levels of income expected, and gradually the supermarkets had been reducing their demand and withdrawing from their commitments as supply reliability failed to improve.

After an end-to-end review by a cold chain consulting company[7] it was found that, of the crop harvested, only 10–15 per cent was making it onto the supermarket shelves, and this usually only had one day of shelf life left after transiting the retailers distribution centre. The loss in yield and shelf life was occurring all the way along the chain: on the farms from heat exposure between picking and packing; while awaiting despatch; on the 10-hour non-refrigerated drive to Bangkok; and while transiting the retailer's distribution centre (DC). Essentially, the project had created production capability, found a market for it – but failed to help the community establish an effective supply chain.

The focus after this review initially turned to increasing the effective yield, and soon after to re-establishing markets, and finding new markets to absorb the higher volumes. New processes were introduced at farm level to get product into the pack-house sooner; simple cooling equipment was installed in the pack-house to pre-cool the herbs before packing; and more effective packaging was introduced to help maintain temperature both in transit and in the DC.

The 10-hour transit to Bangkok, however, was a major obstacle. Refrigerated transport was expensive and difficult to access. As Chang Mai airport was close by, with regular flights to Bangkok, the solution turned out to be airfreight, using specialized thermal covers to maintain the temperature of the pre-chilled produce. Although any initial costing is likely to have assessed this as a much higher cost per carton option than road freight, once the spoilage and loss of shelf life were factored in it became viable. The shift to airfreight also created more market options. As there were direct flights from Chang Mai to Phuket this area was targeted next, and new supply contracts were established with several of the 5-star resorts.

As a result of the process, packing and transport changes, the effective yield on the crops increased to 80 per cent and once this proved to be reliable, higher volume commitments could be made and the new markets accessed. The small producers have been able to maintain reliable supply to these markets for approximately two years.

It is important to note that these initiatives were the result of intervention by an outside agent. Although the initial advice regarding packing and cooling was conducted at no charge, a success fee related to market growth was negotiated. We tend to assume that initiatives of this sort must be funded by governments or donor organizations, but as this case illustrates, there is often a case for harnessing commercial drivers to achieve a result.

This is similar to case studies in Thailand, South Africa, Kenya and Zimbabwe, reviewed by Boselie *et al* (2003), which looked at whether, and how, small producers could compete as suppliers to the growing supermarket trade in their countries. They concluded that although the stringent requirements of the chains usually favoured large producers, if smaller producers overcome key barriers they can be competitive, and in some cases they even had a competitive advantage (especially in highly labour-intensive cropping). They found where small producers had been able to maintain supply relationships with supermarket chains the contributory factors were:

- small producers worked cooperatively and in a coordinated fashion so as to meet quality and volume requirements;

- the supermarket often played a role in organizing the groups of producers and/or providing expertise or physical inputs;
- communication systems were established so that producers could communicate with their customers, at least by telephone or fax (remembering this was written in 2003 – the expectation is now likely to be by e-mail);
- producers had arrangements to chill product or deliver rapidly to a chilled facility;
- and finally, the producers had organized themselves in ways that delivered consistency of supply and quality (which was 'probably most important' in the authors view).

2.2 From subsistence to industrial suppliers in Papua New Guinea

The final case study is a venture initiated by Business for Millennium Development (B4MD). Australian companies and the Australian divisions of several large businesses[8] have committed to finding ways to support the Millennium Development Goals[9] (specific UN-initiated goals to significantly reduce poverty and its impact by 2015) using the commercial skills, and their involvement with the Asia Pacific market:

> B4MD believes that Australian businesses have the opportunity to do much more to reduce poverty while developing business with the emerging markets of the Asia Pacific region (Business for Millennium Development, 2010a).

In this context they have sought specific projects in the Asia Pacific region where their resources, business networks or expertise could be leveraged.

One of the founding companies of B4MD, Oil Search, is a shareholder in a major Liquefied Natural Gas (LNG) project that is being built across the Southern Highlands of Papua New Guinea. This US $15 billion LNG project is forecast to double PNG's Gross Domestic Product within a few years (AAP, 2009). Construction is ramping up, with the first sale of product due in 2013. New roads are being built to support the project, which will open up access to towns and villages that have been inaccessible to normal vehicles in the past.

On a B4MD business mission to PNG in 2009 looking at options for social businesses, the opportunity that the opening up of this traditionally subsistence-farming area and the large increase in the workforce posed, was recognized. Continuing research, and liaison with local communities and the B4MD partners, has resulted in a framework for a new business model that involves local landowners, employs people from the local community and uses the knowledge and skills of the commercial partners. It is:

> modelled as a Social Business Enterprise, where the community is the primary owner and beneficiary and the Australian and multinational businesses lend

their core competencies as key stakeholders...[it aims] to provide long term sustainable income for approximately 7,500 women growers in the Southern Highlands regions. (Business for Millennium Development, 2010b)

A company known as Hailens[10] Fresh Produce (HFP) will be formed to provide an integrated supply chain for fresh fruit and vegetables, poultry and eggs. The initial market is Oil Search work camps, with a business plan to quickly build capacity to supply more project sites as roads are opened to the Gulf Province and within two years to markets in Port Moresby, the capital of PNG. Each of the parties involved has a clear role in providing or building capability in the supply chain:

- The local growers from the regions of Hiwanda, Hides, Nagoli, Tari, Juni, Kumo, Juhu, Kobalu, Benaria and Angore – producers;
- Sygenta – seed and farm extension services;
- Amalpack (Visy J Vin PNG) – packaging supplier;
- Agility Logistics – refrigerated transport and cold storage;
- Goodman Fielder – poultry and egg extension services and training;
- Oil Search – initial market access.

The supply arrangements are to be built on tightly specified contracts detailing products, quantities and timeframes. These contracts are considered by the partners to be necessary to formalize market and supply commitment and to underpin the investment by all parties.

Although the highland areas of PNG are said to have 60,000 traditional gardeners, this highly fertile and productive farmland has not been leveraged in a commercial way in the past. The creation of infrastructure, and the building of production and supply chain capability through models that empower local people, has the potential to significantly improve the wellbeing of these communities.

A final word – the supply chain as an enabler

In this chapter four case studies have been considered, and in each the critical role that the supply chain can play in improving outcomes in developing countries is apparent. In three of these cases proactive initiatives have focused on this opportunity – by contrast the supply chain has not yet been a part of the dialogue on improving outcomes for diabetes sufferers in these incredibly difficult settings.

The lessons are clear. Whether distributing essential medicine in Africa, or creating livelihoods in Papua New Guinea, the supply network can be either an impediment or an enabler. The body of knowledge and the technology that has evolved in the commercial world around supply chain and logistics has a critical place in development. Funding and planning that ignores its importance risks wasting resources; and governments, donors and the private sector have a role to play in facilitating new approaches and developing models to overcome supply chain barriers and to leverage the opportunities emerging.

References

AAP (2009) Aussie corporations take on PNG 29/05/2009; available at: http://tvnz. co.nz/world-news/aussie-corporations-take-png-2761915 [accessed 13 October 2010]

Bennett, S, Randall, T (2010) *Bloomberg Businessweek*, 8 September, **4191**, pp 22–23

Boselie, D, Henson, S and Weatherspoon, D (2003) Supermarket procurement practices in developing countries: redefining the roles of the public and private sectors, *American Journal of Agricultural Economics*, 85(5), pp 1155–61

Business for Millennium Development (2010a) website: http://b4md.com.au/about. asp [accessed 10 October 2010]

Business for Millennium Development (2010b) unpublished briefing note

Ellis, D (2010) *Advancing the Aid Supply Chain: Outcomes from the Supply Chains at the Extreme – Development Aid and Humanitarian Relief Seminar*, Discussion Paper, MGSM, Macquarie University, Sydney 22 February; available at: http://aidsupply.blogspot.com/

International Diabetes Foundation (2002) *Global Access to Insulin and Diabetes Supplies, 2002* reported in *Diabetes Atlas (2nd edn)*; available at: http://eatlas.idf. org/Insulin_and_diabetes_supplies/Access_to_Insulin/ [accessed 19 February 2009]

International Diabetes Federation (2005) *Diabetes Atlas, (2nd edn) 2005*; available at: http://www.eatlas.idf.org/ [accessed 19 January 2009]

International Diabetes Federation (2009) *Diabetes Atlas, (4th edn) 2009*; available at: http://www.diabetesatlas.org/content/africa [accessed 4 October 2010]

LLamasoft (2010) news available at: http://www.llamasoft.com/News/LLamasoft_to_ Develop_Logistics_Module_for_Unified_Health_Model.aspx [accessed 4 October 2010]

Magner, M (2009) 'Supply chain in the developing world' presentation for LAA, *Clinton Foundation*, Adelaide, 31 March

Nolte, E *et al* (2006) Diabetes as a tracer condition in international benchmarking of health systems, *Diabetes Care*, **29**(5), pp 1007–11

PEPFAR (2010) available at: http://www.pepfar.gov/press/79668.htm [accessed 2 October 2010]

SCMS (2010) *From Emergency Relief to Sustained Response*, SCMS in Brief, August 2010; available at: http://scms.pfscm.org/scms [accessed 25 September 2010]

UNAIDS (2008) *Report on the global AIDS epidemic 2008*, August 2008; available at: http://data.unaids.org/pub/GlobalReport/2008/20080715_fs_global_en.pdf [accessed 2 October 2010]

Notes

1 http://www.un.org/millenniumgoals/index.shtml

2 PEPFAR – The United States Presidents Emergency Plan For AIDS Relief.

3 UNAID reports in 2009 indicate a fall in adult and child deaths from AIDS, and reducing numbers of new infections.

4 Supply Chain Management System (SCMS).

5 Inability to access insulin and supplies is considered to be a key causal factor in lower life expectancy. A Global Survey in 2002 (International Diabetes Federation, 2002) found that people with Type 1 diabetes in 30 countries did not have access to insulin 100 per cent of the time, and that in Africa 32 per cent had access for less than 50 per cent of the time.

6 Undiagnosed diabetes accounted for 85 per cent of those with diabetes in studies from South Africa, 80 per cent in Cameroon, 70 per cent in Ghana and over 80 per cent in Tanzania (International Diabetes Federation, 2009).

7 Case study taken from interviews with Chris Cato-Smith, Freshport (a consultant on this study), 24 August 2010 and 30 September 2010.

8 Including BHP Billiton, Visy, IBM, KPMG, Insurance Australia Group, Nestle, Oil Search Ltd, Agility and Macquarie Bank.

9 See: http://www.un.org/millenniumgoals/

10 Hailens is pidgin English for 'Highlands'.

10
Humanitarian logistics professionalism

DAVID M MOORE AND DAVID H TAYLOR

Abstract

This paper considers the important role that logistics/supply chain management has played in improving performance of commercial organizations. It presents the view that humanitarian logistics could adopt and adapt their logistics strategies, especially as military organizations, which have a similar operational deployment ethos, have similarly adapted such approaches. It then considers that professionalism is a key driver of performance improvement. This allows a discussion upon the nature and role of professionalism, leading to the view that knowledge is the basis of professionalism and that this will underpin future performance improvement.

Context and background

Underpinning most, if not all, humanitarian aid operations, is the matter of logistics. Arguably, the measure of successful response in terms of aid relief is whether what is required is actually available, and where and when it is needed. In this respect, the first few days after a disaster has occurred, ie the immediate response, is usually vital.

Whether such criteria of success can be met, will come down to the performance of those involved in planning, organizing, delivering and managing the logistics of aid. The need for efficiency and effectiveness that is prevalent in commercial organizations is exacerbated in the humanitarian aid environment where the expenditure of monies provided by private individuals or public institutions is subject to scrutiny from donors, the general public and the media. The willingness of the ordinary citizen to provide funds on a continual basis will be sorely tested if it can be seen that systemic inefficiencies have arisen and degraded organizational effectiveness, so that aid takes longer to arrive in the disaster area or fails to be distributed once there, as was apparently the case with the recent disaster in Haiti (Whiting, 2010).

To ensure successful and efficient provision of humanitarian aid requires people with commitment, enthusiasm and logistics skills and knowledge. Application of logistics best practices will enable aid agencies to move towards more optimal decision-making, the avoidance of inefficiencies and the minimization, if not complete eradication, of poor performance.

Understanding logistics: commercial best practice; supply chain management as the evolutionary development of logistics

Since the mid-1980s commercial organizations, building upon the earlier successes of Japanese organizations, have utilized *lean* and *agile* philosophies to give themselves an advantage over their competitors. These required organizations to focus upon those activities that added value to their output; if any activity did not add value then management action would be centred on its elimination. By definition, virtually everything that did not add value was to be considered waste. Further, commercial organizations recognized that the whole of the supply chain, ie the linking of processes across organizational boundaries, had to be considered when seeking to eliminate such waste. For optimal effectiveness, processes and activities from the point of origin (for example, raw material procurement or manufacturing) through to the end-users (for example, the consumer) had to be taken into account. Such considerations are the basis for an integrated approach to supply chain management. Supply chain management encompasses the activities, both internal and external to an organization, that cover the previously discrete functions of specification of requirement, procurement, contracting, manufacture, distribution (including stock management), warehousing and transport, plus all the systems required to coordinate and control the smooth flow of goods and services from their point-of-origin to the end-user.

Fundamental to this holistic concept is the fact that logistics is not a 'stand-alone' activity, nor is it the traditionally long-held perception of a low-level, reactive activity that concerns stores and trucks. Through the application of supply chain management, as a developmental extension of logistics, which manages coordination and control of the integrated flow of materials, services and information, commercial organizations have in recent years, reduced their cost base – elimination or considerable reduction of waste – and have been able to compete more and more in the global marketplace. In short, they were able to become efficient and effective (or they went out of business). This can be seen as the norm in most commercial organizations now, but it has developed over a period of time.

Further application of supply chain management: military adaptation – the use of commercial best practice in the defence logistics environment

Military organizations, such as those of the United Kingdom, have recognized the beneficial effects of supply chain management as a developmental extension of logistic activity and have worked hard to emulate the best practice of commercial organizations. Increasingly, *lean* and *agile* philosophies are being utilized successfully in improving military logistics performance.

In the military sense logistics is defined as 'encompassing all actions required to move and maintain forces, including the acquisition and positioning of resources as well as the delivery of these resources to the forces'. The tenets of supply chain management apply particularly well in such a 'total process' perspective but commercial best practices have not been *adopted* without question within the Armed Forces; rather they have been *adapted* and amended to suit the military contextual setting. Indeed, in order to be successful in this adaptation considerable change in respect of military culture, structure and management ethos has been necessary.

This is particularly important, for just as commercial organizations have utilized logistics developments in the form of supply chain management, so too have the military. Military organizations undertake a role that requires them to work as part of multinational, multi-discipline operations that have to be conducted at great range from their home base. The notion of essential links that exist between manufacturers and end-users is conceptually akin to commercial organizations although, importantly, the contextual setting is different. Nevertheless, just as with commercial organizations, for success in military supply chain management there is a need to integrate across organizational boundaries and eliminate (or considerably reduce) waste. This has required a holistic or fully integrated perspective to be utilized.

Further, military organizations have a supply chain that, conceptually, has considerable resonance with humanitarian aid organizations (see Figure 10.1). Military organizations require a port of embarkation in the home base and a port of disembarkation in the operational arena, with subsequent distribution through central, regional and local warehouses. The link between the home base and operational arena is known as the 'coupling bridge'.

FIGURE 10.1 Military organizations' supply chain

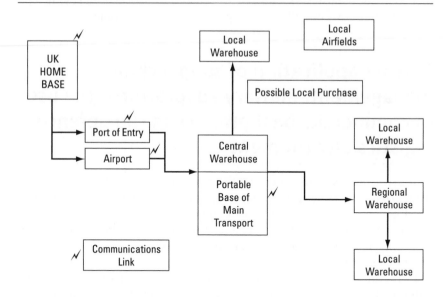

For humanitarian logistics operations the concept is very similar, although 'international transit' is typical of the terminology that could be utilized instead of 'coupling bridge' (see Figure 10.2). Of course, it is frequently seen that military logistic assets, be they human or physical, are deployed to assist in humanitarian operations. Although there is cultural dissonance between military and humanitarian organizations, there is an increasing imperative for them to work more closely together in order to improve the overall performance of supply chain activities particularly in the early phases of disaster response.

Humanitarian logistics: an opportunity to develop and adapt commercial and military approaches

In the same way that military organizations have adapted best practices from commercial supply chain management in order to improve efficiency and gain effective performance, so humanitarian organizations could follow a similar approach. Indeed, the supply chain for humanitarian aid is very similar to that of military organizations. Just as military organizations must prepare for operations (such as war fighting or peacekeeping), so too must humanitarian aid organizations prepare for disaster relief operations. Most

FIGURE 10.2 Humanitarian logistics operations supply chain

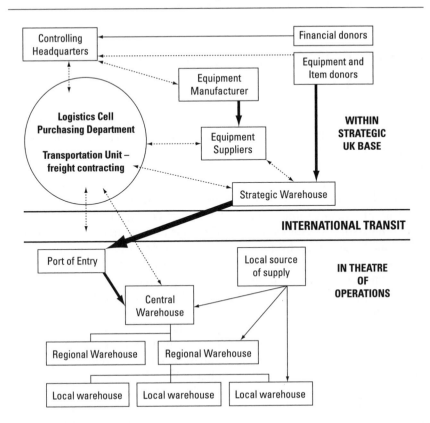

civilian agencies recognize the need for a system that coordinates, through a local and sequential process, all of the aspects related to logistics or supply chain management, ie specification, purchasing, transport, maintenance, stocktaking and integration of the flow of materials, equipment and information. However, the organizational environment of humanitarian aid is particularly challenging, with many players, a mix of complex cultures, political influences, differing interests, structures, systems, procedures and activities.

If the *adaptation* of supply chain management as the evolutionary development of logistics is to be considered in the humanitarian context one further aspect needs to be borne in mind. To be effectively coordinated, ie to reduce waste across functional and organizational boundaries, there needs to be overall strategy and direction if duplication and confusion are to be avoided. While this strategic level is essential, there is also a need for clarity of direction at both tactical and operational levels. At tactical level, effective performance is paramount, while at operational level much will depend upon the skills and talents of individuals 'on the ground' undertaking the minutiae of detail that brings logistics success.

Challenges of, and for, humanitarian logistics

There is a wide variety of challenges in the development of more efficient approaches to humanitarian logistics and supply chain management including strategic, operational, organizational and change management issues.

In any disaster or crisis environment, conventional systems may be unreliable or break down completely. The humanitarian aid logistics systems of organizations need to be robust enough to bridge any gap between existing logistics systems and the devastated areas' infrastructure. This can be achieved by local contracts, cooperation, ingenuity and a flexible approach. Yet in order to enhance efficiency and gain optimum effectiveness in respect of donor financial and material contributions, not only should this happen but also coordination and integration across the organizational boundaries of all aid agencies must be undertaken.

As stated earlier, supply chain management has a wide scope, spanning not only different organizations along the chain but also many different functions within any one organization. In a sense, therefore, logistics is everyone's business rather than the domain of a 'chosen few', which in turn requires at least some education and understanding of people across an organization as to the roles, functions and objectives of logistics. This is the case in commercial organizations, but is exacerbated in humanitarian agencies, which are often geographically dispersed, culturally diverse and dealing with supply chains that are temporary.

However, perhaps the most fundamental challenge in improving logistics and supply chain management in the humanitarian context is the need to gain a proper understanding of the scope and importance of logistics and supply chain management at all levels within the aid community.

From the perspective of logistics professionals, it seems obvious that logistics and supply chain operations are central activities of most aid operations. In disaster response, sourcing products and delivering them in an efficient and timely manner to beneficiaries is not only critical, but is the major focus. Even in less time-critical, on-going development scenarios, sourcing and distributing products is often an essential activity. Added to this, recent research reports (Tomasini and Van Wassenhove, 2006; Whiting, 2010) have indicated that logistics/supply chain costs can account for anything between 40 and 80 per cent of the aid spend. Yet we still have a situation where 'the powers that be' in the aid community do not appear to fully recognize the importance of logistics and supply chain management. Many aid agencies do not have a full-time logistics or supply chain director. Even where such positions do exist, the incumbents may have only limited influence. On the one hand they may not have board-level status and thus find it hard to gain a logistics/supply chain input into the top-level strategy. On the other hand, in some agencies they may only be able to act in an advisory capacity to programme managers who have the ultimate responsibility for achieving aid distribution. At the operational end of the management spectrum, many of the people who are responsible for logistics have no formal logistics training and/or may only be assigned to logistics positions on a temporary basis. Beyond the aid agencies themselves there is a further problem. Major donors, particularly national or transnational government organizations do not appear to understand the centrality of logistics to the aid efforts they support. In consequence there is little evidence that rigorous analysis and reporting of logistics performance is a critical element in the evaluation of funding effectiveness. Furthermore, donors are reluctant to provide funds for the improvement of logistics and supply chain management as monies are normally only allocated to specific events or programmes.

The above comments are not meant as criticism but are presented as a perspective on the current situation. In fact the situation where there is a lack of appreciation of the importance and potential benefits of better logistics and supply chain management is not at all unique to the humanitarian sector. Even today, there are some commercial companies and indeed some commercial sectors, where there is still only a rudimentary knowledge and application of an integrated approach to supply chain management. It must not be forgotten that in reality, appreciation of the benefits of logistics and supply chain management as a key element of business strategy is still relatively new, stretching back only some 20 or 25 years.

An important question then arises as to what provides the impetus for individual organizations or indeed whole sectors to take a more proactive and professional approach to supply chain improvement. Reflection on the development of best practices in supply chain management across different sectors suggests there have been a number of different triggers.

In some sectors it has been directly a result of commercial competition. One or more leading companies may develop a more holistic and determined approach to supply chain activity, which results in significant cost savings and/or service improvements thus giving competitive advantage and improved profits. For example, in food retailing the move to centralized and contracted-out distribution, first adopted by companies such as Sainsbury's in the UK, Wal-Mart in the USA and Carrefour in France in the 1980s, led to dramatic improvements in supply chain management across the retail sector as other companies followed suit. In the automotive industry in the 1990s, the increasing market share gained by Toyota and other Japanese manufacturers as a result of their lean policies, necessitated automotive manufacturers throughout the world to review and upgrade their supply chain operations. In these and other sectors, the increased focus on logistics and supply chain management has been driven by commercial competitive pressures and has resulted in the eventual elevation of the function to a key part of company strategy and operations.

In other situations, governments have taken the initiative and developed programmes for improved supply chain management in order to improve the competitiveness of sectors of industry that they consider to be of national importance. For example, in the UK during the last 10 years, the government has funded major supply chain improvement programmes in the agri-foods sector; similar initiatives have been carried out in Australia. While in sectors such as healthcare and defence, which are funded by public finances, the pressure from governments to reduce costs and improve service has provided the impetus for managers to rigorously analyse supply chain performance

An interesting issue arises in relation to transnational supply chain activity, which is a feature of both humanitarian and commercial operations. The globalization of manufacturing and markets over the last 30 years has led to the development of long, complex international supply chains in many commercial sectors. Such global chains were often developed around lowest cost manufacturing locations, but firms soon realized that unless the whole supply chain was carefully managed, there was significant potential for failures in customer service as well as increased overall costs. This quickly led management to first of all measure overall supply chain performance and then to focus on its systematic improvement. Although humanitarian chains have perhaps always been transnational, there does not appear to have been strong pressure to improve performance as in the commercial world. On the one hand it is sometimes claimed that humanitarian operations cannot afford to worry about cost when human lives are at stake; while on the other hand, there is no real mechanism to evaluate how effective the aid operations have been in terms of the number of lives saved or perhaps more pertinently the number of lives lost through inefficient aid provision.

The question therefore arises as to what might trigger the elevation and improvement of supply chain management in the context of humanitarian aid. Indeed there are a number of factors that seem to mitigate against the development of such triggers. There is no direct competitive imperative arbitrated by consumer choice as in the commercial world. Although competition between agencies does exist, it is focused on obtaining funding, rather than operational performance. The voice of the humanitarian end-user (beneficiaries) is weak, if not unheard. As humanitarian activity is typically transnational, individual national governments have neither the incentive or influence to instigate initiatives to improve supply chain practice. Major donors such as DfID or ECHO, appear to lack an appreciation of the scope and importance of logistics and hence do not exert pressure for improved supply chain performance. The United Nations, through initiatives such as UNJLC and more recently the Logistics Cluster, have started attempts to improve logistics performance in the sector. However, such initiatives are hampered because the UN has no mandate to control or command, but can only try to influence and persuade, which is difficult in the face of the proliferation of aid agencies around the globe.

In the absence of compelling external pressures to improve humanitarian logistics performance, it is suggested that the trigger for improvement might have to come from within the humanitarian logistics community itself. Can the small but increasing band of humanitarian logistics and supply chain managers create a revolution or at least a transformation from within? By increasing professionalism they may not only be able to improve the operational performance of humanitarian supply chains, but may also be able to develop a more compelling argument as to the importance of logistics and supply chain management in order to elevate its status both within the aid agencies themselves and to the wider donor community.

However if professionalization of humanitarian logistics is to provide such an impetus, it begs the question of what exactly does professionalization mean.

Professionalism

The whole idea of 'profession' causes much discussion and debate. For example, 'even the way in which it is theorised is contested' (Freidson, 1994: 14). Yet the concept of 'profession' and that of being 'professional' are highly valued in modern society. Many claim to be professional; it indicates status and grants distinction as to how an individual is perceived. That professions and professionals are important to modern society is emphasized by Schon – 'the professions have become essential to the very functioning of our society... we look to professionals for the definition and solution of our problems and it is through them that we strive for social progress' (Schon, 1987: 3).

Inevitably, there are semantic issues in respect of the word profession and its various derivatives, such as 'professional' and 'professionalism'. In addition, the same word could be perceived as having different meanings. Professional could be seen as a noun, ie belonging to a profession; alternatively, it could mean the manner of undertaking a task, function or activity in a particular manner, ie used an adjective or an adverb in a denotative or connotative application.

Although there may be no absolute definition available for the term 'profession', and certainly none where there is total agreement, there are a number of aspects that are fundamental to any consideration of the topic. These need to be set, albeit briefly, within a historical context that identifies a complex and changing concept that has profound effects upon perception, motivation and performance.

Developing from the 'status professions' of law, medicine and the clergy, 'occupational professions' have grown based on trades or the sciences. Such new professions included, for example, engineers and architects – they straddled the normative, scientific divide and have a syncretic epistemological foundation. The military have been noted as an example of such a profession (Halliday, 1985). Not only did they achieve independence from aristocratic patronage, they were able to select members and exclude outsiders as well as being able to expel incompetent, immoral or unethical members.

During the early 20th century, there was an increasing interest in, and theorizing about, the concept of profession. Sociological analysis can be seen as far back as Flexner (1915), when there was a period of considerable growth in the number of occupations that were claiming to be professions. Frequently, the approach for determining which occupations should be considered as a profession was based upon a number of traits. There is a particular challenge in this however, as there is an abundance of potential criteria upon which such judgements can be made. For example, Millersom (1964) identified 23 criteria stated by 21 authors without a single common feature!

Nevertheless, emerging from all of these criteria, were a number of pertinent characteristics (or traits) broadly based upon service delivery, itself based upon skill and knowledge. Other prominent characteristics included autonomy and responsibility. Included within these characteristics or traits was the need to draw upon a systematic body of knowledge. This typically required a lengthy period of higher education, coupled with further training and application over several years.

To understand the concept of profession is important, as it is the end state – the desired ideal of the professional or professionalism. Hoyle (1980) identifies functionalist approaches to 'professionalism' and notes certain social functions of the professions that are vital to the well-being of society. The functionalist view is summarized by Hoyle as follows:

- A profession is an occupation performing a crucial social function.
- To exercise this function requires a considerable degree of skill and the application of this skill can be performed in situations which are not routine and where new problems and situations may arise.
- A period of socialization into a set of 'professional' values is required.
- The practitioners must draw upon a systematic body of knowledge.
- A period of education is needed to acquire this knowledge.
- As knowledge-based practice is specialized, there is a need for the exercise of 'professional' judgement in respect of appropriate action.
- Although it can be seen that there is debate over the nature of the theorising of 'profession,' and whilst 'profession' can be seen as an essentially contested concept, there is substantial agreement about the general dimensions of 'profession'. (Hoyle and John, 1995)

In summary, these are:

- Normative dimension: oriented towards service with distinctive ethics.

- Evaluative dimension: a comparison of professions to other occupations.
- Cognitive dimension: a body of knowledge and techniques applied in work.

Arguably, consideration of 'profession' in a modern context, ie complex, inter-disciplinary applications, should be grounded in a theory of occupations, because a 'profession' is generically an occupation. From this, there is a view that there is a distinct shift of focus from a static concept of 'profession' as a distinct type of occupation, to the process by which occupations are 'professionalized'. It may also be possible to develop an order of relatively scarce attributes, such as specialist skills and knowledge associated with a particular profession,

At this point it is useful to consider that a wider view of humanitarianism as a whole has its roots in private charity and politically motivated relief. What comes from these traditions is a relationship between the providers and receivers of aid, especially in respect of immediate disaster relief (Walker, 2009). However, this in itself cannot be seen as professionalizing the word 'humanitarianism' as a noun: it might however be accepted as an adjective or adverb – ie describing the manner in which aid was received – if the provision of immediate relief (ie logistics) was undertaken efficiently and effectively. However, there is much evidence that this is not always the case, with initial response to providing disaster relief exhibiting duplication, typically including incorrect stocks, poor communication and not developing good relationships between providers. This is not to criticize intentions. There is no lack of evidence of moral and ethical commitment to assisting those in need. Indeed it is enshrined in international law. But moral and ethical commitment and best intentions are not the nature of professionalism. Performance is the essence of professionalism.

A particular challenge is that the very creation of professionals (as a noun) especially the now prevalent occupational professionals, means a degree of exclusion. Bluntly, one is either in a profession or not. If there is to be a humanitarian logistics profession then there must be recognition of all the players that are encompassed in that environment. At an organizational level these can be many and varied as the essence of supply chain management (and best practice within the construct) is predicated upon a 'total process' perspective that includes many relevant players.

Professionalism in humanitarian logistics practice

Having outlined a contextual and conceptual setting it is necessary to bring these together and consider whether professionalism is present or what needs to be undertaken to enable such accreditation to humanitarian logistics activities.

Although professionalism is essentially a contested topic there are generally accepted tenets that can be applied. Hoyle's fundamentalist view of the end state was highlighted as being vital to the well-being of any professionalization initiatives. In respect of humanitarian logistics and the background and context discussed here they are particularly apt.

- *Social function*:

  There can be no doubt that the humanitarian logistician performs a crucial social function.

- *Judgment in the application of skill*:

  Similarly, Hoyle's view that 'to exercise this function requires a considerable degree of skill and the application of this skill can be performed in situations which are not routine and where new problems and situations may arise', is entirely pertinent.

- *Socialization into a set of professional values*:

  As regards the third tenet, this comes, in respect of humanitarianism generally, with the very nature of wanting to provide relief and assistance to those in need and by learning from others already involved in humanitarian activities. Although there is no doubting the commitment of such people nor the community within which they operate, it may be seen that much of the immediate aid provision in the event of a disaster is not always performed well (examples are numerous but include New Orleans after Hurricane Katrina, the tsunami in SE Asia, the floods in Pakistan, etc). In part this is due to the complexities of trying to develop coordinated and coherent management of all the activities within the concepts of logistics within the difficult contextual setting of humanitarian disasters. However, unless there is some change in the socialization process and inculcation of values that are geared towards elimination of waste and optimization of value, this aspect of such performance is likely to persist. The socialization element of professional will thus require change in behaviours and the development of a culture that sees efficiency and effectiveness as key performance aspects of humanitarian logistics. This in turn requires the necessary knowledge to enable cultural change.

  The remaining tenets of Hoyle's model cover in one form or another the key issue of 'knowledge' and are areas where attention must be focused if professionalism is to be recognized.

- *A systematic body of knowledge:*

  To date, there would not have been a systematic body of knowledge upon which humanitarian logistics practitioners can draw. Development of such a body of knowledge is fundamental to enabling professionalism, but at this stage, there is only the beginning of a recognition of such a need.

  What has distinguished the development of commercial and military logistics is that there is a plethora of knowledge synchronism and distribution, eg books, papers, articles, documents and training and education courses. In the specialist humanitarian logistics area, until recently little had been written and articles that were produced were often not widely published or easily accessible. However, in the past five years or so, this has begun to change. A nascent body of knowledge is emerging, with, at one end of the continuum, publications such as the *Humanitarian Logistics Operating Guide*, focusing on humanitarian logistics at a practical, 'on-the-ground' level; while at the other end of such a scale, there are increasingly pertinent critically analytical papers appearing in relevant academic journals and indeed the appearance of specialist humanitarian logistics publications such as the *International Journal of Humanitarian Logistics*, which published its first edition in 2011.

Much of this stems from the growing recognition of the need to coordinate disaster relief especially in the initial response stage. Institutions such as the Chartered Institute of Logistics and Transport (CILT) and academic providers such as universities have a considerable role to play in developing a suitable body of knowledge. Such institutions can provide objective evidence of the need for improved management of the supply chain, especially the holistic (total process) perspective considered earlier. They can develop methodologies and concepts that assist in the adoption and adaptation of performance-enhancing approaches that are applicable in the humanitarian logistics context. These can then be inculcated into the body of knowledge, which will aid the movement of theory into practice (and indeed vice versa).

There has also been increased input from context-specific organizations, such as the Fritz Institute, Red R UK, the Feinstein Centre and the Humanitarian Logistics Association (HLA) as such organizations have become aware of the need for improved logistics performance. Nevertheless it can be argued that the field of humanitarian logistics and supply chain management is still in its infancy both from the conceptual and theoretical perspectives and from that of practical application. This is akin to the situation faced earlier by other sectors of the economy as already noted.

- *A period of education in order to acquire the knowledge followed by knowledge-based practice exercised with professional judgement:*

In many ways, these tenets bring together all aspects of professionalism. Knowledge is the key to professionalism and there can be no doubt that all professions are built on a period (often lengthy) of time spent in learning and acquiring this knowledge. However, knowledge is not merely gained by a period of education, nor is it gained by just being socialized into a set of core values – nor indeed does having skill in a particular area constitute knowledge. Real knowledge in a professional sense requires the concepts and skills acquired through education to be tested and tempered by application to practical situations.

Gaining knowledge: the basis of professionalism in humanitarian logistics

Consideration of 'profession' as a noun – ie a collective body with self-regulation (etc) – is not yet a reality for those in humanitarian logistics. Although the journey towards such a status has commenced and is indicated by the increasing number of initiatives that are being introduced by institutions and organizations around the world. This can only be applauded as the aim will be to enable enhanced performance in respect of disaster response. Nevertheless, a fundamental element of this journey must be that 'professionalism', in the sense of an adjective or an adverb, is introduced and developed. In other words the manner in which those involved in humanitarian logistics undertake their role and activities must become more efficient and effective, ie professional. This must be accompanied by greater understanding of what needs to be undertaken, how it should be undertaken and why in differing situations differing approaches need to be applied. Further, it requires standardization of processes, clear communication, uniformity of terminology, inter-disciplinary thinking, global best-practice concepts and application. Importantly, it also requires mechanisms and approaches to systematically measure and evaluate humanitarian logistics activity. In short, this understanding requires knowledge.

In the short term this can bring about professionalism in one sense (and improve performance) and it may, in the longer term, bring the concept of a humanitarian profession to fruition. Either way, knowledge underpins the journey towards professionalism.

Knowledge can be gained in a number of ways and, to ensure that optimal benefit is gained, there is a need for a careful balance of training, education and experience. Training can provide those involved with the 'how' to do things. It provides the processes and procedures necessary for activities to be undertaken in the most suitably efficient manner; it is the basis of skill development and can be delivered in a number of pertinent ways. Education will provide the opportunity to understand why things may or may not happen; it is about critical analysis of theories and concepts applied in particular contexts. However, neither training nor education on their own will produce the professionalism; that will deliver enhanced performance, nor is there an exact balance between the two. The knowledge that will enable professionalism comes from education and training, which is balanced by the recognition and utilization of experience.

This can be shown diagrammatically (Figure 10.3). In order to gain cognitive growth in humanitarian logistics professionalism, knowledge

FIGURE 10.3 Knowledge acquisition

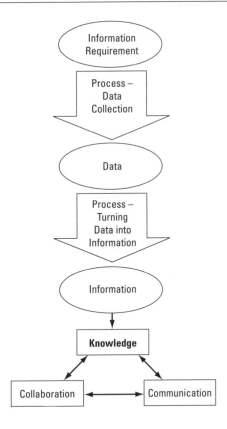

needs to be developed and recorded in the three aforementioned areas. Theories and concepts or propositional knowledge, which will come from education, need to be developed and balanced with how to do things or process knowledge. Put together through a perspective that could be seen as filtering what is relevant and applicable in a range of contingent situations will enable growth and development of knowledge.

However, a major challenge to this is that often in the context of humanitarian logistics, knowledge, or rather information and data, are available but not necessarily utilized. Frequent turnover of personnel at an operating level is one of the reasons that this can occur. Every time humanitarian aid is provided learning takes place. Sometimes the learning is in people's heads, and is lost as they subsequently move to other roles or organizations (especially given the periodic nature of some humanitarian logistics positions); on other occasions it may be recorded in, for example, documents or local operating procedures. However, it is unusual if all of this information or data are readily available to all of the players within the humanitarian environment or indeed if they are recorded in a critically analytical way that can be made available for the creation of more learning opportunities that could lead to the development of greater knowledge. As an example, the IFRC recognized this in its decision that:

> to include knowledge management in its preparedness strategy it was acknowledging that further competencies and value could be created from the lessons learned from previous disasters. The IFRC acknowledged that its supply chain would dramatically improve if it could capitalise on the knowledge possessed by the staff of the Red Cross movement globally. (Tomasini and Van Wassenhove, 2009: 115)

It is not only the IFRC, of course, who have taken such issues into account. For some time the UNJLC and its later incarnation the Logistics Cluster have taken on the mantle of information management in complex disaster/ emergency situations. Although information management in this sense can include communications generally (eg with the media) it has primarily been in bringing logistics information together in a coordinated manner so that data collection and analysis can be undertaken and disseminated in a way so as to assist decision making. This is a crucial activity and can be the basis of future growth of knowledge, but it is still limited in its overall effectiveness and requires considerable commitment from all players within the humanitarian logistics arena.

This can be seen generically in Figure 10.4. The key element is in understanding what is likely to be required in the immediate response to a disaster. Although each disaster is different there are many logistical aspects that are recurring, although the extent and application may vary. Similarly, there have been many situations where information requirements, at least in respect of broad logistics/supply chain concept can be determined. Data at all levels have to be collected; this can include facts from past performance, cost movements, availability of transport, trained personnel, etc. It can be at the operational, tactical or strategic levels. For greatest professional impact it should be comprehensive. This data have to be analysed in accord with the requirements for information and have to be considered on one hand on a generic basis, so that general principles can be developed and determined in respect of information, yet on the other hand must be flexible enough to allow for the contingent situation to be assessed and processes and experience to come into play to seek the right balance to ensure knowledge creation and dissemination. Too often information is available and data can be provided, but this in itself is not knowledge – it is rather facts or figures, which if utilized carefully, can be turned into knowledge. This is the basis of professionalism in humanitarian logistics but it will not be relevant unless it is used to exercise professional judgement, for it is the use and application of that knowledge by humanitarian logisticians that will bring performance improvements.

FIGURE 10.4 Cognitive growth process

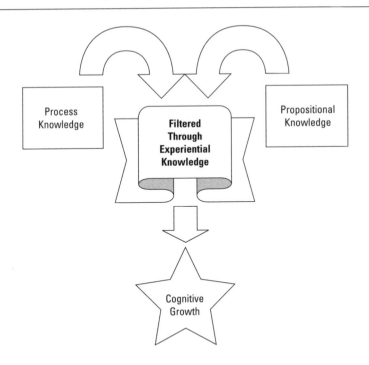

Professionalism – the response for, and of, humanitarian logistics

This chapter has highlighted the growing cognizance in recent years of the need to improve performance of logistics activity. In consequence there have been a number of developments in both the academic and practitioner's spheres aimed at developing the professionalism of humanitarian logistics.

Some 10 years ago the authors of this chapter recognized the potential opportunity to improve the efficiency and effectiveness of humanitarian logistics by utilizing commercial best practice in taking a holistic perspective of the supply chain. This was made more pertinent when taking the military logistics adaptation of commercial best practice into account, where the need to prepare for deployed operations that may or may not happen is a paramount consideration and has resonance and symmetry with the role of humanitarian logistics organizations. Hence we organized a workshop at Cranfield University's Shrivenham campus in the United Kingdom, with key players from government, NGOs, the UN, the military, academic organizations and interested individuals. The aim was to understand key issues and challenges and whether we could provide input to thought-leadership and influence practical applications that could assist in enhancing performance. All those present felt that we could, by working together as a wider humanitarian logistics community, make a positive impact. From this early beginning, one of the outcomes was the creation of Cranfield University/Cardiff University Humanitarian Logistics Initiative (CCHLI), which has subsequently held conferences, published papers and made various conceptual inputs to the topic. The Shrivenham meeting also spawned, with support from the Chartered Institute of Logistics and Transport (CILT) the forum that has now become the Humanitarian Emergency Logistics Professionals (HELP). This organization aims to mobilize the experience and expertise of professional logisticians in the commercial and military sectors to assist in practical applications in the humanitarian sphere. These two entities (both operated on a purely voluntary basis) epitomize the humanitarian ethos, but rather than take an enthusiastic amateur role, their basis is the belief that by working in a coherent coordinated manner, more effective and efficient supply chain performance can be achieved and thereby provide better value for the monies donated by governments and individuals. While this is the aim, the means of achievement stem from better understanding, underpinned by knowledge. Knowledge, and its dissemination, holds the key to better decision making.

Other academic initiatives have also developed, perhaps the most notable of which is the HUMLOG Institute based in Finland. HUMLOG was established in 2007 by a group of Scandinavian universities, to bring together academics and practitioners from around the world for joint research and knowledge exchange. Such initiatives bring an academic perspective that is generally focused on more critical analysis and the development of concepts, themes and ideas. This view of understanding through reflection and abstraction can be balanced with those initiatives and approaches that are being developed in respect of training courses and procedural guides.

The educational contribution has been further enhanced by the development of specific humanitarian logistics modules on undergraduate and postgraduate courses at universities in Europe, North America and Australia; and through analytical research by doctoral students seeking evidence in respect of specific humanitarian logistics hypotheses.

Concurrently with the above developments, other entities have progressed professionalization initiatives: The Fritz Institute in the USA, established after the Asian tsunami of 2005, has focused on improving logistics in the immediate response phase to disaster relief and has worked in conjunction with CILT in the UK, to develop standards and programmes for training logisticians at an operational level.

Initiatives have also been instigated from within the aid community itself. UNJLC and the Logistics Cluster have sought performance improvements through coordination and coherence and have been at the centre of many of the training and development activities. In January 2009, the Humanitarian

Logistics Association (HLA) was established as an association for individual humanitarian logistics practitioners committed to increasing humanitarian logistics effectiveness. At the time of writing, the HLA had some 700 members around the world and was in the process of developing a series of seminars and other educational programmes for members. Its longer term aim is to become *the* recognized professional institute for humanitarian logistics.

Finally it is worth noting that in 2010 in the UK, ELRHA (Enhancing Learning and Research for Humanitarian Assistance) was established with the specific aim of 'Humanitarian Professionalization'. To achieve this ELRHA has a number of objectives including:

- Better coordination among agencies and relief providers, more research, harnessing of training and learning resources as a baseline for the humanitarian workforce generally.

- Agreement on course content with relevant quality measurement, coordination of Master's-level course provision by universities and consensus upon core competencies to enable training consistency.

- The creation of an International Humanitarian Professional Association, as an independent body promoting learning (eg through experience), close relationships with relevant bodies around the globe and the expansion of knowledge that could lead towards wider international accreditation and recognition.

Although ELRHA is not specifically focused on humanitarian logistics, it illustrates many of the key issues and themes that have been discussed in this chapter. This can only be lauded and although it does not cover all of the points that have been discussed, it is an example of how training, education and experience can be brought together as the basis of professionalism. It appears to be more at a practical level and at early stages, which is exactly what is to be expected of a professionalization project (Larson, 1997; Moore, 2004). Similar experiences in other sectors, eg in nursing, teaching and the military, identify that a firm base of training and experience, which is process led, is required to ensure that fundamental skills and competencies can be developed, standardized and delivered to a wide audience. In due course this can be expanded further to include more education, ie critically analytical abstraction including greater research to inform the growing professional area.

Summary

There is a need for improved logistic response to (man-made or natural) disasters. Humanitarian logistics activity is particularly crucial in the vital period immediately after any disaster. By recognizing and utilizing best-practice commercial approaches to logistics, money from donors could be better optimized and greater value achieved. Taking this further, military logistics organizations have taken on broad commercial best practice and adapted this to the environment in which they have to operate. Such environments and the manner in which military and humanitarian logistics organizations deploy have considerable similarities. Despite any cultural dissonance that may exist between them, humanitarian logistics approaches to immediate disaster response, could gain from similar adaptation of commercial best practice just as military organizations have done. There are of course still many challenges for humanitarian logistics, but by taking a professional approach performance could be improved. In practice this is acknowledged and is being actioned both by those responsible for humanitarian logistics and by the wider humanitarian community. However, it is prudent to consider exactly what is meant by professionalism, or indeed derivatives of the word 'profession'.

Humanitarian logistics fits the definition of a profession well, having distinctive ethical underpinning and it can be seen favourably in comparison to other occupations; nevertheless, for cognitive growth and recognition, any profession must be underpinned by a body of knowledge. This has never been more relevant than in the global society in which we now operate. To bring professionalism to this environment will require a number of tenets to be achieved and good progress is already being made. Any discussion of knowledge must recognize the importance of information and/ or data, but must never assume that these are the same things. Information and data have to be analysed and interpreted in order to have meaning and applicability in particular contextual settings, ie to become knowledge.

With this in mind some of the activities that have taken place in recent years have been noted and, from them, often sequential and sometimes concurrent activities have commenced, with a number of committed altruistic entities created. Ultimately these have resulted in organizations that are now actively seeking to develop professionalism in humanitarian activities.

Conclusion

There is a 'groundswell' that is moving the concept of professionalism in humanitarian logistics forward. It will be a matter of time as to whether this will develop into a full-scale profession, ie considered in the sense of a noun. It is more likely that in the short run, professionalism will develop in the sense of an adjective or adverb, in relation to the way in which humanitarian logistics activities are carried out. Indeed this is perhaps to be expected as it is the manner in which most occupational professions emerge and develop. Crucially, professionalism (in either sense of the word) is built upon knowledge and such knowledge must be contextualized based upon three elements, namely process knowledge, propositional knowledge and experiential knowledge. The former can be gained through training and focuses upon the 'how', while the propositional knowledge comes from education, which seeks the 'why' and experience acts as a filter that balances. As a result people can understand how to undertake humanitarian logistics, they understand why it is undertaken in certain ways and can consider alternatives with understanding from personal and anecdotal experience enabling a perspective that will enable performance enhancement. This must be based upon a 'Body of Knowledge' that records, criticizes, codifies and contextualizes what there is to know about the subject area. This is no small task and the various efforts that are under way to professionalize humanitarian logistics will not be easy. However, professionalization will bring performance enhancement, it will bring qualifications, it will bring recognition, but above all it will assist those who need aid.

In contrast to commercial supply chains where, due to competitive forces, 'the voice of the customer' must be heeded, the victims of disaster rarely have an effective mechanism to express their needs, nor do they have any meaningful resort to alternatives if the provision of aid is less than satisfactory. Furthermore there is currently no compelling pressure from key external agencies, be that donors, governments or international agencies for improvements in logistics performance. Nor is there a real appreciation of the importance of logistics at the highest strategic levels in many aid agencies. Therefore, the gauntlet perhaps falls to the humanitarian logistics community itself, to heed the silent cry of the beneficiaries, by striving to become more professional, in order to become more efficient and effective in the delivery of aid and in the subsequent relief of distress and suffering.

References

Flexner, A (1915) Is Social Work a Profession?, in *Studies in Social Work*, 4, New York School of Philanthropy, New York

Freidson, E (1994) *Professionalism Reborn, Theory, Prophecy and Policy*, Polity Press, Cambridge

Halliday, TC (1985) Knowledge mandates: collective influence by scientific, normative and syncretic professions, *British Journal of Sociology*, 36, pp 421–27

Hoyle, E (1980) Professionalisation and deprofessionalisation in education, in E Hoyle and J Megarry (eds), *The Professional Development of Teachers: World yearbook of education*, Kogan Page, London

Hoyle, E and John, PD (1995) *Professional Knowledge and Professional Practice*, Cassel, London

Larson, MS (1997) *The Rise of Professionalism: A social analysis*, University of California Press, Berkley, CA

Millersom, G (1964) *The Qualifying Associations: A study in professionalisation*, Routledge, London

Moore, DM (2004) *Knowledge as the Basis of Professionalism in the Defence Acquisition Community*, EdD thesis, University of Bristol, UK

Moore, DM and Antill, PD (2002) *Logistics for Humanitarian Aid Operations: Meeting the challenges*, in Logistics in the Digital Age, Florence

Schon, D (1987) *Educating the Reflective Practitioner: How professionals think in action*, Basic Books, New York

Tomasini, R and Van Wassenhore, L (2006) 'Overcoming the Barriers to a Cross Sector Partnership', The Conference Board Executive Action Report, INSEAD

Tomasini, R and Van Wassenhove, L (2009) *Humanitarian Logistics*, Palgrave Macmillan, Basingstoke

Van Wassenhore, L (2006) 'Humanitarian Aid Logistics: Supply chain management in high gear', *Journal of the Operational Research Society*, 57, pp 475–89

Walker, P (2009) *What does it mean to be a professional humanitarian?*, Medford, MA: Feinstein International Famine Centre, Tufts University

Whiting, M (2010) The Haiti Earthquake, January 2010, *Focus*, April, **12**(4), pp 26–29

11
Humanitarian logistics
a cultural perspective

RACHEL A DOWTY

Abstract

Culture frequently poses problems for those tasked with sourcing, transporting and/or distributing humanitarian aid. Some problems stem from basic misunderstandings of needs and priorities across cultures, especially when viewed from a Western 'hierarchy of needs'. Attempts to deliver humanitarian aid are also affected by differing standards for public employees, different expectations for social cohesion within a country, and different concepts of time, efficiency, morality and individual initiative. Response to a crisis by multiple organizations, and international policies governing aid ('development assistance') can further complicate the goal of helping others in dire need. Aid takes many forms, and good intentions are no guarantee of good outcomes. Information is the missing ingredient in many humanitarian aid efforts. More knowledge is needed, specifically, local knowledge.

Without sufficient local knowledge, sourcing appropriate food and clothing can present problems, given different cultural mainstays and dominant religions. Successfully transporting humanitarian aid between cultures requires an understanding of not only geographic terrain and weather patterns, but also an understanding of customs, corruption and territorial rights. Even when aid is successfully sourced and transported, distributing it at the final point of delivery can be difficult because of language barriers, past experiences of those requiring the aid, and misunderstood gender roles. However, cultural understandings can potentially help to navigate problems such as waste and delayed delivery of humanitarian aid. Whether the cultural differences are international, organizational or local, they play an integral role in humanitarian logistics. This chapter will review different roles that culture can play in humanitarian operations with regard to problems of sourcing, transport and distribution as well as the role culture may play in solving such problems.

Hierarchy of needs

The hierarchy of needs states that people, no matter who or where they are, must meet their basic needs (which are food, shelter and procreation) before striving to obtain more derived needs (such as self-expression, spiritual fulfillment, smoked salmon, vacation time). Although this may seem logical at first glance, the hierarchy of needs 'collapses once the anthropologist points out that as you go from one culture to another (or even from one social class to another), one person's basic need becomes another person's derived need and vice versa' (Thompson *et al*, 1990: 56).

For example, the World Bank's Basic Needs Program supplied funds to aid villagers in Nepal to re-establish their rice fields that had been decimated. They were shocked when they returned to see the aid money being spent on refurbishing the village temple. The villagers' logic was that good rice production was predicated on a good relationship with their gods, and in order to re-establish a good relationship with their gods, they must first refurbish their temple (Thompson *et al*, 1990). In this case, spiritual fulfilment was prioritized above food production, thus turning the hierarchy of needs on its head.

In humanitarian logistics, such cultural misunderstandings about prioritizing needs can mean the difference between successful or failed relief operations. The possibilities for cultural misunderstanding are endless. Individual initiative in one culture, for example, is insubordination in another. What is categorized as legitimate trade in one culture, for example, may be seen as a betrayal of moral principles in another culture.

A country may be judged by its international trade practices and communication of priorities. People in some developing countries believe that Western corporate culture has aided and abetted corruption in their own country. Kenya president Mwai Kibaki campaigned on an anti-corruption platform in a country where residents commonly paid bribes to police and other government agencies. The biggest target in Kibaki's anti-corruption campaign turned out to be a company registered in Britain (Wrong, 2009). Likewise, critics of the huge Food for Peace programme suggest that it benefits American farmers and the Merchant Marine more than receiving countries, which often lose much of their domestic farming capabilities (Bovard, 1986).

Cultural barometers are also used to measure the effectiveness of humanitarian aid. The 11th-century Jewish scholar Maimonides taught that the best type of philanthropic deed enabled the recipient to achieve economic independence. This is still a widely held viewpoint. Dambisa Moyo uses it to argue against aid efforts, saying that although billions of dollars have been sent to Africa, the number of poor people in the region continues to increase (Moyo, 2009).

The ultimate outcomes of aid programmes may be linked to cross-cultural communication and mutual respect for each other's priorities among people from very different societies, as much as the amount of money spent to initiate change. Cross-cultural problem solving may seem insurmountable, given the number of problems that arise among people from the similar cultural backgrounds who are all apparently addressing the same humanitarian tasks.

Different prioritization between volunteers and other workforces challenge the hierarchy of needs for humanitarian workers as well. Many humanitarian relief efforts involve a large volunteer workforce, especially in matters of sourcing aid and dispersing aid at its final destination. Volunteers may need to work alongside military personnel and other 'professionals' who are being paid to do their work. Because of the value Western culture places on earning money, the professionals may view volunteers as less capable, more likely to cave in under pressure. In the aftermath of Hurricane Katrina, a federal agency noted the 'psychological demands' on volunteers working in a disaster environment. 'Volunteers were often unprepared for the psychological demands that they encountered working in a disaster environment', according to a memo from the US Office of the Inspector General's (OIG) to the Federal Emergency Management Agency (FEMA). 'Some level of counseling needs to be consistently provided both prior to and upon return from deployment to ensure that volunteers can identify signs and symptoms of psychological distress and know how and where to seek additional help when needed' (US OIG, 2007: 3).

Organizations often stereotype one another by function as well as by expertise (or lack thereof) when prioritizing needs. The US Air Force noted differences between its goals in bringing aid to Haiti following the 1991 political upheaval, and the expectations of non-governmental organizations (NGOs). The military's delivery of supplies and emergency medical help was not seen by humanitarian aid organizations as helping people 'in the long run'. 'NGOs usually require some form of minimal payment, payment-in-kind, or an acceptance by the people being supported of long-term medical risks. This can include some means of birth control, proper sanitary conditions, etc' (Hinson, 1998: 8).

People receiving aid also have their own hierarchy of needs in terms of their own recovery, and what recovery means. Their agenda may not coincide with any of the organizations sourcing humanitarian aid. Victims may not want to be represented to the rest of the world by agencies from other countries and cultures. People without clothes might prefer cloth and thread so they can sew the kinds of clothes they feel they ought to be wearing. A community in need may want computers and computer instruction, so that it can structure its own outreach efforts (Brooten, 2003).

Differing measurements for success can create what Emily Chamlee-Wright terms 'signal noise', itself a potential threat to meeting needs to achieve recovery. Signal noise comes from conflicting policies or pronouncements from agencies in charge of recovery efforts. People receiving assistance are victims of signal noise when they are not getting clear messages about their roles in long-term recovery (Chamlee-Wright, 2007).

When volunteer retention depends on matching volunteers to appropriate tasks, it is important that those tasks are set with the perspective of the aid recipients in mind (Falasca *et al*, 2009). Organizational principles have been shown to be important to ensuring good volunteer performance in humanitarian organizations, as volunteers tend to create their own priorities when working in the field and need an organization to focus their priorities (Hilhorst and Schmiemann, 2002).

Differences in prioritization also occur between different organizational cultures that must coordinate to deliver aid successfully, another variable in assigning appropriate tasks. When a humanitarian organization wants to communicate the order of the recipients' needs to a commercial organization, irregular amounts of supplies at irregular intervals can challenge commercial organizations' understandings and erode humanitarian organizations' patience to the point that needs are not met (too much too late, or too little too late, or too much too soon), and ties between organizations that otherwise might have resulted in a valuable cooperative network may be severed or never even established (Beamon 2006).

Sourcing humanitarian aid

Communicating priorities across organizational cultures can be difficult, but communicating aid priorities across international cultures can involve additional complexities (Dowty and Wallace, 2010). Even when communicating, organizations in each culture are seemingly talking about the same thing, it can be a very different thing in the culture from where the item is being sourced and where the item is needed. For example, evacuated Russian soldiers in Eastern Europe during the Second World War did not recognize sliced white bread from America as 'bread' or even as food. They rolled it up in balls and threw it to one another (Tsurikov, 1971).

In the face of the worst food crisis in over a decade, Zambia and Zimbabwe rejected World Food Programme (WFP) maize because it was sourced from American genetically modified crops. The WFP and the United States Department of Agriculture saw no problem with GM maize, but these (and other African countries) forbid any of the unmilled maize to enter their country due to perceived risks on their devastated agricultural economy such as re-planting it, cross-fertilization with local plants, and contamination of cattle feed (Bennett, 2003).

Cultural clashes can also occur in logistical operations serving citizens within the same nation or even local area. For example, Latino residents in California and Cajun disaster victims in Louisiana have suffered from diarrhoea and other digestive problems within a week of consuming the primarily 'anglo cuisine' offered by the American Red Cross (Phillips, 1993).

While such problems also occur internationally (eg the International Red Cross used to offer coffee and doughnuts to starving war refugees), the fact that different cultures reside side by side in the same local area is important to keep in mind when sourcing humanitarian aid for local communities.

Sourcing clothes presents problems across cultures as well, particularly in international aid efforts when clothing is sourced in the West. Following the 2004 Boxing Day tsunami, clothing donations were sent from American organizations such as the Goodwill and the Salvation Army to impacted areas of India and Sri Lanka. Donations were not sorted according to appropriate climate and cultural considerations, resulting in both wasted clothing aid and frustration on the part of aid recipients. Winter coats and evening gowns were hardly useful at all, while religious and gender considerations made other articles (like women's blue jeans) inappropriate. Sentiments such as 'we scrambled the whole heap and still could not get a saree; there were only churidars (trousers) for women' were common following arrival of post-tsunami humanitarian aid (Thomas 2005: 63).

Transporting humanitarian aid

The process of transporting aid from its source location to an international destination involves crossing multiple cultural boundaries. Each cultural crossroad has the potential to usurp or help guide humanitarian aid efforts. A broad understanding of culture as 'a way of doing things' helps illustrate the numerous cultural issues that compound already difficult logistical transport issues (such as mode of transport and geographical terrain). Humanitarian organizations frequently must work through government departments, especially the government of the nation-state receiving the aid. Negotiating government departments and agencies in other areas of the world is rarely 'logical' according to Western notions of governmental hierarchy, and even identification of problems are often perceived differently.

Any grain transported into Zimbabwe, for instance, meets with governmental testing to ascertain whether or not it is genetically modified (GM), and must first be issued a governmental 'certificate' to assure it is not GM grain before the government allows transport into needy areas (Mbohwa, 2008). This can slow down much-needed aid if unexpected by humanitarian relief organizations, and if as the World Food Programme learned in the aforementioned example, funds have already been spent to ship GM grain to Zimbabwe, much of the aid goes to waste. One way to deal with this is to incorporate flexible procedures into international aid missions to accommodate unexpected rituals and procedures, but this is easier said than done (McClintock, 2009).

In the aftermath of the 2006 typhoon Bilis, the group Aid LeChang 7.15 was formed to specifically deliver aid to the Chinese county of LeChang. The group distinguished themselves from other non-governmental organizations (NGOs) by emphasizing that 'commodities must be directly distributed to the hands of beneficiaries' rather than through local governments. A primary reason for this direct distribution circumventing governmental involvement was to minimize loss of available resources through governmental corruption. Still, arguments broke out between the group and local officials over the way transport and distribution of aid is handled (Rao, 2007). A certain proportion of aid is ritually taken by many governments before the rest is allowed to be transported into a certain area, but black market operations also make the task of ensuring that an entire shipment of aid reaches its final destination intact very difficult.

Corruption is an ongoing challenge for humanitarian organizations to manage as part of their everyday culture, especially with regards to transport. In a study where humanitarian agency staff members were interviewed on the topic of corruption, vehicle management was identified 'as an area to corruption in many forms, due to the high value of transport, fuel and spare parts' (Willitts-King and Harvey, 2005: 22). This not only applies to material aid being transported, but also to transporting people themselves. Such corruption can start as mere 'bad habits' in matters such as bookkeeping, but when serving needy populations such habits can quickly become part and parcel of the way things are done.

Distributing humanitarian aid

Corruption also plagues aid distribution:

> Aid deliverers may well be able to report that the right amount of food was distributed to the right number of people, but this says little about whether kickbacks were paid to ensure registration, what proportion of the food went to the local government official at the distribution site, or what bribes local militias demanded so that beneficiaries could get the food home. (Willitts-King and Harvey, 2005: vii)

Beneficiaries who have had past experiences with corrupt and/or violent local militias but who have moved to a different country where they find themselves needing aid can be particularly vulnerable to cultural misunderstandings at distribution sites. After the Loma Prieta earthquake in California, immigrants whose families had been separated by death squads in South American countries found themselves facing governmental distribution centres that were ominously structured similarly to the death camps. Many Latinos did not approach the distribution centres, especially any centre with the word 'federal' attached to it. Problems were so pronounced that FEMA began erecting signs that said 'EMA' (Emergency Management Agency) to try and dispel anxiety in this population enough to where they would come to collect the aid they needed (Phillips, 1993).

However, the absence of federal government mediation in aid distribution can also signal ineffective humanitarian efforts. In a survey taken of aid beneficiaries in Sri Lanka and India after the 2004 Boxing Day tsunami, researchers found that 86 per cent of respondents in India received some kind of assistance from local government within 48 hours, whereas in Sri Lanka this number was 4 per cent. 'Where was the government when all this happened?' survivors in Sri Lanka asked (Thomas and Ramalingam, 2005: 47). Another case of delayed governmental assistance is that of Hurricane Katrina along the Gulf Coast of the United States in 2005. Only one in five people impacted by Katrina recalled receiving aid from the federal government within 48 hours (Fritz Institute, 2006).

Strained inter-governmental relations also hinder humanitarian efforts, making it more difficult to not only distribute aid but also to freely explore ways of bridging cultural divides. In 2001, Western governments put sanctions on Iraq that made it very difficult for Iraqi doctors to obtain current journals, textbooks, other literature and educational materials. The result was a period in which a shortage of doctors coincided with an increase in malnutrition, infectious diseases and cancers from depleted uranium contamination. The Iraqi Medical Association appealed to other countries to (try to) send such materials to them, but many items were confiscated before reaching them (Al-Araji, 2001). In many Muslim areas, women also typically refuse to be examined by men doctors, making women medical workers in higher demand during a time when even male doctors are in shortage.

War and violence, while resulting in the need for more humanitarian aid, also challenge the logistics of distribution practices with regard to cultural expectations. For instance, separation of potable water and groundwater results in toilets and showers being located at opposite sides of the camp from wells and taps. In Darfur, where women and girls are expected to gather firewood, such water arrangements frequently exacerbate the risks women and children already face of sexual assault (from not only militia but also from male humanitarian workers) when they must routinely travel to camp margins (Petchesky and Laurie, 2007). Although violence is also certainly a hazard to aid workers in many parts of the world, bureaucratic demands for obscure or non-existent forms and paperwork probably defeat more operations, a hazard referred to as 'slow death by a thousand paper cuts' (Polgreen, 2007).

In the context of a natural disaster, another example of misguided distribution arrangements such as those in Darfur occurred after the 2004 Boxing Day tsunami. United Nations relief workers distributed non-Halal food in Muslim areas of Thailand, unaware that such a practice is forbidden. To the relief workers this may have seemed fine, but to the beneficiaries, the distribution arrangements made the rations inedible (Lebel *et al*, 2006).

Such arrangements can at least partially be a result of communication problems among humanitarian organizations, governments, and aid recipients. Language barriers are perhaps one of the most common communication problems in dealing with cross-cultural challenges. Even when 'bread' is recognized as such across cultures, humanitarian workers distributing aid must still know the local word for it, if it is not 'bread'. The most common solution proposed to this problem is to have bilingual translators available at each distribution site, but this is easier said than done (Phillips, 1993; Enarson, 2007). It is also important to keep in mind that just because someone can speak a language does not necessarily mean that s/he understands local custom and rituals to the extent that local governments and/or beneficiaries of aid will trust the translator. Establishing inter-personal trust quickly in such situations involves consideration of perceived benefits and risks by all parties involved in the aid mission (Tatham and Kovács, 2010). Thus the cultural position(s) of local people relative to larger governmental structures and to the humanitarian organization play pivotal roles in establishing effective communication of risks and benefits and consequently, aid distribution.

Members of an organization seeking to help people in a remote and unfamiliar territory must decide what changes will bring about the desired improvements, and how change can best be achieved. Nothing can be accomplished without communication, and in many cases aid workers are not able to evaluate the capabilities and objectivity of their native translator. Poor translation, intended or unintended, has had tragic consequences in Afghanistan, where civilians have been mistakenly targeted and killed through translation errors (Mohmand and Jalalzai, 2008).

Humanitarian aid workers are usually aware that problems in cross-cultural communication exist, but may have no way of knowing just how deep the problems go. Communication involves much more than words, particularly in 'high context' cultures (Hall, 1959). Translations are particularly difficult when members of a 'high context' culture are receiving aid from people with a 'low context' culture (Yousef, 1978). 'Low context' cultures recognize the utility of using unambiguous references and allowing grammatical rules to carry a large burden of meaning. While 'low context' Western aid workers are striving to be as concrete as possible, the 'high context' aid recipients may not even be able to recognize attempts at low context communication. The 'low context' aid workers may come away from a mutually unsatisfactory exchange with the impression that the indigenous population is illogical, or preoccupied with etiquette.

Culture mediates not only attempts to communicate, but also attempts to repair faulty communications (Norrick, 1991). Attempts to unsnarl misunderstandings may make the problem even worse, if people with a 'low context' perspective confront the 'high context' group too directly about communication problems (Gudykunst, 1991).

The importance of local knowledge

If the central concerns of administering humanitarian aid are reaching a remote destination, living under primitive conditions, communicating with people from a different culture, or unravelling red tape, then the solutions can be found in travel guides and survival manuals. A cultural perspective on humanitarian aid raises other questions, such as 'How can aid be delivered without unintended, negative, consequences?' Solutions that take cultural differences into account can avoid the sort of tragedy that Hegel characterized as 'the conflict between two rights'.

Whether considering an individual's culture, a group's culture, an organization's culture, or the culture of a geographic area, culture is local. A common statement bandied about by disaster managers is that 'all disasters are local'. Put together, these statements suggest that to use culture as a tool to overcome problems in humanitarian operations, a bottom-up approach, prioritizing local knowledge above standardized operational procedure, has a number of advantages over a top-down approach. First, local knowledge helps identify the primary foods, clothing and shelter used by the beneficiaries. Second, local knowledge helps navigate more direct and/or easier routes of ground and water transport, as well as avoid the weakness of downward accountability responsible for many unreported cases of corruption (Willitts-King and Harvey, 2005). Third, local knowledge can help establish a firm basis for trusting relationships in the face of war and violence, which can also help secure reliable and trusted translators to overcome language and other communication barriers.

Local knowledge also embraces the full context of a disaster. Culture exists in time and must accommodate location. Many of the most intractable humanitarian problems in recent years involve armed conflicts in which local populations are taken hostage and used as bargaining chips. The effectiveness of this strategy has been amplified by modern communications, which bring images of atrocities into homes around the world. Deprivation has become a cultural strategy to compel negotiation or some other humanitarian aid. This 'linkage' introduces political, perhaps even military, objectives into the humanitarian mission (Thornberry, 1996).

In March 1995, the United Nations High Commissioner for Refugees (UNHCR) fought political blackmail by using its own political blackmail to solve the Bihac Blockade in Bosnia. Serbs blocking aid convoys to Moslem areas were informed that as long as the blockade continued, aid to a Serbian area (Krajina) would be suspended (ibid). The strategy highlights some of the incompatibilities of humanitarian missions in the midst of violence and political turmoil.

Today, television images of starving children and zealous church groups compete with financial analyses that paint a discouraging picture of the accomplishments of aid initiatives through the years. Part of the problem is a lack of cultural perspective and local knowledge. Descriptions of humanitarian efforts around the world describe lofty goals such as freedom from hunger, building schools, digging wells and delivering medical care. Cynics point out that a rich country like America cannot even deliver food, education, clean water and medical care to all its own citizens.

Humanitarian assistance during crises is only one type of aid received by developing countries. People involved with these various missions learn a lot, but their insights may not be preserved to assist the next aid group. The population receiving assistance might never be asked to critique the effort. Failures may only be acknowledged when some group thinks it can remedy a situation, or when some other group seeks to discredit the attempt. The Citanduy irrigation project in Java, for example, involved the imposition of a new system of farming, and the creation of water-user associations that were supposed to keep the system functioning. However, the system was imposed on the people who were expected to maintain it, and results have fallen far short of expectations (AID, 1984).

Munificent Western populations, with a belief in quick fixes and the power of money, have tried unsuccessfully to impose a host of improvements on hundreds of countries. Perhaps it is easier to raise money for a very worthy and ambitious goal, such as eradicating malaria, than for a more modest goal, such as improving livestock in a specific location. Perhaps it is easier to raise money for people who are going over the edge of the cliff than for those barely hanging on. The two types of aid are linked on many levels, and share many of the same difficulties. Ignorance of cultural factors in both humanitarian aid and development assistance is a major stumbling block. The problem involves abrasions where the culture of those receiving aid and the culture of aid workers rub the wrong way. Good intentions are no substitute for an awareness that very different beliefs and values can make life meaningful.

Daniel Jordan Smith, author of *A Culture of Corruption: Everyday deception and popular discontent in Nigeria*, described the process of blending into the community he tried to help:

> In my experience in the Peace Corps it quickly became apparent that being an effective volunteer required a great effort to acquire a kind of cultural competence – epitomized by language fluency and eating and enjoying local cuisine, but encompassing a wide range of familiarity with and empathy regarding local traditions, practices and understandings. In addition, just getting to know people and becoming an accepted person in the community turned out to be simultaneously the most treasured aspect of my Peace Corps experience and the crucial factor in being able to do some effective work.
> www.peacecorpswriters.org (interview with Daniel Jordan Smith conducted by John Coyne, 2008)

'Going native' in a developing country to collect local knowledge can be a long and dangerous process. George Packer wrote of his difficulties as a Peace Corps teacher in Togo where he lived with the village chief, in mutual mistrust (Packer, 1988). The cultural anthropologist's method of acquiring local knowledge is an impractical approach for groups seeking to give economic development assistance, much less humanitarian aid workers responding to a disaster. Disaster strikes and aid organizations spring to action. There is no time to study local villages, learn dialects and establish rapport. An approved plan of action is pulled from the file cabinet and is implemented as quickly as possible.

The challenge is to find a practical way of tapping into local knowledge that is relevant to designing successful projects. Perhaps the best way is to start on a very small scale, with projects that address a relatively obvious local need, using local resources. Building on success is easier than building on failure, and success stories spread quickly. For example, the Peace Corps's Africa Rural Connect contest is full of ideas for small projects geared toward specific locations. One contestant proposed 'Strengthening Food Security and Economic Status among Widows and Orphans in Rachuonyo District, Nyanza Province in Kenya through Crossbreed Chicken Farming Project'. This contestant states that the 'indigenous chickens' kept by rural households in Kenya yield comparatively little, in terms of meat and egg production, according to the contestant. More-valuable chickens would be better protected by a 'semi-free range system the contestant hopes that villagers will try. This low-risk experiment could yield valuable information about the impetus and the impediments for change, and open the door for local knowledge that might inform many future endeavors' (see www.arc.peacecorpsconnect.org/contest).

The World Bank is also beginning to invest in greater participation by the communities affected by projects. Regarding experiences in Honduras and Nicaragua, participants in community disaster management report that their 'main conclusion is that participatory risk management brings great benefits in terms of ownership and direct savings in losses from disasters. But community management is a challenge! While the problems vary from locale to locale and sustainability requires patience, great achievements are possible' (Solo *et al*, 2003). The same lessons are being learned in the Philippines: 'the participatory approach for scenario building, risk assessment and action planning can also generate the much needed awareness on issues, and help to build ownership in the risk reduction process' (Bermas-Atrigenio, 2007: 19).

Communities already organized for risk management are likely to be easier to help when humanitarian aid is needed. Local participation also encourages communities to volunteer local knowledge that could be valuable on a number of different fronts. When international relief efforts failed to deliver food to victims of the 2010 Haitian earthquake, local peasant organizations took over and largely met with success (Bell, 2010). During the 2004 tsunami in the Indian Ocean, the residents of Simeulue evacuated 80,500 people up into the hills based on local knowledge about animal behaviour. Only seven people died on Simeulue Island, while the death toll in the rest of Indonesia numbered over 163,700 (Bermas-Atrigenio 2007: 57). The local approach has also gained new respect in the United States, where neighbourhood associations emerged after Hurricane Katrina as the first line of defence in disaster preparedness, evacuation and recovery (Winkler-Schmit, 2008).

Humanitarian aid has failed to reach its potential for relieving human suffering because all too often problems are poorly articulated and solutions are imposed without regard to the cultural imperatives of people in need. The best chance for success, both at home and abroad, lies in a better evaluation of the cultural status quo. Once the complexity of a situation is grasped, then workable solutions and realistic goals can be negotiated.

References

Agency for International Development (AID) (1984) Citanduy I – An illustration of the pitfalls of water and irrigation projects in Southeast Asia, AID, Washington DC, 16 March

Al-Araji, Adnan (2001) Iraqi doctors appeal for help from doctors in other countries, *British Medical Journal*, **323**, 7 July, Letters, p 53

Beamon, Benita M (2006) *Humanitarian relief chains: issues and challenges*, Proceedings of the 34th International Conference on Computers and Industrial Engineering (eds Y Dessouky and MH Patel), **51**(30), pp 77–82

Bell, Beverly (2010) Haitian peasant groups offer humanitarian aid. *Truthout*, Monday, 10 March; available at: http://www.truth-out.org/ haitian-peasant-groups-offer-humanitarian-aid57285

Bennett, J (2003) Food aid logistics and the Southern African emergency, *Forced Migration Review*, **18** (September), pp 28–31

Bermas-Atrigenio, Nancy (2007) Engaging local governments in disaster risk reduction, *Tropical Coasts*, **14**(2) p 19

Bovard, James (1986) The continuing failure of foreign aid, *Cato Policy Analysis* **65** (January); available at: http://www.cato.org/pub_display.php?pub_id=931

Brooten, Lisa B (2003) *Global communications, local conceptions: human rights and the politics of communication among the Burmese opposition-in-exile*, Doctoral dissertation, College of Communications, Ohio University, March, pp 161–66

Chamlee-Wright, Emily (2007) The long road back: signal noise in the post-Katrina context, *The Independent Review*, **12**(2), pp 235–59

Coyne, John (2008) Interview with Daniel Jordan Smith, Peace Corps Writers; transcript available at: http://www.peacecorpswriters.org/pages/2007/0701/ prntvrs701/pv701talk-djsmith.html

Dowty, Rachel A and Wallace, William A (2010) Implications of organizational culture for supply chain disruption and restoration, *International Journal of Production Economics*, **126**(1), pp 57–65

Enarson, Elaine (2007) Identifying and addressing social vulnerabilities, Chapter 13 in *Emergency Management: Principles and practice for local government* (eds) William L Waugh Jr and Kathleen Tierney, International City/county Management Associate, Washington DC, pp 257–79

Falasca, Mauro, Zobel, Christopher W and Fetter, Gary M (2009) *An optimization model for humanitarian relief volunteer management*, Proceedings of the 6th International ISCRAM Conference, (eds) J Landgren and S Jul, Gothenburg, Sweden, May

Fritz Institute (2006) *Hurricane Katrina: perceptions of the affected*, Final Report; available at: http://www.fritzinstitute.org/PDFs/findings/HurricaneKatrina_ Perceptions.pdf

Gudykunst, WB (1991) *Bridging Differences: Effective intergroup communication*, Sage Publications, Thousand Oaks, CA

Hall, ET (1959) *The Silent Language*, Doubleday, New York, p 47

Hilhorst, Dorothea and Schmiemann, Nadja (2002) Humanitarian principles and organizational culture: everyday practice in Médecins Sans Frontiéres-Holland, *Development in Practice*, **12**(3&4), pp 490–500

Hinson, David R (1998) *US military interaction with humanitarian assistance organizations during small-scale contingencies*, Report, April, US Air Force, Air Command and Staff College, Montgomery, AL

Lebel, Louis , Khrutmuang, Supaporn and Manuta, Jesse (2006) Tales from the margins: small fishers in post-tsunami Thailand, *Disaster Prevention and Management*, **15**(1), pp 124–34

Mbohwa, Charles (2008) *Identifying challenges and collaboration areas in humanitarian logistics: a Southern African perspective*, Paper presented at the Rockefeller Foundation Bellagio Center Conference, Bellagio, Lake Como, Italy, 5–9 May; available at: http://hlogistics.som.umass.edu/

McClintock, Andrew (2009) The logistics of humanitarian emergencies: notes from the field, *Journal of Contingencies and Crisis Management*, **17**(4), pp 295–302

Mohmand, Hashem and Jalalzai, Freshta (2008) Mistakes by Afghan translators endanger lives, hamper antiterrorism effort, *Radio Free Europe,* 2 September

Moyo, Dambisa (2009) *Dead Aid: Why aid is not working and how there is another way for Africa*, Farrar, Straus and Giroux, New York

Norrick, NR (1991) On the organization of corrective exchanges in conversation, *Journal of Pragmatics*, **16**, pp 59–83

Packer, George (1988) *The Village of Waiting*, Vintage Books, New York

Petchesky, Rosalind P and Laurie, Melissa (2007) *Gender, health and human rights in sites of political exclusion*, Background Paper prepared for the Women and Gender Equity Knowledge Network of the World Health Organization Commission on Social Determinants of Health, July, 62 pp; available at: http:// www.who.int/social_determinants/resources/gender_health_human_rights_ wgkn_2007.pdf

Phillips, Brenda (1993) Cultural diversity in disasters: sheltering, housing, and long term recovery, *International Journal of Mass Emergencies and Disasters*, **11**(1), pp 99–110

Polgreen, Lydia (2007) Aid to Darfur imperiled, officials say, *New York Times*, 27 March

Rao, XiuHui Rebecca (2007) *Issues and challenges of humanitarian logistics in China*, MSc Operations Management Dissertation, University of Nottingham, 103 pp

Solo, Tova Maria, Godinot, Myriam and Velasco, Osmar (2003) Community participation in disaster management: reflections on recent experiences in Honduras and Nicaragua, in *Thinking Out Loud IV: Innovative case studies on participatory instruments*, Spring, Latin America and the Caribbean Region Civil Society Team: The World Bank, available at: http://www.worldbank.org/ socialaccountability_sourcebook/Regional%20database/Case%20studies/Latin%20 America%20&%20Caribbean/TOL-IV.pdf

Tatham, Peter and Kovács, Gyöngyi (2010) The application of 'swift trust' to humanitarian logistics, *International Journal of Production Economics*, **126**(1), pp 35–45

Thomas, Anisya (2005) Improving aid effectiveness: two studies suggest solutions, *UN Chronicle* **4**, pp 61–63 ; available at: http://www.fritzinstitute.org/PDFs/InTheNews/2006/UNChron_0206.pdf

Thomas, Anisya and Ramalingam, Vimala (2005) Response effectiveness: views of the affected population, *Forced Migration Review*, Special Issue (July), pp 46–47

Thompson, Michael, Ellis, Richard and Wildavsky, Aaron (1990) *Cultural Theory*, Westview Press, Boulder, CA

Thornberry, Cedric (1996) Peacekeepers, humanitarian aid, and civil conflicts, in *After Rwanda: The coordination of United Nations humanitarian assistance* (eds) Jim Whitman and David Pocock, Palgrave Macmillan, Hampshire

Tsurikov, Alexi (1971) Interview conducted by Alice Hicks, Russian Language (research report), State University of New York (SUNY) at Plattsburgh, Faculty Experience

United States Office of the Inspector General (OIG) (2007) Federal Emergency Management Agency's Volunteer Service Program Following Hurricane Katrina, US Department of Homeland Security, June

Willitts-King, Barnaby and Harvey, Paul (2005) *Managing the risks of corruption in humanitarian relief operations*, Final Report, Humanitarian Policy Group, Overseas Development Institute, Study conducted for the UK Department for International Development, March, 64 pp

Winkler-Smith, David (2008) Know thy neighbor, *BestofNewOrleans.com News by Gambit Weekly*, September; available at: http://bestofneworleans.com/gyrobase/Content?imageIndex=3&oid=oid%3A43577

Wrong, Michela (2009) *It's Our Turn To Eat: The story of a Kenyan whistle blower*, Harper Collins, New York

Yousef, FS (1978) Communication patterns: some aspects of nonverbal behavior in intercultural communication, in *Interethnic Communication* (ed) JJ Gumperz, Southern Anthropological Society, pp 49–62

12
The impossible interface?
Combining humanitarian logistics and military supply capabilities

JERSEY SEIPEL

Abstract

In recent years, especially since the Boxing Day tsunami of 2004, interactions and cooperation between military forces and humanitarian aid agencies in the fields of logistics and supply chain management have experienced a slow but steady rise.

The combination of humanitarian assistance and military support is not limited to such unexpected disasters as the 2004 SE Asia tsunami, Kashmir earthquake and Hurricane Katrina (both in 2005) and the Haiti earthquake in 2010, but has also included famine relief and the mitigation of slow-onset disasters such as the Sudan drought of 1992 and the Mozambique food crisis of 2002, as well as peacekeeping operations in the former Yugoslav republic (1992–95) and (to a limited degree) even joint operations in active war zones such as Afghanistan and Iraq.

Furthermore, there can be no doubt that the amalgamation of humanitarian logistics expertise and military capacities, often in the areas of transportation (especially air lift) and security, has helped to save lives and reduce human suffering. Why then, are these interactions not more common?

This chapter considers some of the factors influencing the cooperation, or lack thereof, between humanitarian aid agencies and armed forces and aims to provide an explanation for the absence of mutual support as well as some recommendations for donor agencies, armed forces and the humanitarian non-governmental organizations themselves.

Introduction

When Bernard Couchner and a small group of 'renegade' doctors from the Red Cross founded Médecins sans Frontières (MSF) in 1971, logistics was not at the forefront of their minds. Those were the days of the Biafra War, now a long-forgotten bloodbath in what was then still commonly regarded as the heart of darkness, a fever-ridden cesspit at the end of the world that very few knew anything about and – almost – nobody cared. For those French doctors and nurses the treatment of civilians caught between the front lines was the overriding priority; 'témoignage', the speaking out loud of abuse, rape and murder of innocents, a desperate shout to help the helpless; and drugs and medical supplies were something you begged, borrowed or scratched together from whatever could be found wherever. Antibiotics had to be bought from dubious sources, were donated by sympathetic embassy staff or the odd journalist passing through, and a (constantly interrupted) supply chain was managed by 'the donor community' of families, friends and contacts back home in Europe.

Today MSF is one of the largest and most respected international humanitarian aid agencies; a true 'global player' operating on an annual budget of over 600 million euros, with over 26,000 staff on the payroll and working simultaneously in more than 65 countries around the world. The organization received the Nobel Peace Price 1999 in recognition of its pioneering humanitarian work on several continents.

Its logistic departments are managed by dedicated and experienced professionals. Central warehouses together with pre-positioned units around the globe make it possible to respond to almost any humanitarian crisis within hours. Often credited with the invention of pre-packed, customs cleared, self-containing modules for field hospitals, water treatment and the containment of epidemic diseases, the MSF supply chain is among the most agile in the humanitarian aid scene and has been copied by various other non-governmental organizations (NGOs) over the years. It is characterized by standing agreements with a variety of suppliers and charter transportation agencies, as well as relatively sophisticated information technology (IT) and communication networks. All MSF's equipment is tested and standardized; ensuring that staff members, no matter if in Sierra Leone or Sri Lanka, know what to expect. This reflects MSF's commitment to provide regular training for field logisticians, as well as for logistic coordinators and procurement specialists at headquarter levels.

MSF is, of course, not the only NGO. Long and Wood (1995) counted over 100 major relief agencies worldwide, each with an annual budget over US $ 1 million; Cross (2003) saw over 1,500 international NGOs registered as observers with the UN, while according to Thomas and Kopczack (2005) the top 10 aid agencies had a combined budget of more than US $ 14 billion in 2004. Although an absolute figure is not available, it was estimated in 2000 that there were over 30,000 NGOs operating worldwide (Roberts, 2001: 73) ranging from large and very influential internati[...] aid organizations such as MSF, Oxfam and Save the Chil[...] groups who 'send a cow' (Cross 2003) into a disaster are[...]

Apart from local, national and international NGOs, [...] influence the field of humanitarian assistance and, with[...] the most important organizations is the International R[...] Crescent Movement.

With national societies in over 180 nations and an annual budget exceeding $ 1 billion, 'the Red Cross', as it is commonly known, fields fleets of trucks and aircraft, operates complex supply chains and employs several thousand staff in logistics, supply chain and procurement roles worldwide.

Meanwhile, the United Nations' World Food Programme (WFP) is 'the largest humanitarian logistics operator by far. On any day it has 40 ships on the seas, 20 planes in the air, 1,000 trucks on the ground' (Van Wassenhove, 2006: 488). In addition to its large array of physical assets, transport and storage capacity, WFP is also the principal agency for the United Nations in its role as the lead for the logistics cluster – an approach that aims to achieve improved effectiveness and efficiency across the UN 'family' and beyond.

Humanitarian and military logistics

Humanitarian logistics can be defined as:

> the process of planning, implementing and controlling the efficient, cost-effective flow and storage of goods and materials, as well as related information, from the point of origin to the point of consumption for the purpose of alleviating the suffering of vulnerable people. The function encompasses a range of activities, including preparedness, planning, procurement, transport, warehousing, tracking and tracing and customs clearance. (Thomas and Kopczak, 2005: 2)

Humanitarian supply chain managers such as the heads of logistic departments at several international NGOs (Gustavsson, 2003; Rickard, 2003; Chaikin, 2003), as well as academics and researchers (Van Wassenhove, 2006; Pettit and Beresford, 2005; Beamon and Kotleba, 2006; Kovács and Spens, 2007), have argued over a number of years for improvements in specialized logistics training, better use of technology, increased inter-organizational cooperation, development of specific IT solutions and integrated logistics systems, as well as more coordination of activities. But, as one observer remarked: 'in many cases, aid organisation logistical structures are still in their infancy' and 'logistics activities have, up until recently, been undertaken in a fragmented and sub-optimised manner and based upon outdated logistics philosophies' (Antill, 2001).

Furthermore, the director in charge of the emergency response and disaster mitigation unit of an international NGO concluded that:

> Very little capital (from any source) has been invested in the development and implementation of modern management information systems (MIS), information technology (IT) or logistics systems. Most NGOs lack modern 'systems capacity' in just about any category. Most NGOs have indeed also undervalued the role of logistics, supply chain management and integrated systems support. (Gustavsson, 2003: 7)

All humanitarian aid organizations are, to varying degrees, limited by the funding available to them (be it from private donors, governments or multinational bodies such as the UN or the European Community), and investment in solid logistics capabilities is, in many cases, still seen to be a relatively low priority even though efficient logistics and supply chain management is emerging as not only necessary, but absolutely crucial, for the success of humanitarian aid operations.

This relatively depressing picture of the perceived importance of logistics can usefully be compared to that in the military field where commanders have long understood its vital importance in underpinning the operational capabilities of their forces and, hence, the extent that supply chains influence the capacity to conduct and sustain warfare. Indeed, the word 'logistics' is thought by many to be derived from the French term 'logistique' that was used by military theorists during the 1800s to describe the provisioning of an army and the movement of required material (Thompson, 1996; Sinclair, 1996; Roth, 1999; Prebilic, 2006).

Thus, unlike many humanitarian NGOs, modern Western armies integrate supply chain preparations from the very first stage of their operational planning and will not (and, in reality, can not) deploy without solid logistics backup. As a result, the military asset base includes large numbers of trained specialist personnel; an air, sea road (and, to a limited extent, rail) transportation capacity on a scale that no aid agency can match; associated loading/unloading equipment; mobile storage and repair facilities; and sophisticated communications systems as well as the technicians to maintain all of this.

With these introductory thoughts in mind, and the clear potential benefit that interaction might bring, the question raised in the abstract of this paper is reiterated – why is the engagement between militaries and aid agencies not much more common?

Humanitarian principles and ideology

While aid agencies are sometimes specified according to their main field of activity (such as medical, water and sanitation, or food distribution), academics have recently tried to group these organizations also according to their ideological roots (Tomasini and Van Wassenhove, 2009). This approach distinguishes between faith-based organizations, 'Dunanists' and 'Wilsonians'. Leaving faith-based organizations to one side for the moment, a brief exploration of the other two concepts might be useful as it is a clear pointer that will help determine the likelihood of a specific organization's willingness to cooperate with armed forces in a joint supply chain operation during a humanitarian crisis.

Dunanists encompass humanitarian organizations for which the principles and guidelines of Jean Henri Dunant (the founder of the Red Cross movement in the 19th century) have overriding priority. Apart from the Federation and the Committee of the Red Cross and Red Crescent, this group also includes MSF, Action against Hunger, Oxfam and Save the Children.

By contrast, Tomasini and Van Wassenhove (2009: 24f) argue that Wilsonians (so-named after the US American President Woodrow Wilson) try to 'project US values and influence as a force for good in the world', leading to 'a built-in conflict of interest depending on how much their ideologies influence their agenda'.

That said, all humanitarian aid organizations follow, to varying degrees, four basic principles of action: humanity, neutrality, independence and impartiality.

- Humanity aims to deliver assistance without discrimination.
- Neutrality refers to the provision of aid without taking sides in a conflict.
- Impartiality implies that action is based on needs alone.
- Independence serves to separate the distribution of aid from political, economical, military or other objectives.

Smith (2007) called these principles the basic 'rules of engagement' for NGOs, providing them with a mandate and framework of references under which to operate, as well as influencing the degree of cooperation with other actors such as governments, military organizations or religious institutions.

However, during the last decade there has been increasing pressure and expectations on international NGOs to cooperate with the military emanating from multinational donor coordination agencies such as ECHO (the European Community's Humanitarian Aid Office) and the United Nation's OCHA (Office for the Coordination of Humanitarian Affairs). Indeed, arguably, much of the slow growth in 'joint operations' between humanitarian NGOs and military organizations can be attributed to this pressure, rather than to a genuine recognition by aid organizations of the benefits of cooperation.

Thus, while there is increasing pressure to cooperate more closely with military forces, humanitarian aid organizations fear most of all the loss of neutrality, impartiality and independence that they believe would result from being associated with Western military units and their associated political agenda. For example, Pettit and Beresford (2005: 320) observed that:

> the involvement of the military in the provision of humanitarian aid (HA) is seen by many NGOs as being likely to compromise their neutrality.

As convincing demonstrations of neutrality, impartiality and independence from government agendas are exactly the requirements that enable humanitarian aid agencies to achieve access and assistance to vulnerable populations in the first place, the loss of these attributes strips away the only protection humanitarian aid workers have in, above all, zones of armed conflict.

In order to fulfil their mission, especially in war zones, humanitarian NGOs need to be perceived by all factions involved in an armed struggle to be neutral and not taking sides in a conflict.

Yet by becoming associated with peacekeeping forces and Western military organizations through cooperation in humanitarian aid projects, the four fundamental principles of humanitarian assistance seem to become meaningless. This point is reinforced by General Tim Cross (2003: 204) who, writing about his experiences in Kosovo, commented that:

> State focused, with legitimacy coming from the state, the military are, by definition, political servants and are neither neutral, impartial, or independent.

A similar point is made by Harmer (2008: 528) who suggested that:

> Concerned with overly close association with political and military objectives, humanitarians argue that integrated mission structures threaten to undermine the neutrality and independence of humanitarian action by creating the perception (and possibly constructing a reality) that humanitarian efforts are being subordinated to the political and security goals of UN missions.

Furthermore, Cross (2003: 214) also suggests that:

> The NGO community is not only ignorant of the military but have ingrained suspicions – usually seeing the humanitarian world as their province, an area where only they have the necessary experience to make a difference; they too often regard the military as amateurish and even dangerously incompetent.

From all the above, it should be clear that Dunanists (as well as Wilsonians and faith-based organizations), struggle with balancing their mandate to, on the one hand, assist the victims of disasters and warfare as effectively and efficiently as possible (for example by using military airlift capacity to reach an area of humanitarian operations that might otherwise not be easily accessible), and on the other with their 'rules of engagement' based on the ultimate principles of humanitarian assistance as their principal raison d'être.

A strategic-level decision

In principal, the decision of an international humanitarian aid agency to cooperate or not with military forces will be made by a board of directors, at headquarters far removed from 'ground zero'. Such decision makers, typically with backgrounds in medicine, social science, international law or development studies and often with many years of previous experience as a 'head of mission' or 'country manager', are usually elected by a general assembly composed of all members of the organization in a process of grass-roots democracy. Significantly absent from the major humanitarian aid agencies and international NGOs are directors with a previous service career in the armed forces... as well as logisticians and supply chain managers. Therefore, balancing issues such as the impact on aid appeals, donor expectations, political circumstances and the history and mission of their own organization, the board will make a decision if, where, when and how they will cooperate with a particular country's armed forces.

For military commanders in-country it is important to understand that a Western international NGO's decision to cooperate or not does not rest with the head of mission in the country where the humanitarian crisis is taking place. This is true even though, unlike their military counterparts, the leaders of humanitarian missions are usually given much more operational autonomy over how to achieve their assignment objectives. Rather, such decisions are very much the province of the board of directors (or their equivalent) based in the HQ away from the immediate pressures of the disaster/emergency.

The implication of this is that attempts to achieve policy changes (be this by donors or military organizations), will need to be directed at the strategic decision-making level of humanitarian aid organizations, not their tactical or operational representatives.

It should also be understood that such policy-based decisions are fluid and constantly debated within humanitarian aid organizations. Thus, a seemingly minor change or re-shuffling within the board of directors can sometimes lead to dramatic changes in policies regarding the cooperation (or lack thereof) with the military. While the overall direction is likely to be determined by the broader history of the organization and its Dunanist or Wilsonian roots, the reality is that decisions regarding humanitarian–military joint operations during a specific crisis are often based on previous experience with armed forces during a comparable situation as well as the impact of the disaster or complex emergency itself.

The joint logistics and supply chain interface: function defines form?

Assuming that a humanitarian aid NGO is indeed willing to cooperate with the military, what form is the logistic and supply chain interface between the two parties likely to take?

Pettit and Beresford (2005: 314) concluded that this very much depends on the specific type of crisis-scenario the two actors will face:

> The nature of a particular disaster or emergency largely determines the form of the response and the mix of military and non-military resource allocation.

With this in mind, five broad types of operation can be distinguished: rapid-onset natural disasters; slow-onset natural disasters and famine relief; development programmes; peacekeeping missions; and active war zones; each of which will be briefly discussed.

Natural disasters

The term rapid-onset natural disaster encompasses phenomena such as floods, earthquakes, volcano eruptions, large-scale fires, storms, tsunamis and avalanches. These catastrophic events usually take place suddenly and with little warning and, as a result, the affected population will often be forced to leave the disaster area in great haste and with few possessions. Infrastructure, electricity supply and telecommunication networks will be severely damaged, and area-access restricted by obstacles.

The first response to such emergencies after an initial assessment typically consists of the installation of reception areas for displaced people in a safe zone, screening and registering of survivors, provision of first aid and medical support, shelter, food rations, potable water and sanitary installations.

In this regard, a United Nations Disaster Assessment and Coordination (2006: 372) staff field manual states that:

> The logistical responses in an emergency may be divided into providing for limited needs, such as providing critical medical items, communications equipment, repair items for water supply, sanitation, electrical power, etc., and moving bulk commodities, such as food and shelter or even peoples themselves. It is important to bear in mind that there are a number of other factors that pose constrains on logistics, such as pre-existing logistics infrastructure, political factors, the sheer number of humanitarian actors, the damage caused by the disaster, and sometimes the security environment.

It will be readily appreciated that time is the most critical factor under these circumstances and, in order to establish a supply chain for humanitarian aid as quickly as possible, good communications are a must. As Long and Wood (1995: 216) noted:

> Communications and information systems are of critical importance in controlling the relief operation, especially in emergency situations.

And the director of an emergency response unit agreed that:

> Communication systems are not a core strength for the humanitarian community yet are a critical part of humanitarian operations. In crisis situations, communication… is vital. (Gustavsson, 2003: 7)

As discussed in Chapter 4 of this book, the dependence on real-time communications and data transfer has become even more important with the recent introduction of specialized software for humanitarian supply chain management, including track-and-trace capabilities for relief commodities from suppliers all the way to the victims of a disaster. Examples of such specialized IT platforms currently include the Humanitarian Logistics Software (HELIOS/HLS) developed by the San Francisco-based Fritz Institute, which has been implemented by the International Federation of the Red Cross, the United Nations Logistics Support System (LSS), Compass – a commodity-tracking system used by the World Food Programme, Logistix 7.08 – a fourth generation supply chain software developed in-house by MSF, and SUMA (Supply Management) – a regional Latin American platform supported by the World Health Organization.

As previously mentioned, a number of international NGOs specialize in responding to short-notice crises and have rapid-deployment teams, pre-packed emergency kits in regional warehouses, communications equipment such as satellite telephones and stand-by transport arrangements with air-charter providers available. They are able to mobilize quickly and deploy to any disaster area worldwide within 48 to 72 hours (Chaikin, 2003), but often face the obstacle of the 'last mile problem' (Gustavsson, 2003; Kovács and Spens, 2007) as experience has shown that many areas where parts of the affected population shelter might initially not be accessible, except by helicopter. Similarly, damage to infrastructure such as airports, harbours, roads and bridges might well prevent the delivery of aid from the nearest storage area to the final distribution points, as was clearly the case in the 2010 Haiti earthquake.

Additionally, national 'chapters' of aid organizations (such as the national Red Cross/Red Crescent society) or other NGOs are likely to be affected by the disaster itself and are, initially, unable to operate at full capacity.

Under such conditions national governments often tend to mobilize their armed forces to assist. Equipped with assets such as transport aeroplanes, helicopters, communications equipment, trucks and heavy construction equipment (eg bulldozers and cranes), as well as the personnel trained to operate and repair them, modern armies have successfully repaired infrastructure and re-opened access to disaster areas. Examples include the tsunami on Boxing Day 2004, Hurricane Katrina in August 2005 and the earthquake in Kashmir in October 2005.

Thus, as noted by Cuny (1989: 5):

Civilian authorities turn to the military for help in humanitarian operations for several reasons, amongst which the most obvious may be their physical assets. The military is often regarded as a cornucopia of assistance. Amongst the most sought-after assets are transport (land, sea and air); fuel; communications; commodities including food, building supplies and medicines; tools and equipment; manpower; technical assistance (especially logistics and communications) and facilities.

Under the typical scenario outlined above, it is highly likely that there will be relatively few issues of principal between humanitarian NGOs and military organizations, with the result that logistics and engineering staff from both communities will work side-by-side.

This kind of cooperation is also likely to be less of an issue for national NGOs who wish to coordinate their emergency supply chain with the national military, as staff of both such organizations will already share the same language and cultural background. As an example, Oxfam Australia have developed close ties with the Australian Defence Force in respect of the transport of emergency relief kits to the Pacific islands in the event of a natural disaster there. Similarly, Wilsonian US-American NGOs such as CARE and IRC, who accept a majority of their funding from government sources (Lischer, 2007) seem to welcome cooperation with the US Army in the case of natural disasters.

On the other hand, although some international NGOs tend to accept a limited degree of cooperation with the armed forces under these circumstances – as long as the same forces were not engaged in (civil-) warfare or the suppression of humanitarian rights before the catastrophe – others reject such proposals outright. NGOs in the latter camp fear that the negative impact of even a limited affiliation with any military organization will far outweigh the short-term benefits of joint operations. This position is mainly shared among the largest and most influential western NGOs, such as MSF, Oxfam and Save the Children.

Interestingly, these same organizations are also the ones that currently have the most sophisticated humanitarian logistics systems in place and provide ongoing training for their supply chain staff. It seems that, as a rule of thumb, the more comfortable a Western humanitarian aid agency feels about the reliability of its private funding sources, as well as its logistics and supply chain capabilities, the less likely it will be to cooperate with military organizations.

Such large international NGOs often have sufficient funds available to be able to, for example, charter commercial aircraft rather than opting to use military airlift capacities until such time as UN transport assets (or organizations such as AirServ or Aviation sans Frontières that specialise in provision of air transport for other NGOs) become available. That said, a remarkable exception occurred in the immediate aftermath of the Kashmir earthquake 2005 when, for a short time, MSF accepted US Army military airlift capacity to drop emergency response personnel and supplies by helicopter. This decision was, however, hotly debated in MSF circles and it seems unlikely that it will be accepted as a precedent for further cooperation.

Famine relief

Whereas sudden-onset natural disasters can be typified by their unexpected nature, famines, and especially environmental famines (in contrast to political famines where the withholding of food serves as a weapon), tend to be easier to predict. It follows that the preparation and response time available to the humanitarian community is much longer. Furthermore, with satellite imagery and a wide range of environmental data sources at their disposal, organizations such as WFP are nowadays often able to predict areas of famine two to three months in advance and act accordingly. On the other hand, the prescient observation by Long and Wood (1995: 217) that 'Crop shortfalls can be predicted with some accuracy, although whether the area's political and economic system can, and will, function to address the problem is a different question' remains as valid as when stated over a decade ago.

It also follows that with less time pressure on aid agencies to react to a famine, the potential for military involvement in the relief effort depends largely on the political situation in the larger geographical area. Thus, in collaboration with WFP and some international NGOs, armed forces have been deployed in the past to assist with the air transportation of food and provision of security for warehouses and storage areas. Examples include Somalia, Eritrea and Sudan, where the deployment of (Western) military organizations was largely based on a hope of 'bringing stability to an unstable region'. However, experience has since shown that not only was this optimism largely misplaced, but also that the utilization of military assets alone does not, of itself, lead to success:

> For example, a number of specialists have pointed out that the use of military aircraft to deliver food in Sudan in 1985 delayed vital decisions on alternative methods and obscured the fact that there was no onward delivery system from the airports out to the rural population. (Cuny, 1989: 3)

Thus, whereas purely environmental famine relief operations by humanitarian actors such as took place in Mozambique in 1992 have a relatively good chance of success, when the disaster is aggravated by political and military considerations, the outcome is less certain. For example, South Sudan has seen the intersection of a political famine, peacekeeping operations, and the participation of outside military forces in the relief effort. Consequently the humanitarian dilemma such an armed intervention poses for international NGOs, increases.

Development programmes

This type of humanitarian aid programme is very different from natural disasters. Two main factors that are prevalent in the aftermath of a natural disaster, namely time pressure and large-scale population movements, are absent in development programmes – albeit some degradation of the infrastructure might be present. Also, development programmes normally take place in a relatively secure environment with few threats to aid agency staff. NGOs working in these kinds of projects tend to be on the ground for a considerable amount of time (often years or even decades) and, as a result, are able to develop close ties with their local staff, giving them an advantage in terms of language and cultural aspects. Typical activities include the rebuilding or rehabilitation of infrastructure like roads, bridges, schools, hospitals and water supplies, agriculture development projects, strengthening of public healthcare systems, and education programmes.

In short, with the absence of access restrictions, insecurity and time pressure, there are very few reasons for military forces to be involved in this type of project. Civilian contractors are better suited to provide transportation as well as logistic services and NGOs usually have enough time to set up and manage their humanitarian supply chains.

Peacekeeping operations

Peacekeeping operations, sometimes also called 'operations other then war' or 'peace support missions' by the British armed forces, 'complex contingency operations' or 'stability, security, transition and reconstruction operations' by the US military, and 'peace-building operations' by the Australian Defence Forces (Pettit and Beresford, 2005; Ellsworth, 2006; Smith, 2007) are very complex in nature and failure of the military forces assigned to this role can easily lead to tragedy, as the massacres in Rwanda in 1994 and Bosnia in 1995 have shown. NGO involvement in this type of mission often consists of the delivery of humanitarian aid to civilians caught in the conflict or displaced by fighting. Coordination of the relief effort is normally provided through a joint civilian–military agency, such as NATO's CIMIC (Civilian–Military Coordination), in association with UN OCHA staff.

Operational cooperation between NGOs and military peacekeeping forces is frequently centred on convoy protection and securing areas for NGOs to operate in (Gourlay, 2000). Providing transport, mainly by air and road; information about access restrictions and security threats such as landmines; infrastructure repair (especially of bridges); the set-up of refugee camps, including water distribution points and sanitation facilities; food distribution; and the provision of aerial photography are the main points of interface between peacekeepers and aid organizations (Cuny, 1989; Antill, 2001; Cross, 2003; Wieloch, 2003; Pettit and Beresford, 2005).

In terms of supply chain activities, the temporary storage and subsequent transport of relief items from forward bases to final distribution points often provides the link between humanitarian aid logisticians and uniformed transportation specialists. Nevertheless, there are also a number of reasons why some NGOs will not want to cooperate with the military in this type of operations, as Cross (2003) has shown.

In short, these can be summarized as: a loss of neutrality (and therefore an increased security threat), media profile and/or independence; military security paranoia hindering the two-way transfer of information; a certain obsession on the part of the armed forces with self-protection and exit strategies (as well as arriving too late and leaving too early); the subordination of the humanitarian task to the military mission; and, finally, a lack of understanding by the military of aid work as well as an over-inflated view of their own humanitarian capabilities.

Active war zones

Currently, Iraq and Afghanistan are prime examples of the almost total absence of cooperation between international NGOs and the armed forces of the Western coalition. The reason goes back to the four key NGO principles described above and, as a result, commentators such as Lischer (2007: 23) have observed that:

> military use of quasi-humanitarian 'hearts and minds' operations undermined security and alienated aid organizations.

Even the British NGO–Military Contact Group (2009: 5) concluded that in both countries:

> humanitarian action – saving and protecting the lives of civilians caught up in conflict – can and should be kept separate from the objectives of stabilisation operations.

Furthermore, the same organization (2009: 3) has admitted that:

> one person's stabilisation is another person's war.

Put simply, influential Western NGOs such as MSF, Oxfam and Save the Children have decided not to work together with Western coalition forces in these kinds of operation, as they feel that their humanitarian agenda is incompatible with such cooperation. Understandably, putting aside arguments of principle, security concerns for staff (both national and international) were paramount in this decision (Lischer, 2006; Harmer, 2008).

Thus, while willing to coordinate their humanitarian aid programmes through UN-OCHA to at least some degree, such international NGOs have strictly refused to participate in NATO's CIMIC (Civil–Military Cooperation) contact group. In this scenario, therefore, the opportunity for a successful cooperation between humanitarian and military personal regarding a joint logistic and supply chain interface must currently be rated as practically non-existent.

Recommendations

This chapter has provided a brief overview of the current position and potential areas of development in relation to combined operations of humanitarian aid logisticians and military supply chain specialists. In doing so, it has highlighted the relatively limited common ground, and offered a perspective on the strategic-level decision making processes within humanitarian aid organizations and NGOs. It has underlined the importance of the history, background and self-understanding of these actors in providing a framework of options. That said, the perspective adopted by a particular NGO is likely to reflect the specific nature of a disaster situation and its wider context.

With this in mind, and also in light of the opening remarks in this chapter that outlined the enormous potential contribution that military logistics organizations could bring to bear (in terms of their equipment, trained personnel and speed of response), a number of suggestions for improving the humanitarian/military interface are offered.

Recommendation for donor agencies

To the extent that an improved humanitarian/military interface is perceived to be beneficial from the perspective of those affected by a disaster or emergency, there would seem to be a strong case for donor organizations (such as ECHO) to provide special funding to humanitarian aid organizations who are prepared to interface their logistic operations with military supply chains.

This would help overcome one of the biggest current obstacles for cooperation, which is a lack of knowledge within humanitarian NGOs about procedures and operational flows inside military supply chains and vice versa. Thus such funds would enable improved communication and mutual understanding to be developed through the medium of conferences, coordination and joint training exercises, scenario planning and academic research. Obviously, this should take place prior to a disaster/emergency rather than in the frenetic aftermath, which is not the time at which to attempt to develop the required respect and appreciation of the other's point of view and underlying rationale.

Recommendation for humanitarian aid groups and NGOs

Given that many, particularly Western, military forces have an enviable reputation for providing efficient and effective logistic support, serious consideration should be given to the recruitment into NGOs of former military specialists as logistic coordinators and trainers where they can bring their undoubted expertise of managing what are often equally ad hoc supply networks to bear. They would also be in a position to explain how such military supply chains work, their strengths and weaknesses and the most appropriate means of interfacing with them.

Recommendation for military organizations

Self-evidently, the military should attempt to follow the reverse prescription to that outlined above and establish prior contact and obtain information about humanitarian logistics operations and supply chains, especially in the immediate emergency phase after a large-scale sudden-onset natural disaster.

Rightly or wrongly, military supply chains have a reputation for being inflexible and process-driven; however, the perceived wisdom from the NGO community is that there is a huge benefit in operating as flexibly as possible within the overall organizational mandate. Thus, attempts to shoehorn NGOs into a pre-existing military logistic framework or approach are likely to be rebuffed and fail. So, military logistic organizations must learn to be flexible in such disaster/emergency responses and embrace the unexpected wholeheartedly, keeping the fate of the end-beneficiaries constantly in mind.

It is also important to appreciate that there is a cost to developing and maintaining the interface with humanitarian organizations. This will almost certainly require additional resources and specialist knowledge.

Conclusion

The four principles of humanity, neutrality, impartiality and independence are absolutely fundamental for the self-definition of humanitarian aid agencies. They form the core of their value systems as well as an important part of their raison d'être. On the face of it, therefore, the options for cooperation with military forces seem, at best, very limited, if not to say impossible. Ironically, those INGOs that are currently best positioned to cooperate in terms of advanced logistics and supply chain capabilities are also the ones that are most 'humanitarian' and therefore often exclude such cooperation on fundamental principles.

Thus, until and unless there is a further significant shift in thinking within such organizations, academics as well as military and political leaders would be well advised not to invest too much hope on the viability, as well as the sustainability, of a fully integrated logistics and supply chain interface between military organizations and humanitarian NGOs.

That said, the establishment of an effective humanitarian/military logistics interface is most likely to take place in the emergency phase following a sudden-onset, large-scale, high-impact natural (or technological) disaster as it is on such occasions that the time imperative clearly underpins the enormous potential benefit inherent in military supply chains and their associated equipment and personnel. It follows that humanitarian aid agencies and NGOs that would be willing to enter a temporary supply chain partnership with armed forces should prepare for this scenario through, for example, prior discussion of roles and responsibilities, training exercises and scenario planning.

It may well be that, as a result of positive interactions in such a scenario, aid agencies may feel emboldened to develop a broader relationship that also spans some of the other types of disaster/emergency outlined above – and, in doing so, take positive steps to 'alleviate the suffering of vulnerable people' (Thomas and Kopczak, 2005: 2)

References

Antill, P (2001) *Military involvement in humanitarian aid operations*; Available at: http://www.historyofwar.org/articles/concepts_humanitarian.html

Beamon, BM and Kotleba, SA (2006) Inventory management support systems for emergency humanitarian relief operations in South Sudan, *International Journal of Logistics Management*, **17**(2), pp 187–212

Chaikin, D (2003) Towards improved logistics: challenges and questions for logisticians and managers, *Forced Migration Review*, **18**, p 10

Cross, T (2003) Military/NGO interaction, in *Emergency Relief Operations* (ed Kevin M Kahill), Fordham University Press, New York

Cuny, FC (1989) *Use of the military in humanitarian relief*, available at: http://www.pbs.org/wgbh/pages/frontline/shows/cuny/laptop/humanrelief.html

Ellsworth, JB (2006) SysAdmin: towards Barnett's stabilization and reconstruction force, *The Land Warfare Papers 57*, The Institute of Land Warfare, Arlington, VA

Gourlay, C (2000) Partners apart: managing civil–military co-operation in humanitarian interventions, *Disarmament Forum*, Peacekeeping: Evolution or Extinction? 3, pp 33–44

Gustanvsson, L (2003) Humanitarian Logistics: context and challenges, *Forced Migration Review*, **18**, pp 6–8

Harmer, A (2007) Integrated missions: a threat to humanitarian security?, *International Peacekeeping*, **15**(4), pp 528–39

Harmer, A (2008) 'Integrated Missions: A threat to Humanitarian Security?', *International Peacekeeping*, **15**(4), pp 528–39

Kovács, G and Spens, K (2007) Humanitarian logistics in disaster relief operations, *International Journal of Physical Distribution and Logistics Management*, 37 (2), pp 99–114

Lischer, SK (2007) Military intervention and the humanitarian 'force multiplier', *Global Governance*, 13(1), pp 99–118

Long, DC and Wood, DF (1995) The logistics of famine relief, *Journal of Business Logistics*, 16(1), pp 213–29

NGO–Military Contact Group (2009) *Stabilisation and civil-military relations in humanitarian response*, Conference Report, Foreign and Commonwealth Office, London

Pettit, S and Beresford, A (2005) Emergency relief logistics: an evaluation of military, non-military and composite response models, *International Journal of Logistics: research and applications*, 8(4), pp 313–31

Prebilic, V (2006) Theoretical aspects of military logistics, *Defence and Security Analysis*, 22(2), pp 159–77

Rickard, J (2003) A logisticians plea, *Forced Migration Review*, 18, 9

Roberts, A (2001) NGOs: new gods overseas', *The World in 2001*, The Economist Publications, London

Roth, JP (1999) *The Logistics of the Roman Army at War*, Columbia University Press, New York

Sinclair, J (1996) Logistics, Principles and Practice, in *Military Logistics: A primer on operational, strategic and support level logistics*, M Coles (ed), Australian Defence Studies Centre, Canberra

Smith, MG (2007) Civil–military interaction: building civil society during conflict, *Australian Journal of Multi-disciplinary Engineering*, 6(2), pp 225–36

Thomas, AS and Kopczak, L (2005) *From Logistics to Supply Chain Management*; available at: www.fritzinstitute.org/PDFs/WhitePaper/FromLogisticsto.pdf

Thompson, J (1996) Principles: the disciplines of war, in *Military Logistics: A primer on operational, strategic and support level logistics*, M Coles (ed), Australian Defence Studies Centre, Canberra

Tomasini, R and Van Wassenhove, LN (2009) *Humanitarian Logistics*, Palgrave Macmillan, New York

United Nations Disaster Assessment and Coordination (2006) *UNDAC Field Handbook*, Office for the Coordination of Humanitarian Affairs Field Coordination Support Unit, Geneva

Van Wassenhove, LN (2006) Humanitarian aid logistics: supply chain management in high gear, *Journal of the Operational Research Society*, 57, pp 475–89

Wieloch, R (2003) The humanitarian use of the military, *Forced Migration Review*, 18, pp 32–33

13
Disaster agencies and military forces
not such strange bedfellows after all!

TIM CROSS

British soldiers should be trained to rebuild war-torn countries and not just fight conflicts.
GENERAL SIR RICHARD DANNATT

Abstract

The end of the Cold War saw an alarming increase in the number of complex emergencies around the world, and both inter- and intra-state and ethnic conflicts have erupted on the fringes of Europe, and throughout the Middle East, Africa and Asia. Together with responses to natural disasters around the world, these conflicts have resulted in historically high levels of military commitment, and in military commanders working ever closer with non-military organizations and agencies. Operations in Macedonia/Albania/ Kosovo were somewhat of a turning point, with the UK's 101 Logistic Brigade leading the NATO/KFOR response to the humanitarian crisis that developed in the spring of 1999 in Macedonia, and in assisting the UN/ NGOs in Southern Albania and Kosovo, and NATO's AFOR doing the same in Northern Albania.

This chapter looks at the nature of the military and the non-military 'humanitarian' agencies – the NGOs, the international and governmental organizations – and the psychology that underlies the individuals who work in them; strengths and weaknesses are assessed, before some thoughts on the need to develop a 'joined-up' doctrine are outlined.

Significant differences do exist between the military and humanitarian agencies, both in structure and approach. These reflect their respective missions, expectations, values and perceptions, but above all their psyche and professional ethos. These differences will not disappear, but it is the author's contention that the resulting tensions should be viewed as creative, not disruptive. This is not, or at least should not be, a battle between 'bloody hands' and 'bleeding hearts'. Both sides have weaknesses, but both bring real strengths to bear. The trick is to understand and accept the differences, bring together the positive strengths and focus them on overcoming the crisis, be that man-made or natural. But there is work to be done, particularly in the areas of education, training and doctrine. All of the players must, together, develop a 'joined-up' doctrine to better orchestrate and execute more effective action, and from it develop an integrated training and exchange programme. Through understanding and patient leadership, strong relationships can and should be developed; working together, the two sides of the humanitarian coin have the potential to be a very strong and effective team.

Introduction

In July 2008 the Londonbased *Daily Telegraph* reported that General Sir Richard Dannatt, the then Chief of the General Staff, had used a Westminster speech to propose a shake-up of the way the British Army trained its personnel and ran its operations, putting more focus on reconstruction and development work. His suggestion came amid concern in Whitehall about the way that the British military mission in Afghanistan was fitting into the wider Western effort to develop that country's government and economy.

His speech included the suggestion that military training should be broadened so that service personnel spent time working for local councils to learn how to establish democratic governments in developing countries. The army must, he said, learn to deliver 'civil as well as military effects within areas as diverse as governance, town administration, finance and banking, law and order and sanitation'. To achieve that would mean creating 'permanent cadres of stabilization specialists', which would concentrate on training indigenous forces, and perhaps 'an officer spending a tour with indigenous forces, followed perhaps by an attachment to the Department for International Development (DFID) overseas, or a local council at home or a police force in Africa or elsewhere. The approach could also see British servicemen placed under the direct command of the Foreign Office or DfID.'

To the surprise of many his speech created hardly a stir. While the 8,000 British troops then deployed in Afghanistan included hundreds working on civilian projects as part of provincial reconstruction teams – with the inevitable frictions between the military, DfID and charitable groups – most commentators recognized that the boundaries between the military and non-military had long been blurred. The question was no longer whether the military should be involved in non-military activities, but how better they could do so. And that journey had started 20 years previously.

From cold to hot wars: the growth in humanitarian operations/complex emergencies

The end of the Cold War had seen an alarming increase in the number of complex emergencies around the world as intra-state and ethnic conflicts erupted on the fringes of Europe, and throughout Africa and Asia. Together with responses to natural disasters, these conflicts resulted in historically high levels of military commitment and, like it or like it not, military commanders having to work ever closer with non-military organizations and agencies.

By the mid-1990s the human cost of conflicts and disasters of one sort or another were overwhelming the world's ability to respond. Most of the dozens of conflicts around the world reflected the move away from both territorial disputes between states and wars of de-colonization, to what began to be called 'Wars of Identity'. While conflict has always been essentially tribal, increasingly individuals seemed to identify more with their ethnicity and perceived nationality than with their ruling governments; and many seemed prepared to fight for that identity. Sandwiched between the globe and the individual, the tribe or ethnic group loomed larger. The demise of the Soviet Union and with it, ironically, the relative safety of the Cold War, certainly liberated those who had previously been constrained by Super Power politics, but the result in many cases was catastrophic, with tens of millions becoming refugees and/or 'internally displaced people' (IDPs). Some conflicts, like those in Bosnia, were very apparent; but others, like that in Tajikistan, where the civil war resulted in an estimated 50,000 deaths, 500,000 economic émigrés and 600,000 IDPs, went on almost unnoticed.

Events over the last 10 years have hardly improved matters. Internal conflicts rumble on and, following on from 11 September 2001, large-scale military operations have raged in Iraq and Afghanistan. The percentage of civilian, as compared to military casualties has increased from around 1 in 20 (5 per cent) 100 years ago to probably 9 in every 10 (90 per cent) today, with uncounted millions of civilian lives being lost. Refugees are now pawns in intra-state conflicts, and women, children and the elderly are indiscriminately and deliberately targeted by 'rebel' movements as part of the asymmetric threat to unstable governments.

The turning point

The NATO/KFOR deployment to Macedonia/Albania/Kosovo, known in the UK as Operation AGRICOLA, was something of a defining moment in all of this. The UK's 101 Logistic Brigade led the KFOR response to the humanitarian crisis that developed in the spring of 1999 in Macedonia, assisting the UN/NGOs in Southern Albania and Kosovo. Alongside this was a purpose-built Albanian Force (AFOR), which deployed under the command of a UK General, John Reith, to help the Albanian government deal with the influx of refugees into Northern Albania. In building, and then running, major refugee camps across the region for weeks on end – filling a void which the IOs and NGOs were unable to fill – the deployment highlighted the significant differences in structure and approach that exist between the military and humanitarian agencies.

Those differences remain today; they reflect the respective missions, expectations, values and perceptions, but above all the psyche and professional ethos, of both sides in this debate. And these differences will not disappear. However, I have long argued that the tensions that result should be viewed as creative, not disruptive. This is not, or at least should not be, a battle between 'bloody hands' and 'bleeding hearts'. Both sides have weaknesses, but both bring real strengths to bear. The trick is to understand and accept the differences, bring together the positive strengths and focus them on overcoming the crisis, be that man made or natural.

The players and their roles

We should remember that tensions between the military and non-military players in what are now often called Complex Emergencies is hardly new. The ICRC was born in 1863 out of the Battle of Solferiono, the Save the Children Fund (SCF) in 1919 out of the fallout of the First World War, and OXFAM and the US Committee for Aid and Relief Everywhere (CARE) out of the Second World War in 1942 and 1945 respectively. To a large degree militarism and humanitarianism represent two sides of the same coin, and reflect mankind's inability to manage conflict peacefully. Ben Shephard, in his excellent book, *The Long Road Home – the Aftermath of the 2nd World War* (2010), lays out in graphic and painful detail the way that the Allies dealt with the problems of IDPs and refugees, along with the reconstruction, in post-1945 Europe. Even as the UN Relief and Rehabilitation

Administration (UNRRA) – established in November 1943 with a budget of US \$2 billion – attempted to deal with the enormous numbers of refugees and IDPs left scattered around Europe, there were enormous tensions between the various players. One of Ben's early comments in the book was that: 'the relationship which UNRRA most needed to resolve was that with the military'. It was painfully apparent that even though the Italian Campaign had taught the Allied Generals that dealing with the problems of civilians was an important part of modern warfare, such an understanding did not lead to a smooth relationship with those attempting to rebuild Europe. There is rarely anything new in this world!

There is a generally held view that in complex emergencies there should be a clear distinction between the military and the non-military domains, a view reinforced by the principles of International Humanitarian Law, which attempts to make a clear distinction between combatants and non-combatants, protecting the latter from armed attacks. Nonetheless, with military forces becoming increasingly involved in the provision of relief and services to the local population and the humanitarian community facing increased operational challenges as well as greater risks and threats in the field, various forms of civil–military cooperation/coordination for humanitarian operations have emerged over the last few years. This has inevitably led to an erosion of the separation between the humanitarian and the military space, blurring the lines between the two domains.

There are three primary humanitarian forces – the NGOs, the UN – which Kofi Annan came to personify perhaps more than any other official for generations – and the governmental agencies and international organizations (IOs), most of which have been born out of the liberal democracies of the northern hemisphere. NGOs exist primarily, if not solely, to provide relief from suffering and, in today's world, to try to bring about sustainable development, addressing the failures of governments and society as a whole. They are primarily non-profit organizations motivated by humanitarian and religious values, and are usually independent of government, UN and commercial sectors. Ranging in size from large international and trans-national organizations, to very small local groups who 'send a cow' to Africa or Asia, there has been an explosion in their numbers over the last 30 years. But although worldwide there are now over 1,500 international NGOs registered as 'observers' with the UN, of the hundreds in existence there remains a serious '1st XI', through which perhaps 75 per cent of all emergency aid flows. They are a powerful force in the world, in many cases providing the dynamics for change, and the revolution in communications technology and in networking has only served to strengthen them further, especially in the last five years.

These NGOs operate alongside, and often for, a wide range of governmental and international aid and relief agencies. The UN itself spawned a number in its early years, including the UNHCR and WFP, for although the UN Charter mentions the term NGO in Article 71 such organizations were then relatively few and far between – and they were certainly not the major players they are today. International and governmental aid agencies can be 'multilateral', like the UN or the World Bank, or 'bilateral' like the US Agency for International Development (USAID) or DFID; funded by taxpayers to the tune of billions of pounds per year, these agencies have changed the shape of the world, for good or ill.

My own experiences in this arena go back over 40 years, but the defining time for me was in the Balkans and Iraq. I did three tours in the Balkans in the mid-to-late1990s, the final one in Macedonia, Albania and Kosovo where I led the UK Logistic Brigade in the series of humanitarian and nation-building episodes referred to above – from building refugee camps to re-establishing the railway service, together with aspects of the medical and justice system. Kuwait and Iraq in 1990/91, and Iraq in 2002/03, were on a larger scale; and my Afghanistan experience is restricted to training and preparing troops from the Division I commanded to deploy there from 2004 to 2006 – troops from my Medical, Engineer, Communications and Logistic Brigades among others.

But these last 15 years in particular have convinced me that the question of whether or not the military should be involved in delivering aid is an idle one – by the very nature and scale of these emergencies the reality is that the military will almost always be needed. Whether it is major natural disasters such as those in Pakistan and Haiti, or man-made emergencies such as the Balkans, Iraq, Afghanistan – or even the recent BP oil spillage in the Gulf of Mexico – the military will almost inevitably be engaged in some form or other, so the question is therefore not 'if' but 'how' – how are they to engage, how do we manage the interfaces and the handovers; how do we better train and prepare?

I want to make four points and reach one conclusion.

The good, the bad and the ugly

First, I want to stress that there is no such thing as 'The Military' – any more than there is any such thing as 'The NGO', 'IO' or Government Agency. There are good and bad, effective and ineffective, efficient and inefficient. I would – perhaps unsurprisingly – argue that the British Army is a pretty good, effective and efficient army; although it certainly isn't perfect, the various deployments that we have been engaged in over the last 20 years – from the Balkans/Kosovo and Sierra Leone through to Iraq and Afghanistan – have taught us a great deal; and forced us to reach the sort of conclusions that Richard Dannatt laid out in the speech referred to in the *Telegraph* above.

Over that time I have worked with many other armies; some added real value, but others were certainly less professional and less effective, adding little or no value to what we had been trying to achieve. Beyond that, as we all know perfectly well, there are the various cut-throat, ruthless, crooked and amateur organizations out there who call themselves armies. They are effectively state-sponsored terrorists, and they are certainly not friendly forces in the context of this debate.

But in a similar vein, while I have also worked with many very capable and effective NGOs over the last 20 or so years, I have also worked with completely inefficient and ineffective ones, adding no value whatsoever. Well-meaning they may (or may not) have been, but they did little but stand in the way of progress, and they served those in need very poorly indeed.

It is also important to recognize that in all of this we are not talking about generic, impersonal bureaucracies, but people. All organizations, both military and non-military, are constituted by unique, individual people. Moulded in the womb, raised and nurtured by parents alongside siblings and peers, softened perhaps by family and friends but hardened and tempered by their environment and day-to-day life, through success and failure, rivalries and challenges, these individual people come together within organizations which themselves have identities. The UN agencies and the NGOs are not single organizations; they are a mix, in the same way that military forces around the world are a mix, of professionals and amateurs – again effective and non-effective, efficient and inefficient. In dealing with organizations we are inevitably dealing with their ethos and their psyche, and in order to understand them it seems to me that one must at least have an understanding of their nature, and the nature of the people within them – what drives them. Sun Tzu, some time between 500 and 300 BC in his book *The Art of War*, wrote 'If you know the enemy and know yourself, you need not fear the result of a hundred battles.' The military and non-military organizations are certainly not (or should not be) enemies – although it must be said that military commentators sometimes portray them as such – nonetheless, the principle holds true. To get the best results out of any relationship we must know both ourselves and those we work alongside. When we talk about this issue we do need to recognize that sweeping judgements and assertions are rarely – if ever – helpful!

My own experiences have led me to a few – not particularly unique – conclusions. First, those who work for the humanitarian organizations are suspicious, if not scornful, of governments and institutions representing governments, including the military – and, it has to be said, often with good cause! But their principles of independence, neutrality and impartiality are usually tempered with recognition that there is a 'bottom line'. As they face up to the conflicts between positive principles and negative imperatives – not to legitimize rebel movements, not to contribute to the war effort of either side, not to submit to government controls that interfere with their ability to fulfil their humanitarian mission – there is an understanding that the very process of fulfilling the humanitarian imperative can mean that both neutrality and impartiality are inevitably compromised, and that their involvement does influence a conflict; so their approach is often to 'minimize' rather than 'do no harm'.

In an effort to match their principles, many take real risks and face real hardships. They are prepared to work in dangerous areas and on both sides of a conflict, often moving between and across factional borders/boundaries to places where the cause may seem hopeless but where there is real need. Operating in areas where there may be no front lines, real security or protection, and where access is difficult, they are often vulnerable to warlords and bandits – and many become casualties in the conflict.

And they know their business. Drawn by the desire to alleviate suffering in the world, in the widest sense, and to make a real difference in their chosen area of concern, these organizations are usually committed for the long haul. Many have served in numerous countries/conflicts over many years, and they bring their considerable skills to bear effectively. Most specialize in particular areas of the business, and although they may not have all of the answers, they at least understand most of the questions. And because they are in it for the long term, and they know that they will have to run with any 'solutions'; so they work hard to get it right.

Knowing each other's organizations well, and often having strong individual personal relationships, the humanitarian community are usually pre-disposed to cooperate with one another. They network well. Most of the key NGOs are used to working with the UN. Multinational and multi-lingual organizations such as MSF, World Vision and OXFAM are truly worldwide, with well-established contacts, both between each other and into governments and civil structures. Given devolved responsibility from the home-based headquarters, the representatives on the ground operate under what the military would call 'Mission Command'; they have the authority to make decisions, and do so, being accountable to their donors and fellow workers.

Finally, and very importantly, the UN, NGOs and IOs are good at working with, if not manipulating, the media. With a bias towards drama, crisis and controversy there is a natural alliance. The media often accept the NGO/UN/IO perspective and quote it uncritically, allowing them to publicly voice their concerns and criticisms. And together they can effectively mobilize public opinion. Whatever the rights and wrongs of individual agencies they, together with the media, have become searchlights, illuminating and drawing attention to particular causes and conflicts, and influencing both the participants and the outside world community. Between them they are often the catalyst for a military deployment in the first place. The world is now so inter-dependent and so vulnerable to public opinion mobilized by these humanitarian 'lobbies' that, even where professional instinct and advice argues against intervention, Western governments in particular will often succumb. Global audiences, particularly those in the rich, liberal democracies, demand action of some sort – and humanitarian action, as Alan Roberts, the British historian, has pointed out, is usually much easier to reach agreement on than wider political action. Staying neutral seems not to be an option, as Western foreign policy increasingly includes human rights issues.

That all said, like any organization the non-military agencies are far from perfect and their strengths must be tempered with several harsh realities. They often lack resources, and their lean structures are simply not able to cope with 24-hour operations. They need to find their own accommodation, food, transport, communications, etc, and, unlike the military, often prefer not to operate from the 'field' but from offices and apartments. Even relatively large organizations, such as the UNHCR, have no equivalent of a military brigade headquarters, and their ability to establish and work from a 'Tactical HQ' while maintaining a 'Main HQ' a considerable distance away, is simply beyond them. Travelling light may have advantages, but to sustain operations in all conditions over protracted periods needs a structured command team and the resources to sustain them; there is little evidence within the NGO/IO community of either.

This lack of robustness often leads to a lack of responsiveness, along with a single-issue focus. While bringing tremendous expertise and strengths to bear in their particular fields, several NGOs are very narrowly focused. A lack of understanding or acceptance of wider operational – let alone strategic – issues can (and often does) come across to the military as arrogance; indeed a dogmatic selfishness of their own aims/needs leads to the detriment of others. Not comfortable with pragmatism, there is a constant fear of losing organizational integrity. Cagey about being manipulated, by any side, none want to be 'used' and so, worrying about their independence, they demand their own space and freedom to operate – as they see fit.

Notwithstanding their knowledge of each other, and their willingness to network, there are many rivalries. The NGOs in particular are dependent upon profile and income and they can be fiercely independent and competitive. Running a large humanitarian NGO is big business and most employ public relations men and women whose aim in life is to touch the heartstrings of the rich West. Appealing to the emotions of both governments and the public is a key element of maintaining profile and raising money, but to do so they must be both seen and heard. NGOs can therefore be reluctant to share information with each other and, sadly, some see disasters as 'business opportunities' and put great effort into ensuring that their logo is both large and prominently displayed. The spontaneity and creative nature of the individuals within these organizations can also lead to rivalries, indeed anarchy within them. As the leading international academic in humanitarian studies, Hugo Slim once commented, 'the only consistent factor in NGO approach to cooperation is a lack of consistency'.

Many NGOs are intrinsically hostile to the military and most 'fidget' when the military are around. Their perception of the military is not an unfair caricature, given the range of military forces around the world, and most are prepared to recognize that some military are 'better' than others, with UK forces being generally held in high regard. Few of the individuals are pacifist, and most have no problems with the idea of 'just force'. Nonetheless there is a 'blood-line' between them and the military – whereas the military are prepared to shed blood to bring a conflict to an end most NGOs certainly would not. Linked to a fear of being too closely associated with the military many are not prepared to come to military-led meetings, and those that do are instinctively suspicious – expecting them to be highly structured and for 'orders' to be given. UN/NGO-led meetings run from a mixture of the chaotic and confused through to well-structured and useful, but any idea of punctuality is usually a naïve hope, and it is not in the least bit unusual for mobile phone calls to be made during meetings, with individuals wandering in and out at will. Throughout the humanitarian community there is a noticeable determination not to be controlled, let alone commanded! And the end result is that all too often military resources are not put to best effect.

Accept these realities – and move on

So my second point is that differences do exist, and no amount of wishful thinking will change them; so collectively we must learn to live with the realities. Through an understanding of the strengths, and an acceptance of the weaknesses, strong working relationships can be – and often are – developed, and indeed friendships forged (I am now a director/board member of two international agencies!). In one sense both sides of the 'blood-line' divide are a mixture of 'missionaries, mercenaries and misfits', and both share very similar problems. Often, if not usually, put into and operating within a vacuum, with poor mandates and force structures, each can be humanitarian 'fig leaves' covering neglect. The crowded theatre of operations is made up of uneven actors, with poor- and good-quality players on both sides being asked to make hard moral choices. Often unable to take the decisive action needed, and being put into dangerous situations – self-sacrifice may be the ethic but it is not the objective. Both sides are accountable to donors or governments – who can be very wise after the event and who can be unfairly critical of decisions taken under enormous pressure. These similarities bind the players together. Both get it wrong now and then, but the joint aim must be to develop the natural synergies that exist in order to ensure that the achievements eclipse the failures.

And professional armies generally welcome their involvement in 'humanitarian' deployments. Complex emergencies are demanding, and they provide excellent vehicles for maintaining professionalism, a professionalism needed as much in the early stages of emergency aid provision, disaster relief and humanitarian operations as in peacekeeping, peace enforcement and war-fighting. British soldiers – and others, such as the French – happen to be pretty good at this business, and take great pride in making a difference. They switch easily from one role to another, and psychologically have no difficulty with helping refugees one day and preparing to fight their way out of trouble on another. As far as commanders are concerned these operations provide, at all levels, sufficient uncertainty and friction to ensure that they are well tested. We need commanders who are comfortable with chaos, and the humanitarian community, never mind the situation itself, ensures that there is plenty of that!! Nothing is ever easy on these deployments, and cool heads are needed to bring order out of the chaos.

Although in most circumstances it is important to maintain a clear separation between the roles of the military and humanitarian actors, by distinguishing their respective roles, competences and responsibilities, coordination is crucial; sharing information, clear division of tasks, collaborative planning, etc. Being under the command or complete control of the military should, in principle, not take place, unless in extreme and exceptional circumstances – and only then as a last resort. But coordination and cooperation (the closer form of coordination) are relatively easy to do. Information that might affect the security of civilians and/or humanitarian workers can – and should – be shared, as should locations, plans and intentions; for example, routes and timing of humanitarian convoys and airlifts, mine-action activities, population movements, military relief efforts, etc.

The military usually have the capability to establish a secure environment on the ground within which humanitarian activities can take place in relative safety, but while any civil–military coordination must focus on alleviating human suffering – and the key objective of providing protection and assistance to populations in need is often, if not always, paramount – the potential consequences must nonetheless be thought through. Even the perception of affiliation can jeopardize neutrality and impartiality, and the agencies must strive to maintain their ability to obtain access to all vulnerable populations, in all areas of the complex emergency; they therefore need to be able to negotiate such access with all parties to the conflict. The military can deploy large numbers of people and 'stuff', but beneficiary identification, needs and vulnerability assessment, impartial and neutral distribution of relief aid, monitoring and evaluation – all these and more will remain essential to an effective and successful humanitarian operation, and the assessment of such needs must be independent with assistance given regardless of race, ethnicity, sex/gender, religion, social status, nationality or political affiliation of the recipients. This requires freedom of movement for humanitarian staff – in order to conduct independent assessments, select staff, identify beneficiaries based on their needs, and establish a free flow of information between and within agencies – as well as with the media. A clear distinction must also be maintained between combatants and non-combatants – including the sick, wounded, prisoners of war and ex-combatants who are demobilized. International humanitarian law protects non-combatants by providing immunity from attack and humanitarian workers must never present themselves or their work as part of a military operation; equally, military personnel must not present themselves as 'civilian humanitarian workers'. Those operating within an emergency situation need to be free to identify the most effective and secure approach in the delivery of aid to vulnerable populations; but staff safety might well lead to a decision to seek military-based security. Even so the agencies must avoid becoming dependent on support provided by the military, which may well be time and scale limited. Ultimately, any humanitarian operation – save perhaps a natural disaster situation – using military assets must retain its civilian nature and character.

There is more to this than war-fighting and military victories

My third point is this. Although the bottom line is that the best armies are first and foremost war-fighting organizations, deployed by the state in order to deter or defeat an aggressor, they are increasingly deployed to establish security in a failed or failing state, bring a conflict to an end, or deal with the fallout – planned or unexpected – of any of these operations. All of these cases demand that the military understand the wider implications of a deployment and are prepared for and can deliver a wide range of practical support and assistance to those caught up in the maelstrom. Winning Hearts and Minds is not just a doctrinal principle, it is a practical and important part of achieving what the military call the 'End State' of an operational deployment – however poorly thought through that End Sate may have been by the government who despatched them there in the first place.

There is in other words a Humanitarian Imperative – indeed a Moral Imperative – alongside and indeed embedded within what we might call the 'pure' Military Imperative of an operational deployment. Contrary to popular opinion not all armies are made up of unthinking automatons, keen for a fight and uncaring of the consequences. The reality is far from that. It has been well said that the young men and women who end up in places such as Iraq and Afghanistan are a mixture of missionaries, mercenaries and misfits; and there is some truth in that. Clothed in the outward equipment given them to wear in battle, they are trained to try to become what the image portrays: hard and tough. However, although they may indeed be keen to deal with those bringing about the pain and trouble in the first place, and notwithstanding that relief operations carried out by military forces, even when the intention is purely 'humanitarian', may undermine the overall humanitarian efforts by non-military actors, behind the mask the best military are just as keen as anyone else to provide humanitarian support to those who need it. So getting my soldiers to build refugee camps and help re-build the infrastructure in places such as Kosovo was not a difficult task. Every British regiment on an operational deployment will always be on the lookout for some project or other to support, and they thrive on the opportunity to make a difference. I would argue that the best are therefore the reverse side of the same coin as those who serve in the other state and non-state agencies engaged in these operations.

The independence and civilian nature of humanitarian assistance should of course be emphasized at all times, and a clear distinction must be retained between the identities, functions and roles of humanitarian personnel and those of military forces – ie travel in clearly marked vehicles, clearly mark offices and relief supplies, etc. Weapons should not be allowed on the premises or transportation facilities of humanitarian organizations, and humanitarian personnel should not normally travel in military vehicles, aircraft, etc – except as a last resort or for security reasons – and humanitarian workers should not wear any military uniform-like clothing.

Both sides need each other

Fourth, we need to recognize that for all of the difficulties both sides of this divide bring much-needed capabilities to the emergencies. Generally the military role is to support, not supplant the work of the non-military players; they are there to serve, not to be served. Logistic, medical and engineering support, encompassing the management of airports and seaports, transportation, shelter, route protection and the provision of a secure environment, are all key roles – together with the command and control structures necessary to deliver that capability. Most aid agencies are certainly principled, knowledgeable and committed – but the reality is that they also have very limited resources compared to the military as a whole and they can be slow in responding to the need, as well as being focused on the single issues that drive them.

It was to the US military that the Haitian government turned to run their airspace after the earthquake struck. Controlling the flow of unsolicited and inappropriate cargo into the country was a major issue – indeed the defining issue – and no aid agency had the necessary capacity, and few had – or have – the decision-making and planning capacity, to deal with the mass of related issues. And this often applies, whether in Haiti, Afghanistan or Pakistan after the recent earthquake or current floods. I think I'm correct in saying that there are 900 registered NGOs in Haiti as I write this chapter today. While the UN Cluster system is having an impact, the reality is that whichever one of the dreaded 'C' words we use – Commanding, Controlling, Coordinating, Cooperating – holding such a mass of capability together is simply beyond the capability of many – if not any – non-military organizations. And for governments around the world keeping a track on who is on their soil during these emergencies is a major concern; indeed many are on the point of refusing entry to any organization not registered and prepared to work with all of the other players – military as well as non-military.

So, what? The need for a widely understood doctrine

As noted earlier, rather than debate 'If', we need to discuss 'How': how can we make the best of the combined capabilities? There are many aspects to this but I would argue specifically that we need to start at the strategic level and work our way down.

The first thing we need to produce is an agreed 'Doctrine' by widening the debate on how effective action can best be orchestrated and executed. UK doctrine has developed well throughout the 1990s and the early 21st century, and it is generally held in high regard; nonetheless there is work to be done in the area of the military working alongside the various humanitarian organizations and other governmental departments. There is a constant trail of reports providing frank assessments of why past joint actions have been slow or ineffective, recording tales of poor coordination, missions being duplicated or failing, and humanitarian groups being unsure with whom to work. It is tempting to argue that the UK's involvement over the last 20 years has had a pretty good track record, and there is some truth in that, but the wave of negative press comments that constantly flow rightly touches nerves, and my own experiences confirm that we, too, have much to learn.

Our collective and 'joint' doctrine must reflect agreed principles, on everything from intelligence gathering and analysis, provision of the means, including funding, the roles of the military and the links with and status of non-military aid agencies and civilian contractors. There is a need for an integrated 'campaign plan', covering the political, economic, legal and humanitarian imperatives, alongside the military ones. While inevitably events on the ground will dictate and modify, and commanders will need to respond to these changes, such a campaign plan, prepared jointly by the key players using a framework set within an agreed doctrine will both guide and educate, support and, where necessary, constrain. Linked to ongoing work within the Stabilization and Civil-Affairs Groups, there should be a clearly defined focus for the development of an integrated training and exchange programme, to educate and prepare like-minded people for future deployments. Properly funded, joint education and training programmes are required; the military spend enormous amounts of time educating and training their people; the non-military need to do likewise.

This doctrine should take into account developments within Defence Diplomacy, which was one of the new tasks identified under Conflict Prevention. Early warning and early deployment of forces must be set alongside preventative diplomacy, disarmament and peace-building measures, including focused aid. This broader definition of security policy seems some way off; the ongoing Strategic Defence and Security Review in the UK may well help, but developing the doctrinal debate will bring it closer. The UK's Joint Doctrine Centre should expand its role, developing the principles, practice and procedures that together will make up the doctrine from the military perspective, but the process must be politically driven, and it must give increasing credence to the non-military players. While it is a truism to say that there is no such thing as purely military success in any conflict, this is particularly so in complex emergencies, where military involvement is simply a means to an end. Politics dictates the speed and nature of response, and determines priorities, and it is politicians who need to bring together the key players in a coordinated manner, and allocate the resources as appropriate. Although it would be idle to suggest that it will be easy to establish a single doctrine for complex emergencies, the realities of these deployments means that the DFID, FCO, the MoD and others such as the Department of Trade and Industry (Trade not Aid is increasingly being recognized as a key issue) – and their equivalents elsewhere – must enhance their links and work closer with each other, and with the other key players such as the NGOs, the agencies and the donor community. The natural lead might well lie with DFID, which, for all its many faults is – in my view – a pretty good organization; but some structural change is necessary – to ensure, for example, an ability to plan ahead – and a pan-government, integrated 'Doctrine Centre' is needed to pull all of this together, developing the principles, practice and procedures that together make up the doctrine. One thing is clear, to me at least; if we are to avoid the complete militarization of humanitarian assistance – which would be a grave mistake in my view – then a clear and widely understood doctrine is required quickly.

The example of logistic supply chains

Let me give you a specific example. Although supply chains inevitably underpin almost all humanitarian aid operations, the potential for proactively and strategically managed end-to-end chain has not been pursued with anything like the priority it should have been. There are always far too many supply chains running into the various operational theatres. The Haiti earthquake, the Pacific tsunami, Hurricane Katrina all highlighted the critical role that logistics and the supply chain play in the response to sudden-onset disasters and the timely delivery of relief aid – together with the consequences of bottlenecks and delays.

A recent forum in Sydney discussed the supply chain's role in supporting humanitarian relief, development aid and development initiatives – one of the first times that such a diverse group has convened on this topic. The individuals attending represented NGOs working in relief and development situations, including the Australian Red Cross, the Australian Defence Forces, commercial organizations that support both the NGOs and Defence Forces in humanitarian aid delivery, academics researching humanitarian and development logistics (including one of the editors of this book), and interested private-sector companies and supply chain consultants. The discussions highlighted the simple reality that across these apparently dissimilar organizations there was a common belief – that in many of the response, relief and development situations their organizations encountered, more effective supply chain operations could have a major impact on the outcomes, and that this area had received inadequate recognition and focus. While recognizing the very significant differences across these areas, the organizers believed that there was much to be gained from addressing humanitarian supply chains.

The time for change is now

As we look ahead, military commanders, at all levels, will continue to work closely with non-military organizations; although the scale will inevitably wax and wane in the future, military involvement in complex emergencies is not going to end. This being so, there is work to be done. The humanitarian and military actors have fundamentally different institutional thinking and cultures, characterized by the distinct chain-of-command and clear organizational structures of the military vis-à-vis the diversity of the humanitarian community. The two groups have different mandates, objectives, working methods, and even vocabularies, so it is important that all of the actors fully understand the complex network of humanitarian assistance.

The military, in particular, need to appreciate the cultural and psychological make-up of the non-military players; they need to better understand the ethos and psyche of the various organizations and agencies, and acknowledge the strengths that they bring to such deployments. Effort and resources must go into improving joint capabilities and relationships with the key players, encouraging and participating in a wide doctrinal debate to ensure better and closer cooperation.

And the same applies to the non-military players. Through understanding and patient leadership, strong relationships can, and indeed must, be developed. Working together, the two sides of the humanitarian coin have the potential to be a very strong and effective team. The simple reality is that we live in an inter-connected world and the future fate of many people, all around the globe, caught in the middle of inter-, and increasingly intra-state, violence will depend on mature and professional organizations working hand-in-hand; the stakes are just too high to be left to the inadequate efforts of well-intentioned individuals working in silos and in competition with each other. Fundamental institutional change is required – and it is required now!

14
So where next?
Developments in humanitarian logistics

GYÖNGYI KOVÁCS

Abstract

Upon a review of history and many findings from current humanitarian logistics research and practice, this chapter turns to the future of this field. It is an attempt to answer the question of 'so where next?' Much has happened lately that indicates the maturing of humanitarian logistics, humanitarian supply chain management and, indeed, humanitarian supply networks. Coordination patterns have been developed between agencies and the focus is now turning to collaboration in the humanitarian supply chain and even combining inter-agency coordination with supply chain collaboration through purchasing consortia, sharing of logistics service providers and material suppliers, etc. Humanitarian organizations have also started to develop services they offer each other. Apart from the obvious purchasing economies, the accumulated demand from several agencies gives rise to dedicated product development. Standards are implemented for technologies, products but also (logistical) processes.

Technology for humanitarian logistics is constantly developing, now facilitating a shared pipeline visibility. With visibility comes also the possibility not to only develop performance metrics for the humanitarian supply chain, but also to follow them up. New, meaningful metrics need to be developed for effectiveness, efficiency, but also equity. Besides equity considerations, beneficiaries are becoming active members of the humanitarian supply chain – once the challenge of a secure access to beneficiaries is resolved. Community development is on the agenda as are questions of the sustainability of aid. The latter is considered from aspects of embedding disaster relief in long-term development, in terms of greening the humanitarian supply chain, as well as in designing it with an exit strategy in mind.

Introduction

Humanitarian logistics – both research and practice – has come a long way since the original outcries about the poor management of the 2004 South East Asia tsunami. Back then, criticism of humanitarian logistics practice focused on a lack of coordination of humanitarian efforts, on congested ports and airports, on problems with customs clearance, and on many questionable decisions over which items and services the beneficiaries should be provided with. Research was not in the spotlight, as very few academics had considered the area and there was virtually nothing in the way of investigations of the topic. That logistics should come into focus was triggered by more than a lack of coordination and pipeline problem, rather it was the recognition that it was the main cost driver of humanitarian operations. While Van Wassenhove (2006) put the bar high, suggesting that 80 per cent of the income of humanitarian organizations is spent on logistics, Blansjaar (2009) offers a slightly lower – but still highly significant figure – of 50–60 per cent. It follows, therefore, that improvements in humanitarian logistics performance should translate into a better outreach of the aid and a better level of service to the beneficiaries. But whereas many of the contributions to this book have taken a historical perspective, this chapter seeks to provide a forward view on some of the emerging challenges in humanitarian logistics. In order to achieve this, it will first revisit some of the recent topics in research and practice before outlining some of the key gaps in the research to date, and the important trends in practice.

From inter-agency coordination to relationship building in the supply chain

As highlighted by the 2004 SE Asia tsunami, inter-organizational coordination (or the lack thereof), became one of the prime foci of humanitarian logistics practice and research. The United Nations humanitarian reform programme highlighted the existing inefficiencies, gaps, duplication and overlap. The clear need for inter-agency coordination led to the establishment of different topical clusters, one of which (subsequently called the Log Cluster) was to focus on logistics (GHP, 2006).

Similar movements aimed at improving the coherence and coordination of the post-disaster preparation and response mushroomed across groups of faith-based organizations, and groups of organizations with similar mandates, etc.[1] But also, other dimensions were embraced under the coordination umbrella: humanitarian–private partnerships (in logistics this being particularly prevalent between humanitarian organizations and both global and local logistics service providers), civil–military coordination in its various guises (see Chapters 12 and 13), as well as supply chain collaboration. In practice, these first efforts were very much focused on inter-agency coordination (only), and this was reflected in the relative abundance of scientific articles devoted to this topic.

Inter-agency coordination

Inter-agency groups and clusters were generally pretty well aware of the issues and challenges implicit in their stove-pipe approach to a disaster, but faced the challenge elegantly described in an old saying that 'everybody wants coordination, but nobody wants to be coordinated'. This led to a questioning of the leadership role of cluster leads, and although meetings were designed to be inclusive, in practice only BINGOs (big international non-governmental organizations) and designated aid agencies participated in global meetings. The sheer number of meetings was also something to be coordinated – Völz (2005) quotes 72 per week in Banda Aceh alone upon the 2004 SE Asia tsunami.

Nevertheless, and notwithstanding all the challenges, the humanitarian reform programme has led to the establishment of a joint global hub system (in parallel with the rise of regional hubs for individual organizations[2]) that includes inter-agency warehousing. The *logistical principles of speculation* (or pre-positioning) and *postponement* (eg blank stock that is appropriately labelled immediately prior to dispatch) were employed simultaneously and this allowed the consideration of the topic as part of the humanitarian logistics research agenda (Listou, 2008). In addition, agreement between agencies to conduct joint pre-positioning or warehousing clearly opens up the possibility for the swapping of material supplies, a topic that is currently in the spotlight also in business logistics (cf Kosansky and Shaefer, 2010) – and, indeed, with the potential for exchange of air cargo, shipping or lorry transport slots. At the same time, 'softer' questions of coordination, such as the development of trust between humanitarian field workers (Tatham and Kovács, 2010), have started to be addressed.

Inevitably, roles and responsibilities became somewhat clearer over time. As a result, in the aftermath of Cyclone Nargis (August 2008), the Log Cluster operated alongside the UNJLC[3] and UNHAS[4] (including secondees from 10 humanitarian organizations as well as three commercial logistics service providers) in a Global Logistics Cell that provided services used by 39 humanitarian organizations (Logistics Cluster, 2009). Furthermore, the

Log Cluster used their experiences in responding to this disaster as the basis for the agenda in their subsequent 'lessons learned' global meeting of October 2008 in Brindisi. This recognized the importance of harmonizing the plethora of pre-existing templates used for ordering and tracking items as well as a GIS-T system for assessing transport infrastructure while delivering aid. Templates and technology were key to the opening sharing of online information (albeit it was accepted that this might need to be somewhat restricted in complex emergencies). In parallel, recognizing customs procedures as a potentially significant and life-threatening source of delay, a project was initiated to harmonize customs procedures for disaster relief.

Turning the clock forward to 2010, the development of standards and templates[5] continues to be key for humanitarian operations, and this has led the Log Cluster to develop and publish a Logistics Operational Guide (the 'LOG'[6]). That said, meetings are but one way to coordinate logistical efforts and it is clear that issues such as duplications of effort, prioritization of scheduled arrivals and distribution could be resolved more effectively through an improvement of pipeline visibility across humanitarian organizations. With the development of humanitarian logistics software (such as HLS for the IFRC or HELIOS, as its light version, for broader use[7]), the door is open to the standardization of the underpinning processes of disaster relief operations and, thus, to the improvement of pipeline visibility not just within but also across different humanitarian organizations. But although *process standardization* and *pipeline visibility* are appearing on the agenda of at least the larger humanitarian organizations, (see Chapter 3), research on these topics is unquestionably lagging behind. Furthermore, associated issues such as *product and packaging standardization, modularization* that would facilitate joint/shared transportation, have yet to be addressed in humanitarian practice and research.

New dimensions to coordinate

With the increasing recognition of the need for inter-agency coordination and the tentative steps towards its improved achievement, comes a move to consider other dimensions of coordination. This builds on the many partnerships between humanitarian organizations and global logistics service providers (LSPs) that have been established and researched in the past years.[8] However, the focus is moving on to cross-learning from these partnerships and also to their local rather than global dimension. The importance of strengthening local economies – as previously discussed in global vs local sourcing in humanitarian supply chains (Jahre and Spens, 2007) and a recent 'hot topic' in humanitarian logistics research (Kovács and Spens, 2008) – has also been embraced in relationships with LSPs. Thus Mattila (2008) found that humanitarian organizations have started to move away from global partnerships to a policy of establishing such arrangements with regional or local LSPs. In reality, it is argued that *global partnerships are complementary to local ones*, and are established in parallel to deal with inbound vs outbound logistics activities.

A further dimension of coordination is constantly gaining in importance. *Humanitarian logistics has moved on towards humanitarian supply chain management*, which demands that organizations take a more strategic dimension and associated view of suppliers and customers. As discussed in the first chapter of this book, such a development follows the history of logistics and supply chain management in general with a first extension towards suppliers and then a rediscovery of the role of beneficiaries in the humanitarian supply chain.

As a result of this process, new questions have emerged. First, should a (material) donor be seen as a supplier or a customer that needs to be satisfied (or both)? Historically, funding schemes and fundraising activities have been the focus of considerable attention within humanitarian organizations, and while their concerns for accountability and transparency are laudable, the extent of activities related to seeking funding and reporting to funding institutions inevitably shifts their attention away from beneficiaries. Furthermore, (and as discussed in Chapter 2), the design of funding schemes has a clear impact on the design of humanitarian operations and the humanitarian supply chain. New, *basket funding* schemes have the potential to address many of these issues by providing supplementary funding to a problem area (a region, disaster or activity) and thereby enabling the logistical principles of postponement and speculation to be embraced. However, much remains to be achieved in terms of developing an organization's understanding of the optimal mode of operation for the humanitarian supply chain and, in particular, for consideration of *supply chain performance in terms not only of effectiveness and efficiency but also equity* (see Chapter 4). In this respect, after lengthy discussion of (external) aid effectiveness vs (internal) performance measures in the humanitarian supply chain, research has recently embraced the equity dimension from public services to this context (Balcik *et al*, 2010).

Second, are beneficiaries to be seen as 'customers' even though they lack traditional purchasing power (Kovács and Spens, 2008)? There are (hopefully) no repeat purchases, and beneficiaries can rarely choose between items and services and rarely select a particular supplier. Beneficiary preference has, therefore, sometimes been treated as irrelevant (cf Beamon and Kotleba, 2006)! That said, new developments of practice such as cash components in aid are bringing back the purchasing power and customer role of beneficiaries. This also fits well with research *rediscovering the customer service dimension* of the supply chain management framework for humanitarian supply chains (Oloruntoba and Gray, 2009). What is more, beneficiaries can be, and have been, incorporated as active members of the humanitarian supply chain in, for example, reconstruction supply chains (Kovács *et al*, 2010).

Last but not least, how does the humanitarian context impact on commercial suppliers and vice versa? Much of the context is similar to fields such as public healthcare, education and public services in general, thus research and practice in these fields can also be beneficial to humanitarian supply chains (and again, vice versa). A crucial difference between public services and humanitarian supply chains is, however, the need to develop relationships with suppliers just in case. In other words, supplier relationships in the humanitarian context are rarely built on the basis of a frequent economic transaction but are *dormant (or latent) relationships*. As in the case of inventory pre-positioning, future demands are uncertain, and suppliers are needed with a capacity at the time of need (Whybark, 2007). This implies that suppliers are expected to set aside other orders when needed, and can even be expected to delimit their own partner organizations and companies to those that comply with humanitarian principles. However, notwithstanding these constraints, many companies have welcomed humanitarian organizations as their customers for a variety of reasons. Even though much of this activity takes place under the umbrella of corporate responsibility (Kovács, 2008), the reality is that the humanitarian 'industry' is booming (Thomas and Fritz, 2006). Companies ranging from the pharmaceutical industry to packaging manufacturers have even started to *develop tailor-made products for humanitarian purposes*. An example of this is Clip-Lok's containers that are convertible to latrines. But after much discussion in which the motives of companies vs humanitarian organizations to enter partnerships was scrutinized, the debate has turned towards aspects of relationship building in the humanitarian supply chain (Larson, 2011).

Inter-agency coordination can also be mixed with supply chain relationships. Pipeline visibility and joint stock aside, inter-agency *purchasing consortia* (such as the UK-based Inter-Agency Procurement Group) have helped to achieve purchasing economies at the same time as avoiding the double-booking of manufacturing capacities. In addition, purchasing consortia enable the swapping of supplier capacities depending on the particular short-term financial situation of different humanitarian organizations. Aggregating volumes over several organizations also aids the creation of a positive atmosphere for further product development for humanitarian purposes. Indeed, joint supplier platforms (such as Innovasjon Norge) can work as incubators for this kind of product development. In summary, the focus on coordination has shifted from inter-agency coordination to relationship building in the humanitarian supply chain, and further to a mix of the two.[9]

Technology development and the pragmatism of humanitarian operations research (OR)

Technology development has also entered a new era as more and more humanitarian organizations are not just developing logistics information systems – eg IFRC's fleet management system and World Vision International's tracking system – but are also opening them up for use/lease by other humanitarian organizations. The novelty does not necessarily lie in the development of such technologies but, rather, in the *services* humanitarian organizations have started to offer each other. However, service management research has yet to discover the area of humanitarian logistics and supply chain management.

New technology development projects embrace questions of interoperability across organizations, systems and, indeed, people. For example, RFID for humanitarian logistics need not only deal with questions of technological feasibility, system interoperability, propriety and user rights but also, inter-operability across different types of humanitarian organizations (eg the health and shelter clusters), including organizations that operate in different phases of disaster relief (from search and rescue operations to long-term development). Social media applications and the like have also entered the scene through applications including searching for missing relatives to matching donations with demand (eg ALAN's AidMatrix[10]).

With technology comes improved data – not only historical but, increasingly, with minimal time lag. This, in turn, gives rise to the potential use of dynamic operations management models in humanitarian logistics. This new trend in research embraces the slogans of 'doing good with good OR' as well as 'compassionate operations'. What has not been possible before due to a lack of input data (and many authors have previously been criticized for modelling away reality by assuming the existence of demand data, or worse, assuming constant demand) may, indeed, be possible in the future. Yet it continues to be of huge importance that operations management and operations research scholars appreciate the constraints of the actual operational theatre of humanitarian logistics. As Van Wassenhove (2010) emphasized in his tutorial on humanitarian logistics at the ALIO/INFORMS conference in 2010, 'good' OR for humanitarian logistics is pragmatic and, hence, focuses on context-driven, simple and applicable solutions. In other words, the humanitarian OM/OR models of the near future should focus on decision support rather than finding optimal or near-optimal solutions. *The challenge of humanitarian OM/ OR research therefore lies in working with contextual constraints* and consciously building these into proposed models.

Questioning disaster taxonomies and the humanitarian-development divide

Take any article in humanitarian logistics prior to 2009 and it will start with a long discussion of types of disaster, phases of disaster relief and the various taxonomies combining the two. Notwithstanding the additional challenges that a complex emergency' brings (such as questions of *security*, the use of armed forces, *access* to the other group(s) of beneficiaries) when compared with a natural disaster (Listou, 2008), taxonomies can be misleading and their use for logistical purposes has been questioned. Kovács and Spens (2009) tried to categorize the typical disasters in Ghana according to a natural vs man-made and slow-onset vs rapid-onset divide, but came to the conclusion that a number of 'natural' disasters can have their root causes in human activity, such as bush fires leading to deforestation, depletion of fertile soils and, ultimately, food shortages, famine as well as internally displaced persons (IDPs) – indeed, some would argue that there is no such thing as a natural disaster, rather it is the decision of humans to, for example, live in a particular earthquake zone (Haiti) or deltaic region (Bangladesh) that places them at risk. Similarly, climate-change related disasters – although on the rise (Suarez, 2009) – equally defy such categorizations. Thus, rather than looking at the phases of disaster relief per se, Tatham and Kovács (2007) saw shifts in major transportation modes as defining moments. Other than that, general timelines are important in order to determine who is involved at which point in time in disaster relief activities (Beresford and Pettit, 2011) or to pinpoint which activities an organization actually considers.

Units of analysis – taking the strategic view

As for different types of supply chains, McLachlin *et al* (2009) differentiate between for-profit and not-for-profit and interrupted vs not interrupted environments, placing disaster relief in the not-for-profit but interrupted quadrant. Although this categorization is interesting from a supply chain management perspective, it needs to be borne in mind that interruptions are seen as such from a local perspective (a particular disaster in a region), while global humanitarian organizations can take an aggregate view on demand for their services. The much discussed surge in demand thus only takes place in certain locations at a particular point in time, while global aggregate demand is much smoother. This brings the advantage to BINGOs who do not just operate globally, but also on a scale that enables long-term relationships in the supply chain, fosters product development for humanitarian purposes and allows for purchasing economies – especially if combined with inter-agency purchasing consortia. That said, operations in the field are often carried out by so-called 'implementing partners' of BINGOs, which has largely been neglected in supply chain design research so far. This view again calls for more attention to the strategic aspects of *global humanitarian supply chain management* – or, as the title of the book suggests, global humanitarian supply network management – and away from the fragmented treatment of each disaster as a unique case. After all, disasters are not just events in the highly uncertain risk category of supply chain risk management but the very *raison d'être* for humanitarian organizations (Kovács and Tatham, 2009). Besides learning from specific cases, humanitarian logistics research could therefore benefit from more comparative cases (such as longitudinal studies, as in Gatignon *et al*, 2010) and those that take a more strategic view. Initial examples that are moving in this direction have begun to emerge, including a review of critical success factors (Pettit and Beresford, 2009) as well as the cost drivers of humanitarian logistics (Tatham *et al*, 2010a).

Taking such a strategic view readdresses questions of urgency and speed that have long been advocated as the ultimate performance indicators in humanitarian logistics (to the extent that Beamon (1999) has put lead times at an ideal of zero). A focus on lead times and responsiveness has earned humanitarian supply chains the label of being 'most agile' (cf Oloruntoba and Gray, 2006) or 'fully flexible' (Gattorna, 2009). Although responsiveness and resilience will always remain important concepts in the humanitarian context, an aggregate view extends the previous short-term focus on immediate response to a disaster to planning and preparedness on the global scale. The urgency tag on humanitarian operations can, however, be counterproductive as, for example, humanitarian aid delivered by sea is often not considered urgent enough to be exempt from customs delays – regardless of whether such sea transportation may actually be quicker, cheaper and more accessible than air transportation. This, in part, led to the dismissal of the sea-basing concept in the Ring of Fire even though it would have been more time-, as well as cost-, efficient. Indeed, customs processes all over the globe would need to readdress questions of urgency and lead times from a logistical point of view.[11]

Addressing sustainability

The focus on particular phases of disaster relief is naturally fostered by organizational mandates and the policy makers generally divide between humanitarian (or emergency) relief and development. Mandates can, indeed, differentiate between relief and development (in food relief between the domains of WFP and FAO), but humanitarian organizations have started to attempt to *bridge the gap between short-term relief activities and long-term development* (again in food aid, the International Alliance Against Hunger brings together WFP, FAO and IFAD for just this reason[12]). Moreover, humanitarian organizations have long taken on tasks that relate to (regional economic) development, and considerations of the sustainability of aid (humanitarian or development aid) have led to a blurring of this divide. Besides, disasters often take place in developing countries[13] where humanitarian and development activities overlap. For example, the 2008 cholera outbreak in Zimbabwe came at a time when international humanitarian and development agencies were already present in the country to support the national public healthcare system. Thus, humanitarian and development activities need to be considered jointly, and disaster relief needs to be embedded in long-term development. Research has yet to attend to the gaps in between, and the practicalities of considering the long-term effects of humanitarian activities. Most importantly, *humanitarian supply chain design needs to address questions of sustainability* from the very moment of the activating humanitarian efforts.

Sustainability has multiple meanings in the humanitarian context. It can be applied in relation to sustaining an operation, ie maintaining aid through continuous funding (financial continuity) and/or embedding it within development activities (*long-term development*). It can also be understood as designing the humanitarian supply chain in a way that facilitates its continuation in the region after humanitarian organizations have left (*sustainable exit strategy*). Supply chain design can also consider sustainability from the perspective of community development through local sourcing, capacity building and engagement of beneficiaries. Thus, Kovács *et al* (2010) present a case of *community-based supply chain design* where beneficiaries become active members of the reconstruction supply chain. This approach contributes to beneficiary empowerment, helping to ensure community ownership of the reconstruction process, as well as to the local economy in general. Additionally, community-based supply chain design can incorporate aspects of peace-building (Anderson, 1999). But humanitarian supply chains have yet to embrace the challenges of becoming 'green'.

That said, green humanitarian logistics projects have begun to focus on issues such as transportation emissions although, arguably, there is little choice in the mode of 'last mile' transport and the emissions it causes – albeit, in an ideal world, maintenance regimes for vehicle fleets would improve along with the associated reduction in harmful emissions. In addition, however, there are enormous opportunities for reducing the environmental impacts in other areas of the supply chain. Inbound transportation accounts for much of logistics costs (up to 60 per cent in some cases) as items are moved around the globe. Not all these items need to be shipped in this way, and local sourcing is not just a matter of strengthening local economies but it also helps in cutting transport costs as well as emissions. But other activities in the field (from warehousing to camp management) also have serious environmental impacts. Non-degradable materials in the field have further environmental implications, particularly as there is an almost total absence of reverse logistics processes. Furthermore, some organizations may still bring unsolicited items to the field,[14] although increasingly organizations have started to manage in-kind donations, soliciting them as they are actually needed – a prime example being the American Red Cross who will actively contact manufacturers and seek specific donations (towels, nappies, tents, etc). Nonetheless, all items given to beneficiaries remain in the field, and even large units such as field hospitals are commonly donated to the host country of the disaster relief operation. Most importantly, however, *greening the humanitarian supply chain* requires aid organizations to look beyond field activities to the supply chain to choices of suppliers, materials, manufacturing processes as well as transportation links (Sarkis *et al*, 2010). Indeed, given that many natural disasters can be associated with climate change (eg the 2010 flooding in Pakistan) and the whole subject of climate change adaptation and related early warning systems have been high on the agenda of humanitarian organizations for many years, surprisingly little attention has been paid to greening the relief supply chain itself.

Besides climate change, urbanization also impacts on humanitarian supply chains. Already by 2009, it has been estimated that 50.5 per cent of the world's population lived in cities, and this percentage is expected to rise (UN DESA, 2010). Urbanization increases the vulnerability of populations in and to disasters as more people are exposed simultaneously and, as urban dwellers, have relatively few mitigation and coping strategies (Suarez, 2009). Even if the number of disasters were to decrease (though trends point to the opposite), urbanization boosts their impact. From a sustainability perspective, *early warning systems*, enforcement of more stringent and robust building standards along with a reinforced focus on *preparedness* in the humanitarian supply chain are emphasized once again. Indeed, in this regard it is instructive to compare the impact of the earthquakes in Haiti (January 2010) and Chile (February 2010). Although the latter was some 300 times more powerful, the death toll was less than 1,000 (with around one-third of this mortality actually being caused by a post-earthquake tsunami), compared with the 230,000 killed in Haiti. And although both quakes struck urban areas, Chile has a stricter regime of building codes that are relatively rigorously enforced (Bilham, 2010).

Concluding remarks

New trends also bring new challenges in humanitarian logistics. First, the whole field of humanitarian logistics has broadened from a narrow focus on operations in particular disasters to strategic considerations of how best to operate a (sustainable) humanitarian supply chain. Calls for more coordination have been (partly) answered across agencies, and these are now being extended to the humanitarian supply chain itself, not least as a means of improving visibility *across* supply chains. More and more key logistics principles from postponement and speculation to standardization and modularization as well as the adaptation and development of products and services for humanitarian purposes are to be found in the best-of-breed humanitarian supply chains. In other words, the discipline is maturing, which is also visible in first academic attempts of dedicated theory development (see Jahre *et al*, 2009). Clusters, communities of practice, platforms and associations (most notably the Humanitarian Logistics Association) have developed to foster the professionalization of the field and have resulted in the development of specialized training programmes, certificates and education programmes. This has, in turn, shone a spotlight on the skills and attributes required by successful humanitarian logisticians (Tatham *et al*, 2010b). In short, humanitarian logistics research has become more institutionalized with institutional partnerships and with new outlets of research results. Apart from many recent special issues in logistics and supply chain management journals, a new, dedicated outlet has also been launched: the *Journal of Humanitarian Logistics and Supply Chain Management*. Ideally, it will serve as a scientific journal that can contribute with theoretical developments but also with a pragmatic approach to the improvement of humanitarian logistics practice.

References

Anderson, MB (1999) *Do No Harm: How aid can support peace – or war*, Lynne Rienner Publishers, Boulder, CO

Balcik, B, Iravani, S and Smilowitz, K (2010) A review of equity in nonprofit and public sector: a vehicle routing perspective, in *Wiley Encyclopaedia of Operations Research and Management Science*, (ed) JJ Cochran, John Wiley & Sons, Chichester, Sussex

Beamon, B (1999) Humanitarian relief chains: issues and challenges, *Proceedings of the 34th International Conference on Computers and Industrial Engineering*, San Francisco, CA, pp 77–82

Beamon, B and Kotleba, S (2006) Inventory management support systems for emergency humanitarian relief operations in South Sudan, *International Journal of Logistics Management*, 17(2), pp 187–212

Beresford, A and Pettit, S (2011) Humanitarian aid logistics: the Wenchuan and Haiti earthquakes compared, in *Relief Supply Chain Management for Disasters: Humanitarian, Aid and Emergency Logistics*, (eds) G Kovács and KM Spens, IGI Global, Hershey, PA

Bilham, R (2010) Lessons from the Haiti Earthquake, *Nature*, **463** (Feb), pp 878–79

Blansjaar, M (2009) Logistics vs supply chain management in disaster relief, *Lecture in the PhD course on Supply Chain Management in Disaster Relief*, August, Helsinki, Finland

Gatignon, A, Van Wassenhove, LN and Charles, A (2010) The Yogyakarta earthquake: humanitarian relief through IFRC's decentralized supply chain, *International Journal of Production Economics*, **126**, pp 102–10

Gattorna, J (ed) (2009) *Dynamic Supply Chain Alignment*, Gower, Farnham, Surrey

Global Humanitarian Platform (GHP) (2006) A brief overview of the humanitarian reforms; available at: http://www.globalhumanitarianplatform.org/doc00001833.html [accessed 29 July 2010]

Jahre, M and Spens, K (2007) Buy global or go local – that's the question, *Proceedings of the International Humanitarian Logistics Symposium*, (ed) P Tatham, Faringdon, London

Jahre, M, Jensen, L-M and Listou, T (2009) Theory development in humanitarian logistics: a framework and three cases, *Management Research News*, 32(11), pp 1008–23

Kosansky, A and Schaefer, T (2010) Should you swap commodities with your competitors?, *Supply Chain Quarterly*, Q2/2010, pp 42–47

Kovács, G (2008) Katastrofe logistik – en case om nødhjælp (Corporate social responsibility in the supply chain – the case of humanitarian aid, in Danish), in *Corporate Social Responsibility Børsens Ledelseshåndbog*, (eds) JS Arlbjørn, AM Christiansen, D van Liempd and HB Jørgensen, Børsen Forum A/S, Copenhagen, chapter 11.2, pp 1–10

Kovács, G and Spens, K (2008) Humanitarian logistics revisited, in *Northern Lights in Logistics and Supply Chain Management*, (eds) JS Arlbjørn, Á Halldórsson, M Jahre and K Spens, CBS Press, Copenhagen, Denmark, chapter 13, pp 217–32

Kovács, G and Spens, K (2009) Identifying challenges in humanitarian logistics, *International Journal of Physical Distribution and Logistics Management*, 39 (6), pp 506–28

Kovács, G and Tatham, P (2009) Responding to disruptions in the supply network – from dormant to action, *Journal of Business Logistics*, 30(2), pp 215–29

Kovács, G, Matopoulos, A and Hayes, O (2010): A community-based approach to supply chain design, *International Journal of Logistics: Research and Applications*, 13(5), pp 1–12

Larson, P (2011) Strategic partners and strange bedfellows: relationship building in the humanitarian supply chain, in *Relief Supply Chain Management for Disasters: Humanitarian, Aid and Emergency Logistics*, (eds) G Kovács and KM Spens, IGI Global, Hershey PA

Linnerooth-Bayer, J, Mechler, R and Pflug, G (2005) Refocusing disaster aid, *Science*, 309, 12 August, pp 1044–46

Listou, T (2008) Postponement and speculation in non-commercial supply chains, *Supply Chain Forum: an International Journal*, 9(2), pp 56–64

Logistics Cluster (2009) Minutes & Meetings, *Global Logistics Cluster Meeting – Brindisi – October 2008*; available at: http://www.logcluster.org/about/logistics-cluster/meeting/global-logistics-cluster-meeting-3-4-octobre-2008, last update 9 Dec 2009 [accessed 27 July 2010]

Mattila, J (2008) Humanitära organisationers val av tredjepartslogistikpartner (TPL partner selection in humanitarian organizations), Master's thesis, Hanken School of Economics, Helsinki, Finland

McLachlin, R, Larson, PD and Khan, S (2009) Not-for-profit supply chains in interrupted environments: The case of a faith-based humanitarian relief organization, *Management Research News*, 32(11), pp 1050–64

Oloruntoba, R and Gray, R (2006) Humanitarian aid: an agile supply chain?, *Supply Chain Management: an International Journal*, 11(2), pp 115–20

Oloruntoba, R and Gray, R (2009) Customer service in emergency relief chains, *International Journal of Physical Distribution and Logistics Management*, **39** (6), pp 486–505

Pettit, S and Beresford, A (2009) Critical success factors in the context of humanitarian aid supply chains, *International Journal of Physical Distribution and Logistics Management*, **39**(6), pp 450–68

Sarkis, J, Spens, K and Kovács, G (2010) A study on barriers to greening the relief supply chain, in *Relief Supply Chain Management for Disasters: Humanitarian, Aid and Emergency Logistics*, (eds) G Kovács and KM Spens, IGI Global, Hershey, PA

Suarez, P (2009) Linking climate knowledge and decisions: humanitarian challenges, *The Pardee Papers*, **7** (December)

Tatham, PH and Kovács, G (2007) The humanitarian supply network in rapid onset disasters, *Proceedings of the 19th Annual Conference for Nordic Researchers in Logistics*, (eds) Á Halldórsson and G Stefánsson, NOFOMA 2007, Reykjavík, Iceland, pp 1059–74

Tatham, PH and Kovács, G (2010) The application of 'swift trust' to humanitarian logistics, *International Journal of Production Economics*, **126**(1), pp 35–45

Tatham, PH, Haavisto, I, Kovács, G, Beresford, A and Pettit, S (2010a) The logistic cost drivers of disaster relief, *LRN 2010 conference proceedings*, Leeds, UK, pp 650–59

Tatham, PH, Kovács, G and Larson, PD (2010b) What skills and attributes are needed by humanitarian logisticians – a perspective drawn from international disaster relief agencies, *Operations in Emerging Economies, POMS 2010 conference*, Vancouver, Canada, paper 015-0179

Thomas, A and Fritz, L (2006) Disaster Relief, Inc. *Harvard Business Review*, November, pp 114–22

Tomasini, RM and Van Wassenhove, LN (2009) From preparedness to partnerships: case study research on humanitarian logistics, *International Transactions in Operational Research*, **16**, pp 549–59

UN DESA (2010) World urbanization prospects. The 2009 Revision. Highlights. ESA/P/WP/215, Department of Economic and Social Affairs, Population Division; available at: http://esa.un.org/unpd/wup/Documents/WUP2009_Highlights_Final.pdf [accessed 30 July 2010]

Van Wassenhove, LN (2006) Humanitarian aid logistics: supply chain management in high gear, *Journal of the Operational Research Society*, **57**(5), pp 475–89

Van Wassenhove, LN (2010) Humanitarian logistics tutorial, *ALIO/INFORMS conference*, June, Buenos Aires, Argentina

Völz, C (2005) Humanitarian coordination in Indonesia: an NGO viewpoint, *Forced Migration Review*, Special Issue, July, pp 26–27

Whybark, DC (2007) Issues in managing disaster relief inventories, *International Journal of Production Economics*, **108**(1–2), pp 228–35

Notes

1 Not surprisingly, coordination became one of four (or five) initial topics to be addressed by the HUMLOG Group as decided in their Geneva meeting in 2007. The other topics were funding (see also Chapter 2), needs assessment

(Chapter 3) and performance measurement (Chapter 4), as well as, arguably, organizational learning.

2 A similar hub system and, thus, decentralized supply chain design has been established by the International Federation of Red Cross and Red Crescent Societies (IFRC) since 2006 (see Gatignon *et al*, 2010). Interestingly, these regional hubs (both those of the UN and the IFRC) overlap with the geographical locations of similar systems used by commercial logistics service providers.

3 United Nations Joint Logistics Centre.

4 United Nations Humanitarian Air Service.

5 Templates have also been developed for needs assessment, eg HELP and CILT's 'HELPNAT' template.

6 Available at: http://log.logcluster.org/ [accessed 29 July 2010]

7 The Humanitarian Logistics Software (HLS) of the Fritz Institute has been adopted by the International Federation of Red Cross and Red Crescent Societies (IFRC) and continues to be developed and implemented as the Helios software across organizations such as Oxfam, World Vision International, etc.

8 A series of INSEAD teaching cases addresses partnerships between LSPs and humanitarian organizations – see also Tomasini and van Wassenhove (2009).

9 The mix of inter-agency coordination with supply chain collaboration (re-) introduces and re-emphasises a network view of humanitarian supply chains. A taxonomy of projects, chains and networks in humanitarian logistics can be found in Jahre *et al* (2009).

10 See: http://www.aidmatrix.org/alan/index.html [accessed 29 July 2010]

11 Customs and modal shift are areas in which logistics performance indicators are still subordinate to political constraints in humanitarian logistics.

12 The three organizations are the World Food Programme (WFP), the Food and Agriculture Organization (FAO) and the International Fund for Agricultural Development (IFAD). These are the so-called 'Rome-based agencies', though several other NGOs have joined the alliance since. More information can be found at: http://www.iaahp.net/ [accessed 29 July 2010]

13 Linnerooth-Bayer *et al* (2005) present statistics on the discrepancies between death tolls from natural disasters based on country income, but the differences are even higher if one would consider complex emergencies and internal conflicts as well. Unfortunately, not even EM-DAT compiles data on such disasters despite that natural disasters account for about 6 per cent of humanitarian activities (according to Van Wassenhove, 2006).

14 Until recently, it had appeared that this trend was decreasing – perhaps as a result of publicity explaining the downside of such donations. However, it is clear from reports in the wake of the January 2010 earthquake in Haiti that it still remains a difficult area. In any event, there are no reliable statistics on the matter.

Index

NB: page numbers in *italic* indicate figures or tables

ABI/INFORM Global™ database 17
Academy of Management (ANZAM) 3
supply chain special interest group 3
Action against Hunger 219
Action Aid 129
Action Contre La Faim (ACF) 13
ADRA 129
Afghanistan 208, 227, 234, 235, 245
Africa 121–40
   challenges of humanitarian logistics 134–36
   contingency planning 127–28
   disaster risk management 127–28
   human capacity building 133–343
   nature/incidence of disasters 123–24
   scope/role of humanitarian logistics 124
   sustainable development 123–24
   training in disaster management 133–34
   role of technology 131–33
Africa Regional Strategy for Disaster Risk
   Reduction 128, 136
Africa Union (AU) 128, 129
   New Partnership for Africa's Development
     (NEPAD) 128
'agility' 4, 125, 257
aid agencies 16, 20, 39, 41, 229
   accountability 73
   aims 202–03
   annual expenditure 2
   expenditure on logistics 66
   feedback on performance 77
   financial indicators 42
   funding and 36–41
   funding cost percentage 42
   local knowledge 208–12
   logistical capabilities 4
   overhead costs 42
   quality indicators 41
   role 245
   visibility 41–42
   volunteers 203
   see also humanitarian logistics, NGOs
aid workers 22

AÏDA project (Advancing ICT for Disaster Risk
   Management in Africa) 132
AirServ 224
Albania 26
American Red Cross 144, 204, 259
Annan, Kofi 237
armed forces 52, 188, 229
   co-operation with humanitarian aid
     agencies 215–31, 233–48
   need for joint doctrine 246–47
   peacekeeping operations 226–27, 242
   role in disasters 52 , 166, 243–44, 245
   supply chain management and 181–82, *182*
Australian Defence Forces 224, 226, 247
Australian Red Cross 247
Aviation sans Frontières 224

Bangladesh 256
Biafra War 216
Bill and Melinda Gates Foundation 167
BINGOs (big international non-governmental
   organisations 251, 256–57
BP 5
Bosnia 235
Buffet, Warren 167
Bush, George 167
business process reengineering 5

Care International 129
CARE USA 21, 224, 236
Caritas 12
catastrophic event 18–19
Central Emergency Response Fund (CERF) 34
Chad 93
Chamlee-Wright, Emily 203–04
Chartered Institute of Logistics and Transport
   (CILT) 191, 196
Chile earthquake 259
Cisco 8
Clinton HIV/AIDS Initiative (CHAI) 167, 168
Clinton, Bill 26
Cold War 235

Common Humanitarian Funds (CHFs) 34
communications system 10
Concern 62
connectivity 7
Consortium of British Humanitarian Agencies
(CBHA) 61–62
contingency planning 127–28
inter-agency 130
corporate social responsibility (CSR) 28
corruption 206
Couchner, Bernard 216
Cranfield University/Cardiff University
Logistics Initiative (CCHLI) 196
Cross, General Tim 220
cultural clashes 204–05
cultural perspectives 201–14
Cyclone Nargis 251

Dannatt, General Sir Richard 233, 234–35,
238
Darfur 37, 207
Dell Computer 20
demand/event-driven responsiveness 4
Democratic Republic of Congo (DRC) 92
Department for International Development
(DFID) 234, 247
development aid/programmes 19, 23, 24, 25,
226, 256
diabetes 170–73
deaths from 170
insulin supply 170–72
disaster
definition 122
man-made 122, 238
natural 1, 19, 22, 33, 122, 222–25, 238
types 122
Disaster Impact Index (DII) 78
disaster relief 19, 23, 24, 25
beneficiaries 253
efficiency 125–26
importance of logistics 104
needs assessment 116–17
response programmes 50
speed of response 125
supply chain planning and 50–52
see also armed forces, humanitarian
logistics
disaster taxonomies 256
distribution 206–08
donor agencies 228
'Dunanists' 219, 220, 221
Dunant, Jean Henri 219

ECHO (European Community's Humanitarian
Aid Office) 219, 228
ELRHA (Enhancing Learning and Research for
Humanitarian Assistance) 197
Emergency Response Funds (ERFs) 34

empowerment aid model 29

famine relief 225
fast-moving consumer goods (FCMG) retail
business 2
Feinstein Centre 191
Fenton, George 9
Florida 145
Florida Department of Emergency Management
(FDEM) 142, 145–58, 159
Comprehensive Emergency Management
Plan (CEMP) 152–53
County Point of Distribution (POD) 149
County Staging Areas (CSA) 149
human resources 149–50
information and communication 154–58,
157
Logistics Staging Area (LSA) 148–49
planning and coordination 150–54
role of private sector 153
State Emergency Response Team
(SERT) 146, 149–50, 152, 160
State Emergency Operations Center
(SEOC) 147, 154
State Logistics Response Center
(SLRC) 147–48, 152
State Mobilization Area (SMA) 148
State Resource Management Network
(SRMN) 156–57
supply chain infrastructure 147–48
temporary facilities 148–49
Vendor Managed Inventory (VMI) 158–59
Food Agriculture Organization (FAO) 257
Food for Peace programme 202
4PL (Fourth Party Logistics) provider 8
Fritz Institute 54, 59, 60, 61, 76, 115, 124,
131, 191, 196, 223
Fritz, Lynn 54
fund management 40
funding systems 33–47
accountability 35
allocation to emergencies 38
allocation to resources and activities 39,
41
donations and 35
donor agencies 228
flexibility 38–40
fluctuation and predictability 37
governments and 35
humanitarian relief and 34
impact on disaster response 36–41
incentives provided by donors 41–42
links with logistic systems
management 40
shortcomings 43
speed/timing 37–38
structure of 35
volume 36–37

genetically modified (GM) crops 204, 205
German Red Cross 12
Ghana 133
Global Fund 167, 168
global warming 24
globalization 186
Good Humanitarian Donorship (2003) 43
Goodhand, Mike 9
Goodwill, the 205
Gujarat earthquake 38

Hagan, Chuck 158, 161
Hailens Fresh Produce 176
Haiti earthquake disaster (2010) 49, 66, 203,
        211, 215, 245, 247, 256, 259
Helios Foundation 60–61
Helios project 51, 54–57, 252
        Oxfam GB and 58–59
hierarchy of needs 201, 202–04
HIV/AIDS
        fight against 166–69
Hoyle, E 188, 189–90
humanitarian-development divide 256
Humanitarian Emergency Logistics
        Professionals (HELP) 196
Humanitarian Imperative 244
humanitarian logistics 67
        Africa 121–40
        Challenges 184–92
        Cluster Approach and 85–101
        commercial approaches 182–84
        coordination 252–54
        critical success factors 125–26
        cultural perspective 201–14
        definition 67, 76, 125, 217
        developments in 249–60
        'green' 258
        knowledge acquisition 192–95, 193
        inter-agency communication, collaboration
                and co-ordination 129–31
        lessons learned from South East Asia
                Tsunami 112–16
        military organizations 181–82, 182,
                218–19
        professionalism 187–98
        professionalization 116, 260
        training 133–34
        United States 141–63
        see also supply chains, supply networks
humanitarian logisticians (HL) 2, 16
        fundamental tenets 190–91
Humanitarian Logistics Association (HLA) 75,
        191, 196–97, 260
Humanitarian Logistics Conference (HLC)
        (2004) 52
Humanitarian Logistics Software (HLS) 54,
        71, 223, 252
        See also Helios

humanitarian/military cooperation 12,
        215–31, 233–48
        joint logistics supply chain 222–28
humanitarian operations research (OR) 255
humanitarian principles/ideology 219–21
        humanity 219, 229
        impartiality 219, 220, 229
        independence 219, 220, 229
        neutrality 219, 220, 229
Humanitarian Response Depots (HRDs) 49,
        92
Humanitarian Response Review (HRR) 89–91,
        112, 117
'humanitarian space' 29
Humanitarian Supply Chain Solutions
        (HSCS) 54
Humanitarian Track and Trace (HTT) 54
humanitarianism 189
'HUMLOG initiative 3, 13, 14
Hurricane Katrina 66, 87, 142, 144, 190, 196,
        203, 207, 215, 223, 247
Hurricane Mitch 37

Information systems 255
information technology 47–63, 249, 252
        Africa 131–33
        see also Helios, Oxfam GB
inter-agency coordination 251–52
Inter-Agency Procurement Group (UK) 254
internally displaced persons (IDPs) 256
International Assistance Mission 28
International Council for Science (ICSU 77
International Diabetes Foundation (IDF) 170
International Federation of the Red Cross and
        Red Crescent Movement (IFRC) 35,
        54, 194, 205, 219, 223
        balanced scorecard 75
        Disaster Relief Emergency Fund 38
        fleet management system 255
        Humanitarian Logistic software 54, 71
        Logistic Resources and Mobilization
                Department (LRMD) 74–75
        origins 236
        use of metrics 71, 74–75
International Fund for Agricultural
        Development (IFAD) 263
International Medical Corps (IMC) 60–61
International Organisation for Migration
        (IOM) 111
International Rescue Committee (IRC) 61,
        224
Inventory management 126
Iraq 227, 25
Iraqi Medical Association 207

Java 210
John Snow International 167
Joint Doctrine Centre (UK) 246–47

Journal of Humanitarian Logistics and Supply Chain Management 260
just-in-time (JIT) 5

Kashmir earthquake (2005) 215, 223, 224–25
Kenya 202, 211
Kenya Red Cross 61
Kibaki, Mwai 202
Ksovo 244

language barriers 207–08
Lead Logistics Provider 8
Li & Fung 8
Life Quality Index (LQI) 78
local knowledge, importance of 208–12
logistic metrics *see* metrics
logistics *see* humanitarian logistics
Logisticx9 223
Loma Rrieta earthquake, California 206

Maimonides 202
Médecins sans Frontières (MSF) 12, 216–17, 219, 224–25, 227, 240
media, the 240
Merlin 60, 62
metrics 10–11, 65–84
  academic perspectives 70–72
  appeal coverage 71–72
  assessment accuracy 72
  donation-to-delivery time 72
  effectiveness of supply network 73–74
  financial efficiency 72, 77
  healthcare 78–79, 80
  human wellbeing 77–79, 80
  impact monitoring 71
  measurement frameworks 71
  outcomes 70
  outputs 72
  performance measures 68–70
  practitioner perspectives 73–76
  recipient's perspective 76–79
military intelligence 25
military organizations *see* armed forces
Millennium Development Goals (MDGs) 24, 166
'Mission Command' 240
Moyo, Dambisa 202
Mozambique 25
  food crisis (2002)
  Disaster Management Authority 128

National Guard 143
NATO 5
  CIMIC (Civilian-Military Co-ordination) 226, 227
  KFOR deployment (Operation Agricola) 236
natural disasters 1, 19, 22, 33, 222–25, 238

needs assessment 135
Nepal 202
New Partnership for Africa's Development (NEPAD) 128
New York City 143
NGO-Military Contact Group (UK) 227
non-governmental organizations (NGOs) 20, 229, 237
  combined budget 217
  competitiveness 241
  co-operation with armed forces 222–28, 239
  development aid and 27
  hostility to armed forces 241–42
  need for joint doctrine 246–47
  neutrality 220
  number of 217
  purpose 237
  view of logistics 218
  see also BINGOs

Obama, Barack 167
101 Logistic Brigade 236
Oxfam Australia 224
Oxfam 10, 21, 129, 219, 224, 227, 236
  history/background 48
  Humanitarian Investment Plan (HIP) 56
  'Integrating Logistics in Project Planning and Management' (ILPPM) 51, 56–60
  process redesign 56–57
  Tamina concept 57
  User Reference Group 58

Packer, George 210
Pakistan 190, 245
  flooding (2010) 259
Papua New Guinea 175–76
  economic development 175–76
  Liquified Natural Gas (LNG) project 175
Peace Corps 210, 211
PEPFAR 167, 168, 168
performance measurement 68–70
  challenges for NGOs 76
  commercial supply networks 68–69
  not-for-profit supply networks 69–70
  see also metrics
processes, management 6, 11
profession 187–89
  definition 187–88
  functionalist view 188, 190–91
  occupational 187–88
  status 187
professionalism 187–98
  education 191–92
  knowledge 190–91, 192–95, *193*
  social function 190

skills 190
values 190
professionalization 12, 199, 260

Red Cross/Red Crescent 18, 25, 27, 216, 217, 219, 223, 223
see also International Federation of the Red Cross and Red Crescent Movement (IFRC)
Red R UK 191
refugees 235
Reith, General John 26
relationship management theory 130
research 29, 41
resource misallocations 43
risk categories/factors 9, 16
disasters and 24
disruption 19
operational 19
security of 16
types 18
risk management 9, 20, 126
barriers to 27
compensatory 24, 25
prospective 24–25
Roberts, Alan 240

Sainsbury's 185
Salvation Army 205
Save the Children 62, 219, 224, 227, 26
Shell 5
Shephard, Ben 236, 237
'signal noise' 203
Slim ,Hugo 241
Smith, Daniel Jordan 210
South African National Disaster Management Centre (MDMC) 132
South East Asia tsunami disaster (2004) 2, 11, 26, 37, 49, 89, 103–41, 190, 207, 211, 215, 223, 247, 250
background 104–07
communications networks 110–11
co-ordination problems 251
cost of 105
Department of Disaster Prevention and Mitigation at the Ministry of Interior (DDPMMI) 107
impact 105
lessons learned 112–16
number of casualties 105, 106
planning 108
responses to 105–12, 205
Thailand 109
South Sudan 225
Soviet Union 235
Sphere Standards 73
Strategic Defence and Security Review (UK) 246
Sudan drought (1992) 215

Sun Tzu 239
suppliers 254
supply chain risk management (SCRM) 16–31, 50–52
humanitarian world and 23–27
literature review 17–20
postponement strategy 20
proactive planning 19
research findings 29
supply chain risk evaluation and management (SCREAM) 19, 20
supply chains 8, 26, 130, 247–48
costs 184
diabetes 170–73
differences between commercial and humanitarian 21
dormant/active 24
economic development and 173–76
enabler of development 165–78
humanitarian 33–34, 182–84, 183
integration 28
interrupted/non interrupted 256
lean/agile 180, 181
military organizations 181–82, 182
preparing for disruptions 19–20
profit/not for profit 256
relationships 254–55
security of 16
strategies for fighting AIDS/HIV 168–69
types 22
see also humanitarian logistics, information technology,
supply network management (SNM) *see* humanitarian logistics
supply networks 3–7
demand and event driven 4–5
globalization 17–18
network-based 4–5
process-oriented 6
sustainability 13
virtually integrated 7
see also supply chains
sustainability 257–59

Taiwan earthquake (1999) 20
Tajikistan 235
Tear Fund 62
Thailand 173–75
economic development 173–75
'The Continuum' 23
transport 205–06
Total 5
Toyota 185
tsunami disaster *see* South East Asia tsunami disaster
Tsunami Evaluation Coalition (TEC) 77

United Nations (UN) 27, 237

Charter 237–38
co-operation with NGOs 242
Development Programme (UNDP) 22, 24
High Commissioner for Refugees
    (UNHCR) 209, 237, 241
Human Development Index (HDI) 78
Humanitarian Air Service (UNHAS) 251,
    263
Humanitarian Response Depot
    (UNHRD) 6
Humanitarian Response Review
    (HRR) 89–91, 112–13, 117
Inter Agency Standing Committee
    (IASC) 113
Joint Logistics Center (UNJLC) 88–89,
    186, 194, 196, 251
Millennium Development Goals
    (MDGs) 24, 166
Office for the Coordination of
    Humanitarian Affairs
    (UNOCHA) 49, 88, 226
United Nations Cluster Approach 11, 85–101,
    245
    cluster co-ordination role 49
    cluster responsibilities 114
    cost 92
    functional sectors 91–92
    Emergency Preparedness and Response
        Working Group (EPRWG) 88
    Humanitarian Response Review
        (HRR) 89–91
    impact 91
    International Strategy for Disaster
        Reduction (UN/ISDR) Unit 134
    lead organisation responsibilities 114
    Logistics (Log) Cluster 87, 115–16, 186,
        194, 196, 250, 251, 252
    Logistics Operational Guide (LOG) 252
    Logistics Support System (LSS) 223
    organization of disaster assistance/
        response 96
    Relief and Rehabilitation Administration
        (UNRRA) 236–37
    review of (2010) 94
    roll-out 92
    US perspectives 91, 95–98
United States (US)
    alignment with Cluster Approach 97
    Air Force 203
    approach to disaster relief 95–98
    Department of Homeland Security
        (DHS) 143–44
    Disaster Assessment Response Teams
        (DARTs) 96

Federal Emergency Management Agency
    (FEMA) 95, 96
Florida 145–58
    humanitarian logistics 141–63
    hurricanes 141, 142
    National Incident Management System
        (NIMS) 144
    National Response Framework (NRF) 144
    Office for the Coordination of
        Humanitarian Affairs) 219
    Office of Foreign Disaster Assistance
        (OFDA) 95, 96
    organization of disaster response/
        assistance 96
    overview of disaster emergency
        response 143–45
    role of private/commercial sector 144
    terrorist attacks 141, 142
    see also Florida Department of Emergency
        Management (FDEM)
UPS 8
urbanization 259
USAID (US Agency for International
    Development) 95, 96, 97, 167, 238

vendor-managed inventory (VMI) 6

Wal-Mart 8, 185
war zones 227–28
'Wars of Identity' 235
Wilson, Woodrow 219
'Wilsonians' 219, 220, 221
World Bank 35, 211, 238
    Basic Needs Program 202
    Multi-Country HIV/AIDS Program for
        Africa (MAP) 167
World Economic Forum 19
World Food Programme (WFP) 6, 22, 49, 89,
    205, 217, 223, 225, 237, 257
    Augmented Logistics Intervention Team for
        Emergencies 95
    Logistics Cluster lead 91–92, 94, 111, 113,
        115–16
    South East Asia Tsunami 111, 115
World Health Organization (WHO) 79, 171
    International Classification of Functioning,
        Disability and Health (ICF) 79
World Vision International (WVI) 21, 22, 60,
    61, 129, 240
    tracking system 255

Zambia 204
Zara 5
Zimbabwe 204, 205, 258